pcAnywhere® For Dum

T5-CQE-227

pcAnywhere Quick Connection Guide

To begin a pcAnywhere remote control session, you must first launch pcAnywhere on the host computer and then dial the host from the remote.

To launch pcAnywhere on the host computer:

1. Open the pcAnywhere program on the host by double-clicking the pcAnywhere icon on the desktop.

2. Click the Be A Host PC button on the pcAnywhere Action bar.

3. Right-click the icon for the connection item that contains the appropriate phone number or network address, connection device, and security information.

4. Select Launch Host from the pop-up menu.

To dial the host computer from the remote PC:

1. Open the pcAnywhere program on the remote computer by double-clicking the pcAnywhere icon on the desktop.

2. Click the Remote Control button on the pcAnywhere Action bar.

3. Double-click the icon for the connection item that contains the appropriate phone number or network address, connection device, and security information.

   A status box appears telling you that pcAnywhere is dialing, and then the host screen appears on the remote desktop.

pcAnywhere Jargon

Caller

A caller is someone given the right to access a host computer and initiate a pcAnywhere remote control session. Each caller is assigned a login name and password that identifies it to the host. When you initially set up a host connection item, you must identify the callers who have permission to access it.

Connection device

The hardware you use to make a connection between two computers. This can be network cabling, a modem, or a serial cable between two computers.

Connection item

A type of file, represented by an icon on the pcAnywhere desktop, that contains the information required to make a connection, such as the type of hardware used, the phone number or network address, and security information.

Host

A computer that contains files or applications accessed by the remote computer during a remote control session. The remote PC controls the host during the remote control session.

pcAnywhere® For Dummies®

Cheat Sheet

pcAnywhere Online Toolbar

Full Screen

Online Options

Auto Transfer

Chat

Save Screen

Switch to Voice

Restart Host

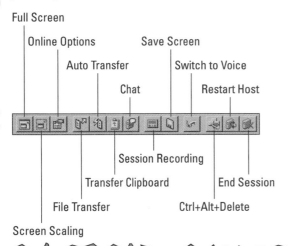

Session Recording

Transfer Clipboard

End Session

File Transfer

Ctrl+Alt+Delete

Screen Scaling

pcAnywhere Support Options

The Symantec Web site offers articles in the Knowledge Base, a Troubleshooter wizard, FAQ's, and other support features. Point your browser to the following site:

www.symantec.com

To purchase pcAnywhere:

http://shop.symantec.com/

To obtain a free trial version of pcAnywhere:

http://shop.symantec.com/trialware/

Telephone Support: This option allows you to chat with a live technician (prices are current as of the time this book went to press):

1-900-646-0006 — $2.95 a minute (charged on a per-minute basis; first minute free)
1-900-927-4012 — $29.95 (U.S.) (Charged on a per-incident basis)

For Dummies®: Bestselling Book Series for Beginners

pcAnywhere® FOR DUMMIES®

pcAnywhere® FOR DUMMIES®

by Jill Gilbert

IDG BOOKS WORLDWIDE

IDG Books Worldwide, Inc.
An International Data Group Company

Foster City, CA ◆ Chicago, IL ◆ Indianapolis, IN ◆ New York, NY

pcAnywhere® For Dummies®

Published by
IDG Books Worldwide, Inc.
An International Data Group Company
919 E. Hillsdale Blvd.
Suite 400
Foster City, CA 94404
www.idgbooks.com (IDG Books Worldwide Web site)
www.dummies.com (Dummies Press Web site)

Library of Congress Catalog Card No.: 99-67526

ISBN: 0-7645-0680-3

Printed in the United States of America

10 9 8 7 6 5 4 3 2 1

1B/RS/QR/QQ/IN

Distributed in the United States by IDG Books Worldwide, Inc.

Distributed by CDG Books Canada Inc. for Canada; by Transworld Publishers Limited in the United Kingdom; by IDG Norge Books for Norway; by IDG Sweden Books for Sweden; by IDG Books Australia Publishing Corporation Pty. Ltd. for Australia and New Zealand; by TransQuest Publishers Pte Ltd. for Singapore, Malaysia, Thailand, Indonesia, and Hong Kong; by Gotop Information Inc. for Taiwan; by ICG Muse, Inc. for Japan; by Intersoft for South Africa; by Eyrolles for France; by International Thomson Publishing for Germany, Austria and Switzerland; by Distribuidora Cuspide for Argentina; by LR International for Brazil; by Galileo Libros for Chile; by Ediciones ZETA S.C.R. Ltda. for Peru; by WS Computer Publishing Corporation, Inc., for the Philippines; by Contemporanea de Ediciones for Venezuela; by Express Computer Distributors for the Caribbean and West Indies; by Micronesia Media Distributor, Inc. for Micronesia; by Chips Computadoras S.A. de C.V. for Mexico; by Editorial Norma de Panama S.A. for Panama; by American Bookshops for Finland.

For general information on IDG Books Worldwide's books in the U.S., please call our Consumer Customer Service department at 800-762-2974. For reseller information, including discounts and premium sales, please call our Reseller Customer Service department at 800-434-3422.

For information on where to purchase IDG Books Worldwide's books outside the U.S., please contact our International Sales department at 317-596-5530 or fax 317-572-4002.

For consumer information on foreign language translations, please contact our Customer Service department at 1-800-434-3422, fax 317-572-4002, or e-mail rights@idgbooks.com.

For information on licensing foreign or domestic rights, please phone +1-650-653-7098.

For sales inquiries and special prices for bulk quantities, please contact our Sales department at 800-762-2974 or write to the address above.

For information on using IDG Books Worldwide's books in the classroom or for ordering examination copies, please contact our Educational Sales department at 800-434-2086 or fax 317-572-4005.

For press review copies, author interviews, or other publicity information, please contact our Public Relations department at 650-653-7000 or fax 650-653-7500.

For authorization to photocopy items for corporate, personal, or educational use, please contact Copyright Clearance Center, 222 Rosewood Drive, Danvers, MA 01923, or fax 978-750-4470.

is a registered trademark under exclusive license to IDG Books Worldwide, Inc. from International Data Group, Inc.

About the Author

Jill Gilbert is a Certified Public Accountant who holds Masters degrees in accountancy and taxation, as well as a law degree. She is currently completing her training to become a Microsoft Certified Systems Engineer. Jill first used pcAnywhere while on maternity leave.

ABOUT IDG BOOKS WORLDWIDE

Welcome to the world of IDG Books Worldwide.

IDG Books Worldwide, Inc., is a subsidiary of International Data Group, the world's largest publisher of computer-related information and the leading global provider of information services on information technology. IDG was founded more than 30 years ago by Patrick J. McGovern and now employs more than 9,000 people worldwide. IDG publishes more than 290 computer publications in over 75 countries. More than 90 million people read one or more IDG publications each month.

Launched in 1990, IDG Books Worldwide is today the #1 publisher of best-selling computer books in the United States. We are proud to have received eight awards from the Computer Press Association in recognition of editorial excellence and three from Computer Currents' First Annual Readers' Choice Awards. Our best-selling *...For Dummies®* series has more than 50 million copies in print with translations in 31 languages. IDG Books Worldwide, through a joint venture with IDG's Hi-Tech Beijing, became the first U.S. publisher to publish a computer book in the People's Republic of China. In record time, IDG Books Worldwide has become the first choice for millions of readers around the world who want to learn how to better manage their businesses.

Our mission is simple: Every one of our books is designed to bring extra value and skill-building instructions to the reader. Our books are written by experts who understand and care about our readers. The knowledge base of our editorial staff comes from years of experience in publishing, education, and journalism — experience we use to produce books to carry us into the new millennium. In short, we care about books, so we attract the best people. We devote special attention to details such as audience, interior design, use of icons, and illustrations. And because we use an efficient process of authoring, editing, and desktop publishing our books electronically, we can spend more time ensuring superior content and less time on the technicalities of making books.

You can count on our commitment to deliver high-quality books at competitive prices on topics you want to read about. At IDG Books Worldwide, we continue in the IDG tradition of delivering quality for more than 30 years. You'll find no better book on a subject than one from IDG Books Worldwide.

John Kilcullen
Chairman and CEO
IDG Books Worldwide, Inc.

Steven Berkowitz
President and Publisher
IDG Books Worldwide, Inc.

VIII WINNER

Eighth Annual
Computer Press
Awards ≥1992

IX WINNER

Ninth Annual
Computer Press
Awards ≥1993

X WINNER

Tenth Annual
Computer Press
Awards ≥1994

XI WINNER

Eleventh Annual
Computer Press
Awards ≥1995

IDG is the world's leading IT media, research and exposition company. Founded in 1964, IDG had 1997 revenues of $2.05 billion and has more than 9,000 employees worldwide. IDG offers the widest range of media options that reach IT buyers in 75 countries representing 95% of worldwide IT spending. IDG's diverse product and services portfolio spans six key areas including print publishing, online publishing, expositions and conferences, market research, education and training, and global marketing services. More than 90 million people read one or more of IDG's 290 magazines and newspapers, including IDG's leading global brands — Computerworld, PC World, Network World, Macworld and the Channel World family of publications. IDG Books Worldwide is one of the fastest-growing computer book publishers in the world, with more than 700 titles in 36 languages. The "...For Dummies®" series alone has more than 50 million copies in print. IDG offers online users the largest network of technology-specific Web sites around the world through IDG.net (http://www.idg.net), which comprises more than 225 targeted Web sites in 55 countries worldwide. International Data Corporation (IDC) is the world's largest provider of information technology data, analysis and consulting, with research centers in over 41 countries and more than 400 research analysts worldwide. IDG World Expo is a leading producer of more than 168 globally branded conferences and expositions in 35 countries including E3 (Electronic Entertainment Expo), Macworld Expo, ComNet, Windows World Expo, ICE (Internet Commerce Expo), Agenda, DEMO, and Spotlight. IDG's training subsidiary, ExecuTrain, is the world's largest computer training company, with more than 230 locations worldwide and 785 training courses. IDG Marketing Services helps industry-leading IT companies build international brand recognition by developing global integrated marketing programs via IDG's print, online and exposition products worldwide. Further information about the company can be found at www.idg.com.   1/24/99

Dedication

To Dan, Tara, Julia, Daniel, and happy telecommuters everywhere.

Author's Acknowledgments

Thanks to my great editors at IDG Books Worldwide, Inc., — Jodi Jensen and Jeremy Zucker — people who know how to write great books and will take the time to teach you stuff. Nettie has named her twins after you two.

Thanks to the Symantec technical support people who patiently answered all my questions and to my technical editor, Jeff Wiedenfeld, for his thorough review of my manuscript.

Thanks to Ed Adams, Martine Edwards, and David Fugate for this opportunity.

And, finally, thanks to Barb at St. Francis Childrens' center for letting me have her coffee.

Publisher's Acknowledgments

We're proud of this book; please register your comments through our IDG Books Worldwide Online Registration Form located at `http://my2cents.dummies.com`.

Some of the people who helped bring this book to market include the following:

Acquisitions, Editorial, and Media Development

Senior Project Editor: Jodi Jensen

Acquisitions Editor: Ed Adams

Copy Editors: Christine Berman, Jeremy Zucker

Technical Editor: Jeff Wiedenfeld

Editorial Manager: Leah Cameron

Editorial Assistant: Beth Parlon

Production

Project Coordinator: Regina Snyder

Layout and Graphics: Karl Brandt, Barry Offringa, Jill Piscitelli, Brent Savage, Janet Seib, Brian Torwelle, Dan Whetstine

Proofreaders: Corey Bowen, John Greenough, Christine Sabooni, Marianne Santy

Indexer: Rachel Rice

Special Help
Amanda Foxworth

General and Administrative

IDG Books Worldwide, Inc.: John Kilcullen, CEO; Steven Berkowitz, President and Publisher

IDG Books Technology Publishing Group: Richard Swadley, Senior Vice President and Publisher; Walter Bruce III, Vice President and Associate Publisher; Joseph Wikert, Associate Publisher; Mary Bednarek, Branded Product Development Director; Mary Corder, Editorial Director; Barry Pruett, Publishing Manager; Michelle Baxter, Publishing Manager

IDG Books Consumer Publishing Group: Roland Elgey, Senior Vice President and Publisher; Kathleen A. Welton, Vice President and Publisher; Kevin Thornton, Acquisitions Manager; Kristin A. Cocks, Editorial Director

IDG Books Internet Publishing Group: Brenda McLaughlin, Senior Vice President and Publisher; Diane Graves Steele, Vice President and Associate Publisher; Sofia Marchant, Online Marketing Manager

IDG Books Production for Dummies Press: Debbie Stailey, Associate Director of Production; Cindy L. Phipps, Manager of Project Coordination, Production Proofreading, and Indexing; Tony Augsburger, Manager of Prepress, Reprints, and Systems; Laura Carpenter, Production Control Manager; Shelley Lea, Supervisor of Graphics and Design; Debbie J. Gates, Production Systems Specialist; Robert Springer, Supervisor of Proofreading; Kathie Schutte, Production Supervisor

Dummies Packaging and Book Design: Patty Page, Manager, Promotions Marketing

◆

The publisher would like to give special thanks to Patrick J. McGovern, without whom this book would not have been possible.

◆

Contents at a Glance

Cartoons at a Glance

By Rich Tennant

"Oh sure, it's nice working at home, except my boss drives by every morning and blasts his horn to make sure I'm awake."

page 57

"I AM pushing, but the 'Enter' key seems to be stuck!"

page 7

"NOW JUST WHEN THE HECK DID I INTEGRATE THAT INTO THE SYSTEM?"

page 161

"You the guy having trouble staying connected to the network?"

page 243

Ever the innovator, Larry beta-tests the Personal Belt Buckle Assistant/Wireless Fax

Hold on a second, Stu, I'm getting a fax.

page 211

Fax: 978-546-7747
E-mail: richtennant@the5thwave.com
World Wide Web: www.the5thwave.com

Table of Contents

Introduction

● ●

*p*cAnywhere liberates you.

pcAnywhere is a program that enables you to choose your own workplace and make the work come to you. Picture it — dialing into your office computer from a beach cabana or that mountain cabin. Or, if you're a network administrator, think of the convenience of being able to see what's happening on someone else's screen and then troubleshoot their problem from wherever you may be. All it takes to earn this kind of freedom is a modest investment of your time as you figure out how to use pcAnywhere.

The purpose of this book is to help you learn the fundamentals of pcAnywhere as quickly as possible so that you can effortlessly connect two geographically distant computers.

You can use pcAnywhere to access a computer in your primary workplace while you're somewhere else, troubleshoot another computer on the network, transfer files, or synchronize changes made on one computer so that the other computer has the same version of the file. This book is intended to provide you with clear, simple directions to establish and troubleshoot these critical connections.

About This Book

This book is a reference source — not a tutorial. I didn't write it with the intention that you would read it from cover to cover. But I did write it to give you the information you need to successfully use pcAnywhere. The chapters are divided into clearly labeled parts intended to help you handle any pcAnywhere task that you want to perform. The structure of this book enables you to read only what you need to know, when you need to know it.

Conventions Used in This Book

In this book, I've used certain stylistic features over and over. You can expect these conventions, and you may even look forward to them.

I've placed new words pertaining to pcAnywhere in italics and explained what the term means in the surrounding text. You can also find these terms in the glossary at the back of the book. I've included some terms in the glossary that aren't specific to pcAnywhere — just because I thought you might need to know 'em, and it might be nice to find them all in one convenient place. For example, I don't assume that everyone knows what a *protocol* is, so I included that in the glossary, too.

When I walk you through a process or task, I provide numbered steps that appear in bold type. Any time within one of those numbered steps that I ask you to type some text, the text that you are to type appears in a regular font (not bold) so that you can see it easily.

What You Don't Have to Read

You'll find some technical background material in sidebars sprinkled throughout the book. You can find some technical information (the geeky stuff) that you may or may not care to read in a sidebar marked by a Technical Stuff icon. Read them at your leisure. Intellectual curiosity is definitely a good quality, but I don't expect all of you to have the time or inclination to read this material. I'm pretty sure that most of you just want to find out what you need to know to get your work accomplished as painlessly and quickly as possible.

A few sidebars cover technical, but fairly basic, stuff that I can't assume that all pcAnywhere users know. Understanding the fundamentals is important, and these particular sidebars are intended for the novice PC user, not the network administrator or multi-degreed guru.

Foolish Assumptions

The biggest assumption I make about you is that I cannot accurately make any assumptions. You may be a network administrator or you may be someone who needs help shutting off your computer.

If you're the latter — don't worry. There are plenty of sidebars to soothe you, glossary definitions to enlighten you, and icons — lots of icons — to guide you along the way.

Icons Used in This Book

Icons, strewn like bread crumbs all over this book, are designed to help you follow the path to the perfect pcAnywhere connection.

I use the following icons throughout this book:

This icon reminds you of a relevant concept or procedure that you may otherwise overlook or identifies a concept that I told you about earlier and I just want to be sure you picked up. You'll want to store these gems away in your brain for future retrieval.

When you see this icon, you know that I'm offering some troubleshooting insight or a suggestion to help you solve a nagging problem.

Occasionally, I use this icon to point out something extra special you get with pcAnywhere or because you bought this book.

This icon identifies something that saves you time or generally just makes you look smarter.

This is the icon that points out additional information for the intellectually curious (or geek wanna-bes).

You'll see lots of new terms set off in italics throughout the book. But occasionally, for an especially important term, I'll drop in this icon to make sure that you don't miss it.

This icon signifies something that I found particularly interesting or relevant and thought that you might also like to know.

When you see this icon, be sure to read the accompanying material carefully. I consider this one a beacon alerting you to potential trouble.

This icons reminds you to make sure that you understand this particular text before moving on.

How This Book Is Organized

I've divided this book into five logical sections, or partitions, as we say in the computer world.

Part I: pcAnywhere, Anytime, for Anybody

Part I gives you a jump-start on the basics and tells you everything you need to know before you actually start working with pcAnywhere. You find answers to the following questions:

- What can you do with pcAnywhere?
- What are the system requirements for installing pcAnywhere?
- How do you install pcAnywhere on an individual PC or across an entire network?
- What is remote control and how does it work?

Part II: Moving Files over Phone Lines

This chapter introduces you to the key "players" in a remote control session — the host and remote computers. You also learn how to begin a session. Concepts covered in this part include the following:

- The role of the host computer and how it's configured.
- The role of the remote computer and how it's configured.
- How to establish a connection between the host and remote PCs.

Part III: For Network Administrators Only

This section covers topics of special interest to those supreme beings charged with administering a network (of course, you're welcome to join us even if you just want to know more about this stuff). Topics include the following:

- How to use pcAnywhere as a powerful diagnostic tool.
- How to add security features to your communication sessions.
- How to configure a gateway.

Part IV: To Infinity and Beyond — Advanced Program Features

So you're bored with the basics and want to try something new and exciting? Part IV covers the following:

- ✔ Automating pcAnywhere tasks by writing script commands.
- ✔ Exploring online services that may yield information that you can't get to by surfing the Net.

Part V: The Part of Tens

Every *For Dummies* book includes this signature section. I like to think that I've taken it to new heights by offering you the following:

- ✔ Ten troubleshooting tips — any one of which justifies the cost of this book.
- ✔ Ten useful utilities, such as connecting to the Symantec LiveUpdate server, or recording and playing back remote communication sessions.
- ✔ Ten reasons to wander the Symantec Web site — there's pure gold in those Web pages, and I lead you right to it.

Glossary

This glossary is a comprehensive list of pcAnywhere terms, as well as frequently used technical terms you currently may only kind of understand. You might even consider skimming the glossary to quiz yourself when you think you're pretty adept with pcAnywhere.

Where To Go from Here

Now you're ready to use this book. Look over the table of contents and find something that catches your attention or a topic that you think can help you solve a problem. You can find information on just about any task that you would want to do in pcAnywhere. Soon you'll be a pcAnywhere pro.

Good luck, and happy remote computing!

Part I

pcAnywhere, Anytime, for Anybody

The 5th Wave   By Rich Tennant

"I **AM** pushing, but the 'Enter' key seems to be stuck!"

In this part . . .

In Part I, the features of pcAnywhere are paraded across the catwalk for you to ogle and admire. But this section is more than a fashion show. It's also a reality check.

I cover the basic technical concepts required to understand how this program works. I make sure that you're working with the right hardware, and that you truly understand what each component is supposed to do. By the end of this part, you'll be able to install pcAnywhere on an individual PC or across an entire network.

Chapter 1

The Power of pcAnywhere

*R*emember how the world changed when PCs were first introduced and computers no longer took up an entire room? Suddenly, there was a computer on everybody's desktop. And now, pcAnywhere lets you take that desktop just about anywhere in the world — all you need is a telephone line. As with the advent of personal computers, pcAnywhere can change how and where you spend your working hours.

For an overview of the capabilities and features offered by pcAnywhere, consider the hypothetical case of Nettie Workmeister. Nettie is a network administrator for a law firm of 200 attorneys. She's been using pcAnywhere to help her troubleshoot the law firm's network for years — and to help her balance motherhood with a fulfilling career. Wherever Nettie may be when her beeper goes off — whether she's at a soccer game or the PTA bake sale — she can use pcAnywhere to dial into the network and troubleshoot the problem.

In this chapter, you witness — through Nettie's eyes — the full range of pcAnywhere's remote computing features and capabilities. Pay close attention as we follow Nettie and her laptop to the delivery room, where she simultaneously troubleshoots a major network crisis and gives birth.

The Miracle of Remote Control

Nettie calls her husband from the office to tell him that it's "time." As she heads for the door, she pokes her head into the office of the managing partner to let him know that she needs to start her maternity leave — now! His face turns ashen. What will they do without her? Is Nettie's assistant up to the challenge?

Patiently — between her controlled breathing exercises — Nettie assures him that her assistant is quite capable. Nettie also tells him that, with the help of pcAnywhere, she'll be in constant contact with the firm's network during her maternity leave.

She explains to the worried partner (who's so upset that he's paused his putting practice) that pcAnywhere uses the concept of remote control, which, she assures him, is much faster than the traditional remote networking she had to rely on when she was on maternity leave with her last child.

Nettie explains that with traditional remote networking, every command has to travel from her laptop over the phone line to the network's server computer. This process is slow because standard telephone lines aren't designed for the fast data transmission that Nettie needs to diagnose and troubleshoot network problems. (Don't worry, I explain all the details of remote control, remote networking, and the differences between the two in Chapter 5.)

With pcAnywhere's *remote control* feature, Nettie explains, she can dial into a computer in the office (referred to as a *host*) and take control of it. The host can be a server on the network, a regular workstation on the network, or a stand-alone (non-networked) computer. When Nettie dials into the host PC from her remote PC, her remote PC takes controls of the host PC. Because Nettie is in control of the host PC, she operates it and executes commands on it as though she were seated in front of it.

Just as Nettie finishes her short lesson on the virtues of pcAnywhere, her water breaks. The managing partner is mortified.

Before Leaving the Office

As Nettie well knows, before she can use pcAnywhere to establish a remote connection to a host computer, she has to be sure that pcAnywhere is running on the host computer. Otherwise, she won't be able to make the remote connection.

So before Nettie heads for the hospital, she does the following:

- ✔ She opens the pcAnywhere program on the host computer and clicks the button on the pcAnywhere desktop labeled Be A Host PC, as shown in Figure 1-1.

- ✔ Several icons appear on Nettie's laptop screen. These icons are actually shortcuts to files on the host computer. These icons contain settings, such as Nettie's password, that enable Nettie to remotely connect to the host PC at the office. These icons are called *host connection items,* and I tell you lots more about them in Chapter 5.

✔ Nettie right-clicks the icon that contains the settings that she wants to use for her remote connection and then selects Launch Host from the pop-up menu that appears.

✔ The pcAnywhere desktop disappears from the host screen, but a tiny pcAnywhere icon on the Windows taskbar tells Nettie that the host is now ready and waiting for a connection from a remote computer.

It's a simple task to launch pcAnywhere on the host. And that's a good thing. Nettie's contractions are now ten minutes apart.

Be A Host PC button   Host connection items

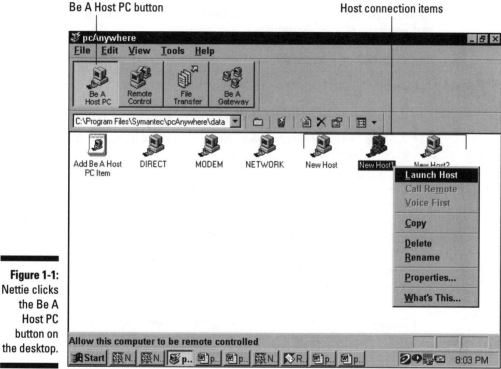

Figure 1-1:
Nettie clicks
the Be A
Host PC
button on
the desktop.

Dialing in from Another Place

Nettie has just arrived at the hospital. Her husband carries her overnight case of toiletry items, but she insists on holding onto her laptop as she's wheeled down the hospital corridor. The managing partner has already paged her — there's a major problem on the network.

The first thing that Nettie does, after she's been checked into the birthing room, is yank the bedside phone out of the jack in the wall. The perky young delivery room nurse starts to protest, but Nettie brushes her aside. Nettie's pager is beeping loudly, and she knows that she must establish a remote control connection immediately.

Nettie plugs her laptop into the phone jack on the wall and calls the office on her cell phone. It's a crisis. The managing partner has entered his Windows NT password incorrectly three times in a row and, as a result, is locked out of the network. He cannot access the documents he needs for a meeting with the firm's largest client. Nettie tells him she'll dial into the network server computer, which contains the central database of user passwords and permissions. Nettie can then restore the partner's access to the network. (But first she has to have an epidural.)

How does Nettie dial into the network? Fortunately (because the contractions are now six minutes apart), it's a simple process. Nettie does the following:

✔ She boots up her laptop and opens the pcAnywhere program.

✔ As soon as the program opens, Nettie clicks the button at the top of her screen that's labeled Remote Control, as shown in Figure 1-2.

✔ Several icons appear on the desktop. These icons are called *remote control connection items*. (I talk about them in detail in Chapter 5.) Each remote control connection item is actually a shortcut to a file containing all the information that pcAnywhere needs to establish a remote control connection to the host computer, such as the type of modem to use and the phone number to dial.

✔ Nettie double-clicks the icon for the remote control connection item labeled Connect to Server. A status box appears, as shown in Figure 1-3, telling Nettie that pcAnywhere is connecting.

✔ After the connection is successfully established, the desktop for the host computer at the office appears on the screen of Nettie's laptop. Her on-screen view is now the same as if she were sitting directly in front of the host computer.

Remote Control button

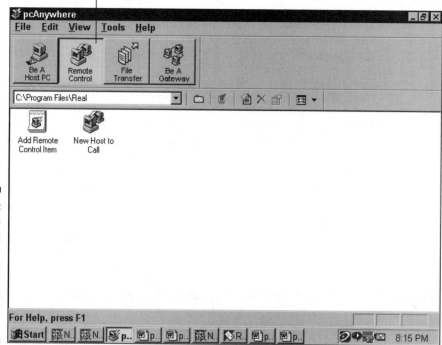

Figure 1-2:
Nettie
begins a
remote con-
trol session
by clicking
the Remote
Control
button.

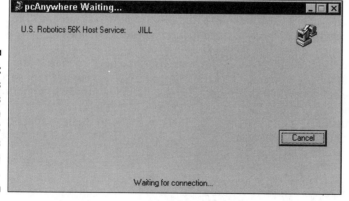

Figure 1-3:
This status
box appears
on the
remote PC
when it's
dialing the
host PC.

Because Nettie has control of the host computer, which in this case is a
server on the network, she can now access the managing partner's user
account and reconfigure the information so that he's no longer locked out.
She manages to do so and throw the laptop to her husband just as the doctor
yells "Push!"

What To Do After You Connect

After Nettie dialed the host on her laptop and established a connection, the host desktop appeared on her screen. She could access the same files and applications she could access if she were sitting in front of the host computer.

Nettie, during her remote communication session, elected to do the following two additional things on the host computer:

- ✔ She enabled an option on the remote PC that blanked out operations on the host PC's screen so that people passing by back at the law firm did not see that the managing partner had again forgotten his password. When the Blank Host Screen option is enabled, no one can see what's happening on the host computer during a remote control session.

- ✔ Nettie also exercised an option to lock the keyboard on the host so that someone walking by couldn't sit down at the keyboard and interfere with her important task. (I talk about these features in detail in Chapter 4.)

Transferring and Updating Files

A couple of other pcAnywhere features make Nettie's life as a network administrator much easier:

- ✔ The ability to transfer files between computers
- ✔ The ability to synchronize updates made to files on one computer, so that both computers have the most recent changes

Nettie and the lawyers at her firm use pcAnywhere each morning to update files that they've changed on their laptops. Nettie also uses these features to perform major file-transfer operations across the network, sometimes involving the law firm's branch offices in other cities. (In Chapter 8, I tell you how to transfer files and synchronize changes made to them so that all computers have the same versions.)

Postpartum pcAnywhere

Along with solving her manager's crisis of the moment and never losing access to her network, Nettie has just given birth to healthy twins — Jodi and Jeremy. She is happy, proud, and grateful to pcAnywhere for helping her fulfill these important roles in her life:

- ✔ **Telecommuter:** As a telecommuter, Nettie works at home and is able to establish a secure and reliable connection to the workplace. She can also establish connections from multiple or changing locations. (See Chapter 9 for more about setting connection items for changing locations.) pcAnywhere also allows Nettie to quickly transfer and synchronize files.

- ✔ **Network administrator:** As a network administrator, Nettie can use pcAnywhere to perform large-scale file transfer and synchronization operations. Nettie can also use pcAnywhere to provide convenient access to a server that is off-site. (In Chapter 14, I explain how to use scripts to automate synchronization and file-transfer processes so that you can even perform them at night, unattended.)

- ✔ **Help desk operator:** After her maternity leave, when Nettie is back at the office, she can enjoy the convenience of being able to troubleshoot and change the settings on computers (including a server) on a local or wide area network without ever leaving her desk.

pcAnywhere is not *just* a software program. For Nettie Workmeister, and many like her, remote computing has become a way of life.

That's why Nettie takes time from her busy schedule to regularly visit the Symantec Web site at www.symantec.com. At the Web site, she finds troubleshooting tips, articles to increase her knowledge about the program, updates, and product news. In fact, Nettie knows that if she's having a problem with pcAnywhere, it's likely that someone else has had it too. So the Web site is the first place she looks for a solution. (In Chapter 17, I provide more suggestions about what you'll find on the Symantec Web site.)

Nettie also regularly uses the pcAnywhere LiveUpdate feature. This utility, which I discuss in Chapter 16, allows Nettie to directly connect to Symantec's LiveUpdate server where she can select and download the latest software updates.

So read on. Throughout the rest of this book, I walk you through the details of using pcAnywhere. Whether you're a telecommuter, network administrator, help desk operator, or just someone who occasionally wants the convenience of accessing your office computer from home, I hope that you discover, as Nettie has, how pcAnywhere can free you from the confines of your office and add a new dimension of convenience to your life.

Chapter 2

Let's Hit the Road!

. . . .

In This Chapter

▶ Checking for system compatibility

▶ Installing pcAnywhere on a single PC

▶ Performing a network installation

▶ Wandering the pcAnywhere desktop

▶ Getting help: pcAnywhere problem solvers

. . . .

*E*very great software adventure begins with the installation! Before pcAnywhere can take *you* anywhere, you need to get it running. Installing it on a single computer is a breeze. But configuring it on an entire network can be tricky; it's one of those things best left to a network administrator (or someone with similar expertise).

You also need to get yourself up and running by familiarizing yourself with the pcAnywhere desktop — its menus, toolbars, and icons. This is not particularly difficult because pcAnywhere doesn't have a lot of different desktop elements. For the most part, pcAnywhere gives its icons, menu items, and wizards commonsense names that actually describe their functions.

If you do run into an installation glitch, pcAnywhere offers an array of Help options for both the casual telecommuter and the technically savvy network administrator. Some of these options are free for the viewing (or listening). Others can be downright pricey. In this chapter, I walk you through installing pcAnywhere and also help you to discover how to make the most of the self-help freebies.

pcAnywhere System Requirements

pcAnywhere requires a relatively modest 32 megabytes (MB) of hard drive space to install. The program consists of 221 files located in 6 folders. Other minimum hardware requirements for the latest version of the program are as follows:

    ✔ Microprocessor with a speed of 486 or higher

    ✔ 16MB RAM (20MB are recommended)

    ✔ VGA (or higher resolution) video adapter

    ✔ CD-ROM drive

    ✔ Microsoft Windows 95, 98, or NT operating system

Typical versus Custom Installation Options

pcAnywhere offers two installation options: Typical and Custom. Most users can opt for the Typical installation option, even if their computer is on a network. The Custom installation option lets you choose which pcAnywhere features you want to install and is especially useful for large networks. By using the Custom installation option, you can customize the pcAnywhere installation for networked environments in which you want to create centrally stored application files and preconfigured pcAnywhere settings. I discuss network installations later in this chapter, in the section "Custom Installation by a Network Administrator."

Performing a Typical Installation

The Typical installation option is the choice of most telecommuters who work in small offices, even if the office computer is connected to a network.

To perform a Typical installation of pcAnywhere, follow these steps:

1. **Launch Windows 95, 98, or NT on your computer.**

2. **Insert the pcAnywhere CD into the CD-ROM drive.**

   This is *all* you need to do if the Windows AutoPlay feature is enabled on your system. You see the initial installation screen, and you can skip to Step 6.

   If the installation screen does not appear soon after you insert the CD, however, it means that the AutoPlay feature is not enabled on your system. Proceed to the next step to begin the installation process manually.

3. **To start the installation manually, go to the Windows Start menu and choose <u>R</u>un.**

4. **In the Run dialog box, type** d:\setup.exe **in the Open text box (see Figure 2-1).**

   Replace *d* with the drive letter for your system if your CD-ROM drive isn't drive D. (If you don't know the letter, see how your CD-ROM drive is listed when you click the My Computer icon on your desktop.)

Figure 2-1:
Type the
setup
command
to begin the
installation
manually.

Letter for CD-ROM drive

5. **Click OK.**

   Now the installation process should proceed, with that reassuring little hum of the computer reading the pcAnywhere CD.

   The initial installation screen appears.

6. **Click the Install Current Software button (see Figure 2-2).**

   A screen similar to the initial screen appears, but this screen offers you additional installation buttons.

7. **Click the pcAnywhere 9.0 button.**

   The installation shield status bar appears, followed by a warning screen telling you to exit all other Windows programs that are running.

8. **Close any open programs and click Next.**

   You are now provided with the option of choosing either a Typical or Custom installation, as shown in Figure 2-3.

9. **Click the Typical installation button.**

10. **Type your licensing information (that is, your company name and other user identification information) on the screen that follows and click Next.**

11. **Click Yes to accept the software licensing terms.**

12. **On the next screen, click Next to accept the displayed program folder; click Browse if you want to install the program in a different folder.**

Click here to begin installation

Figure 2-2:
The first
screen
of the
installation
interface.

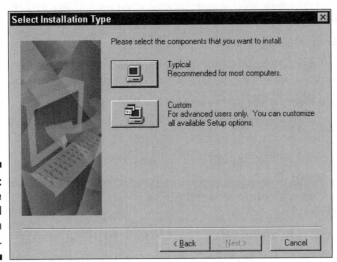

Figure 2-3:
Select the
Typical
installation
button.

13. Click Next to continue the installation and create subfolders.

These subfolders are described in the "Strange new subfolders on your system" sidebar later in this chapter.

The Symantec Support Solutions box appears, as shown in Figure 2-4, and explains the various pcAnywhere technical support options available to you. These options are discussed in the section "Whole Lotta Help," later in this chapter.

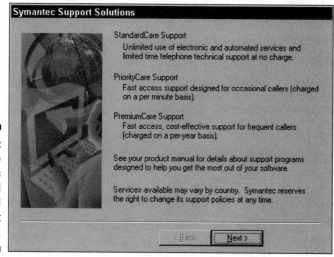

Figure 2-4:
pcAnywhere
offers
several
technical
support
options.

14. Review the next three screens of information that tell you how to contact Symantec via Internet or telephone; click Next to progress through each of the three screens.

The registration screen appears, as shown in Figure 2-5.

15. Type the required information on the next few screens or click Skip to bypass registering for now.

After you have registered, the Additional Options dialog box appears, as shown in Figure 2-6.

If you skip the registration process now, remember to go back and do it later. Registered pcAnywhere users receive important product updates and discounts on future software purchases. To register after installation, go to the Help menu and choose About pcAnywhere to open a dialog box with a Register Now button.

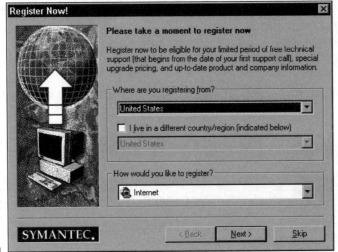

Figure 2-5:
Register
your soft-
ware by
using this
screen.

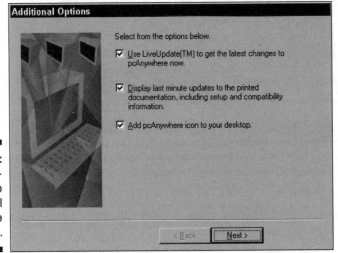

Figure 2-6:
You'll proba-
bly want to
select all
these
options.

16. **In the Additional Options dialog box, it's a good idea to click to put a check mark in the boxes next to *all* the following options:**

   • **Use LiveUpdate to get the latest changes to pcAnywhere now:** This option connects you automatically to the Symantec LiveUpdate server and enables you to select the options you want at the conclusion of the installation. (I discuss the LiveUpdate feature in Chapters 16 and 17.)

- **Display last-minute updates to the printed documentation, including setup and compatibility information:** This option enables you to print supplements to your user manual.

- **Add pcAnywhere icon to your desktop:** This option places a pcAnywhere icon right on your Windows desktop.

17. **Click Next**

 The Readme.txt dialog box pops up on your screen.

18. **After reading the information in the Readme.txt dialog box, close the box by clicking the X in the upper-right corner.**

19. **If you enabled LiveUpdate in Step 15, the LiveUpdate dialog box appears automatically (see Figure 2-7). If you did not enable this option, the Setup Complete dialog box appears and you can skip to Step 21.**

Figure 2-7: The LiveUpdate dialog box helps you connect to the Symantec LiveUpdate server.

From the drop-down box at the bottom of the screen, choose how you want to connect to the LiveUpdate server. You can connect to it using either your modem or the Internet.

As you can see in Figure 2-7, the drop-down box offers an option to have pcAnywhere find your connection device automatically. This option is not recommended for initial setup, but it can be useful for troubleshooting. (I talk more about this subject in Chapter 16.)

Strange new subfolders on your system

During installation, pcAnywhere files are copied into the folder you've specified, and the following subfolders are created:

✔ **Data:** This folder contains connection item information and any scripts you've created.

✔ **Download:** This folder contains files downloaded from an online service during installation.

✔ **Migration:** You need the files in this folder if you plan to migrate to Windows 2000.

20. **Click Next.**

    The latest pcAnywhere software updates begin downloading to your computer, directly from the Symantec LiveUpdate server. When the LiveUpdate downloading is complete, the Setup Complete dialog box appears telling you that you have successfully completed the installation process.

21. **Click to select the Yes, I Want to Restart My Computer Now check box, and then click Finish.**

Custom Installation by a Network Administrator

Installing pcAnywhere on a network can be a complicated process because networks tend to be as different as families. Some network families welcome the addition of a new software product, each member computer embracing it without conflict. Other network families require a little therapy (in the form of some technical tweaking).

You probably shouldn't attempt a network installation of pcAnywhere if you don't have some previous network administration experience. You just never know what conflicts you may encounter. In recognition of the many idiosyncrasies and software conflicts a network administrator has to deal with, Symantec has ever so thoughtfully provided a special Administrator Guide on the pcAnywhere CD-ROM. I strongly recommend that you print this guide and study it carefully before you attempt a network installation. You can also refer to it for troubleshooting help after your installation.

First . . . the right version

Don't attempt to do a Custom installation on a network (as discussed in the next section) unless you have the network version of the software. It won't work.

If you're installing pcAnywhere on ten or more workstations, you'll want to purchase the site license package. The site license enables you to create a special installation file that individual users can access on the network and use to install pcAnywhere on their own workstations.

The site license also offers several other benefits worth considering, including the following:

- **pcAconfig Utility:** Enables you to customize the installation process and distribute the customized installation across the network so that workstations will have the settings, options, and permissions that you want them to have.

- **LiveUpdate Administrator:** Enables the network administrator to centrally manage and select update options for workstations on the network.

- **Norton System Center v3.1:** Streamlines the process of distributing and updating other Symantec software products (such as its popular antivirus software) across the network.

Abracadabra! Administration magic!

After you've obtained the special site license version of the software required for networks of ten or more computers, you can amaze your friends and colleagues by

- Installing pcAnywhere on a network drive using a shared file that all users on the network can access and use to install and run the program on their own PCs

- Preconfiguring the pcAnywhere installation and application options that you want everyone on the network to use

- Adding user licenses to pcAnywhere (after you pay for them, of course)

Although the installation wizard refers to a specialized network installation as a Custom Installation, the Administrator's Guide refers to it as an Advanced Installation.

Installing pcAnywhere on a network

Gone are the days when the poor slave of a network administrator moved from office to office, performing the necessary software installations on each computer. In these modern times, the network administrator can create a pcAnywhere *workstation installation directory* on a shared network drive that everyone can get to, as discussed in the "Drive me crazy" sidebar that follows. Workstation users can then install pcAnywhere on their own machines by accessing the workstation installation directory setup file on the shared drive and following the prompt screens — just as they would if they were installing software on a stand-alone computer. It's all self-service now!

To install pcAnywhere on a network, follow these steps:

1. **Be sure that you have the network version of pcAnywhere.**

   You can install pcAnywhere on individual workstations on the network without purchasing the network version of the software, but if you are installing it on more than ten machines, the network version is usually more economical.

Drive me crazy

If you're installing pcAnywhere on a network workstation, it's helpful to understand a little about drives in general.

A *drive* is an electromechanical device used for viewing floppy disks, CD-ROMs, and tapes. Drives can be located on your local machine or on a remote machine elsewhere on the network. If a drive is located on another computer on the network, but you can access it from your computer, it's referred to as a *shared network drive*.

Drives are often divided into *partitions*. Partitions are each given a letter, so that they can be identified easily. The entire drive can be a single partition, or it can be divided into multiple partitions, each of which operates as a separate drive. For example, the C, D, and E drives can all reside on the same hard drive.

The process of assigning a letter to a drive, or referring to the drive by its letter, is called *mapping a drive.* On a network, an administrator can use drive mapping to reference remote drives and directories.

In the case of a shared pcAnywhere network directory, you're given access to a drive on a computer somewhere on the network. That drive is set up to be *shared,* which means that you and other users on the network all have access to it. The shared drive contains a pcAnywhere file that has the installation options that everyone on your network is supposed to be using. By mapping a drive to the shared installation file, you can install pcAnywhere on your computer without bugging your network administrator. You'll be sure to have the same version of pcAnywhere with the same updates that everyone else on the network is using.

2. **Insert the pcAnywhere CD-ROM into the computer's CD-ROM drive.**

3. **Choose Start⇨Run.**

   The Run dialog box opens.

4. **In the Open text box, type** d:\setup/a **(where *d* is the letter of the CD-ROM drive).**

5. **Click OK.**

   The Select Installation Type dialog box appears.

6. **Click the Custom Installation button.**

   The Select Components dialog box appears, as shown in Figure 2-8. Most likely, you will want to select all three of the options offered in this dialog box:

   - **pcAnywhere:** This option is always grayed and selected.

   - **Allow pcAnywhere to be Remotely Managed:** Select this option if you want to be able to make updates to the pcAnywhere installation file and have these changes take effect on all computers on the network on which pcAnywhere is installed.

   - **pcAnywhere Host Administrator:** This option installs a utility that lets the network administrator update, change, and manage the versions of pcAnywhere installed on computers across the network. (To use this feature, you must also select the Allow pcAnywhere to be Remotely Managed option.)

7. **After you have chosen the appropriate options, click Next.**

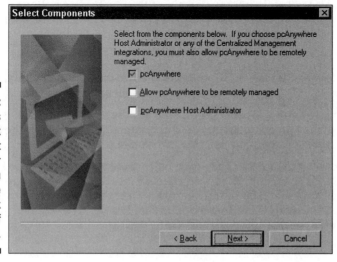

Figure 2-8:
This dialog box does not appear unless you have the network version of pcAnywhere.

8. **Type your licensing information (that is, your company name and other user identification information) on the screen that follows and click <u>N</u>ext.**

9. **Click <u>Y</u>es to accept the software licensing terms.**

10. **Create or select the network folder into which you want to install pcAnywhere. Then click <u>N</u>ext to copy the installation files into the folder you've created or selected.**

Use all capital letters or all lowercase when you name the network folder. If you use mixed case, the lowercase *pc* in pcAnywhere virtually ensures calls to the help desk complaining of `Invalid filename` error messages.

Be sure to make this file accessible to all users on the network. Obvious, yes. But easy to forget.

11. **Review the next three screens of information that tell you how to contact Symantec via Internet or telephone; click <u>N</u>ext to progress through each of the three screens.**

The Registration screen appears.

12. **Click <u>S</u>kip to bypass registering for now or type the required registration information on the next few screens.**

If you elect to skip now and register later, you can access the registration screen at any time from the Help menu.

After you register (or indicate that you want to do it later), the Additional Options dialog box appears.

13. **Select the LiveUpdate options that you want to enable and click <u>N</u>ext.**

If you need more information about the LiveUpdate options presented in this dialog box, refer back to Step 16 of the Typical installation, earlier in the chapter.

The Readme.txt dialog box pops up on your screen.

14. **After reading the information in the Readme.txt dialog box, close the box by clicking the X in the upper-right corner.**

15. **If you enabled LiveUpdate in Step 13, the LiveUpdate dialog box appears automatically. If you did not enable this option, the Setup Complete dialog box appears and you can skip to Step 17.**

From the drop-down box at the bottom of the screen, choose how you want to connect to the LiveUpdate server. You can connect to it using either your modem or the Internet. (The Symantec Web site suggests that you do *not* choose the option that lets pcAnywhere find your connection device automatically.)

16. **Click <u>N</u>ext.**

When the LiveUpdate downloading is complete, the Setup Complete dialog box appears telling you that you successfully completed the installation process.

17. **Click to select the Yes, I Want to Restart My Computer Now check box, and click Finish.**

The network installation creates two new subfolders on your system:

✔ **Data:** This subfolder contains all the connection item configuration information.

✔ **Setup:** This subfolder contains the setup.exe file that actually installs pcAnywhere on the individual workstations.

The First Time You Launch pcAnywhere

Symantec
pcAnywhere

The pcAnywhere installation process automatically places an icon on your Windows desktop. All you need to do to launch the program is double-click that icon.

The *very* first time you open pcAnywhere, you'll be treated to the pcAnywhere Smart Setup Wizard. To use the wizard, follow these steps:

1. **In the Smart Setup Wizard initial screen, select your modem type from the Modem drop-down list (see Figure 2-9).**

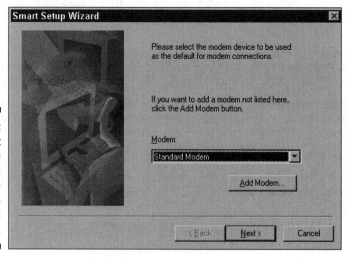

Figure 2-9:
The Smart
Setup
Wizard
appears the
first time
you launch
pcAnywhere.

If your modem is not listed in the drop-down list, click the Add Modem button and browse for your modem type. If you have an internal modem and you aren't sure what type, check the reference manual for your PC for this information. If your modem does not appear on the pcAnywhere browse list, select the Standard modem option from the drop-down list.

This is a rare situation, but if your modem type isn't listed, and when you try to make a connection you get an error message that says that pcAnywhere can't locate your modem, check the Symantec Web site for information about the compatibility of your modem type, including alternative software drivers that you can use. You may also need to contact the manufacturer for an updated driver that's compatible with pcAnywhere. In Chapter 15, I talk more about problems caused by incompatible modems — particularly a modem using Windows Internet Naming Service (WINS) Software.

 2. **Click Next.**

    A second Smart Setup Wizard screen appears.

 3. **Unless a network administrator instructs you otherwise, select TCP/IP from the drop-down list box in the center of the screen (see Figure 2-10).**

 4. **Click Next.**

    Another Smart Setup Wizard screen appears.

 5. **Select LPT1 from the drop-down menu, unless a network administrator instructs you otherwise.**

 6. **Click Next.**

    Another Smart Setup Wizard dialog box appears, as shown in Figure 2-11. This dialog box advises you to password protect pcAnywhere from unauthorized access.

 7. **Enter your login name (any name you want to use to identify yourself) in the Login Name text box and your password in the Password text box. Type your password again in the Confirm Password text box.**

    The Specify a Login Name and Password check box is selected by default. You can de-select it if you don't want to password protect pcAnywhere from unauthorized access.

 8. **Click Next.**

    A screen appears telling you that you've successfully completed the Smart Setup Wizard.

 9. **Click Finish to exit the wizard.**

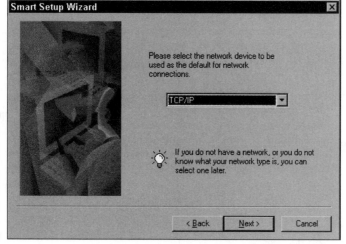

Figure 2-10:
TCP/IP is
the most
commonly
used
network
protocol.

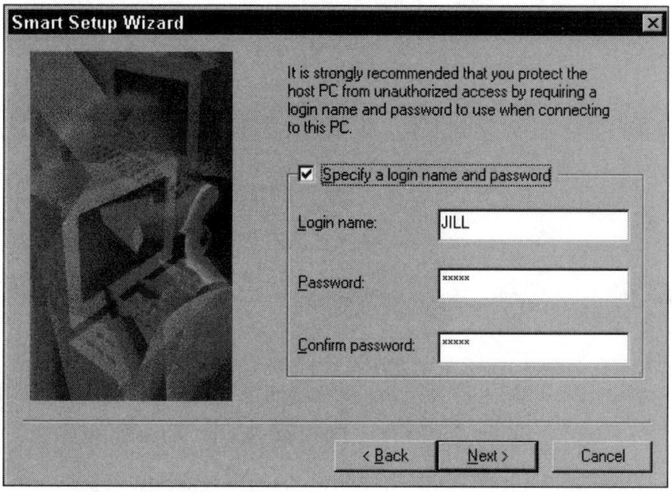

Figure 2-11:
Type a login
name and
password
on this
screen.

Touring the pcAnywhere Desktop

Now that you have pcAnywhere installed, it's time to do some exploring. The pcAnywhere user interface is deceptively austere. The standard menu bar, which you can see just under the pcAnywhere title bar in Figure 2-12, contains just five choices. The Action bar, located directly beneath the menu bar, consists of a mere four buttons. And, finally, across the bottom of the screen, you can see the Status bar.

Menu bar┐   Action bar

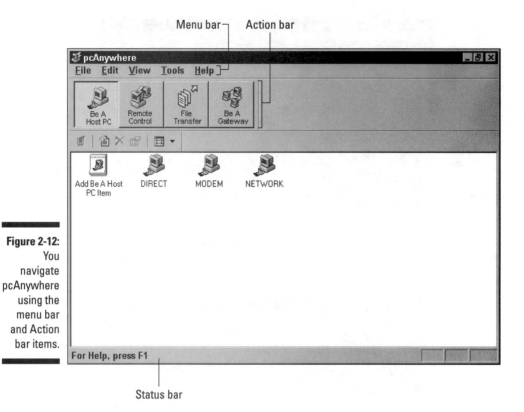

Figure 2-12:
You
navigate
pcAnywhere
using the
menu bar
and Action
bar items.

Status bar

Ordering off the menu

The pcAnywhere menu bar is similar to menu bars found in other Windows-based programs. There are, however, a few caveats worth mentioning.

You use the File menu to manage files: create, delete, and rename, as well as to configure the properties of files. In pcAnywhere, the type of files you work with are called *connection items*. These files contain connection information. For example, a separate file is generally maintained for each hardware device you use to connect to another computer. Each connection item is represented on the desktop by a separate icon and name, and each connection item contains information about the device being used to make the connection, along with the commands or options used during the communication session.

The View menu is definitely worth taking a look at before you begin working with pcAnywhere. You can use it to arrange your desktop in a way that fits your personal preferences.

The View menu, shown in Figure 2-13, is divided into the following five sections:

- **Display section:** The top portion of the menu enables you to choose which bars you want displayed. Make sure that a check mark is placed next to all three of the options in this first section so that the Action bar, Status bar, and Toolbar all appear on your screen.

- **Action button commands section:** The second section of the menu contains commands that correspond to those on the Action bar, which is discussed in the next section, "About the Action bar."

- **Icon information section:** The third section of the menu lets you control the size of the icons appearing on your pcAnywhere desktop. Select the Details option to display additional information on-screen, such as the connection port or device and the caller/user folder (see Figure 2-14).

- **Arrange Icons:** This command lets you arrange the icons that appear on your screen by name, connection, network host, or phone number.

- **Refresh:** This command reloads (or refreshes) the current screen. If you've moved the icons on your desktop around as you've worked, you can choose this command to restore the icons to their original positions.

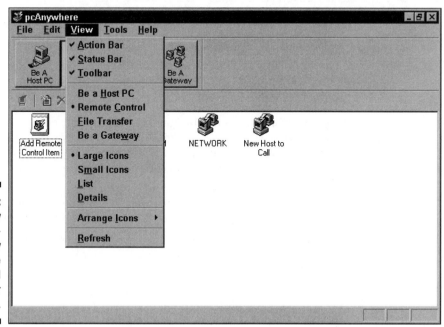

Figure 2-13: The View menu determines how things are displayed on your desktop.

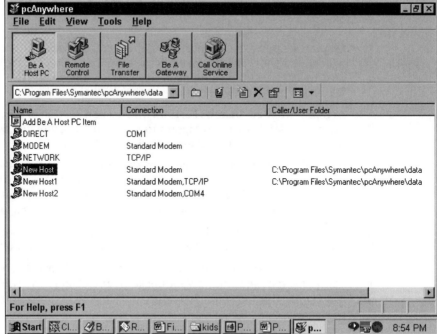

About the Action bar

The standard pcAnywhere Action bar, located just below the menu bar, boasts four *action buttons*. Take a look at what each button does:

- ✔ **Be A Host PC:** You use this button to establish your computer as a pcAnywhere *host*. A host is a computer accessed by one or more other computers, called *remote users*. (I discuss host configuration in detail in Chapter 4 and how to configure remote users in Chapter 5.)

- ✔ **Remote Control:** You use this button to bring up a list of computers that you can actually control from your computer. When you click the button, an icon appears for each computer that you can control remotely.

- ✔ **File Transfer:** You use this button when you want to connect to any properly configured host computer and transfer files from it to the computer at which you are sitting.

- ✔ **Be A Gateway:** You use this button when you want to allow a remote user to dial up your computer and use your computer's modem to connect to the rest of the local area network (LAN). (See Chapter 12 to find out more about gateways.)

They're not icons — they're items

pcAnywhere uses the terms *icon* and *item* interchangeably, and so does this book. The editors let me get away with this because pcAnywhere icons always, *always* represent a connection item file. In pcAnywhere land, icons are never, ever, ever, used for any other purpose. So if you see a pcAnywhere icon, you know that a connection item file is lurking underneath.

Whole Lotta Help

pcAnywhere offers an on-screen Help database, a bunch of electronic manuals on your installation disc, a nifty Web site with automated support, and some potentially pricey (but potentially worthwhile) paid technical support. This section discusses the options for getting an answer in the order that I recommend that you pursue them.

Current prices for technical support (at the time this book went to press) are $29.95 per incident or $2.95 a minute, depending on which option you choose. Just think, the price of this book could be less than one call to technical support!

First, try the Help menu

You'll find approximately 100 pages of useful source material under the Help database, including an extensive glossary. Access this information by opening the Help menu from the pcAnywhere desktop. You can then search the Help database using three different methods:

- ✔ **Table of contents search (book icon):** Enables you to view topics about pcAnywhere, organized in a table of contents.

- ✔ **Key word index (key icon):** Enables you to peruse an alphabetical index of key words.

- ✔ **Find (binocular icon):** Enables you to perform a full-text search for words contained in the Help files. The first time you use the Find feature, you are presented with the Find Setup Wizard, as shown in Figure 2-15. The Find Setup Wizard creates a database of all the key words in your Help files. You can maximize or minimize the search capabilities depending on the space you have available on your system. If you select the Customize option, you can specify whether you want to include the standard database, a special database for administrators, or both. The default is both.

Figure 2-15:
The Find
Setup
Wizard
creates a
database of
all words
in your
Help files.

pcAnywhere also provides you with a convenient Glossary feature. To use the pcAnywhere Glossary, follow these steps:

1. **From the pcAnywhere desktop, select Help from the main menu.**

   The pcAnywhere Help window opens.

2. **From the Help menu, click the book icon (for a table of contents search).**

3. **Scroll to the end of the list of topics, as shown in Figure 2-16.**

4. **Double-click the last topic, which is labeled Reference.**

5. **Click the pcAnywhere Glossary icon.**

   A glossary index appears on the right side of the screen.

6. **Under the Glossary Definitions heading, click the first letter of the term you want to look up.**

7. **Find your term on the list of words beginning with that letter, and click it to display a definition.**

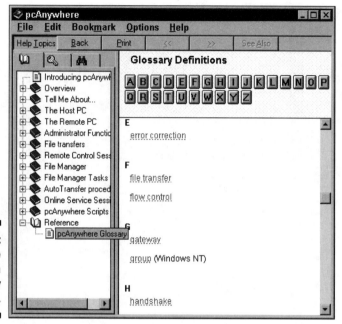

Figure 2-16:
pcAnywhere
provides a
glossary
feature.

Manuals on the CD-ROM

pcAnywhere includes the following three great resource manuals on the CD-ROM installation disc:

- ✔ **Administrator Guide:** Contains valuable information for network administrators, including how to install pcAnywhere on the network and how to configure user and security options.

- ✔ **Creating Scripts Guide:** Provides an in-depth explanation and index of the language used to create and edit *script* files, which are files containing specialized commands and routines. (See Chapter 14 to learn about scripts.)

- ✔ **Technical White Papers:** A series of technical articles on setup, configuration, and advanced features and services of pcAnywhere.

To access these manuals, place your CD-ROM in the CD-ROM drive and click the View Manuals option, as shown in Figure 2-17.

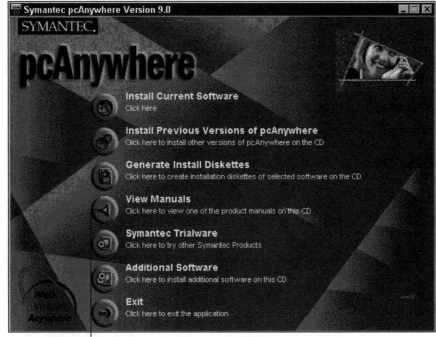

Figure 2-17:
The
pcAnywhere
installation
CD contains
resource
manuals.

Click here to view manuals

If the installation screen doesn't appear right away, the AutoPlay feature may not be enabled on your system. To start the installation manually, choose Start⇨Run. In the Run dialog box, type **d:\setup.exe**. (Replace *d* with the proper drive letter if your CD-ROM drive uses a different letter. If you don't know the letter, see how your CD-ROM drive is listed under My Computer.)

Answers on the Web

Symantec boasts that its Web site has been deemed one of the ten best support sites on the Net. This is not surprising. The Web site includes comprehensive answers to frequently asked questions and enough articles on esoteric topics — such as encryption — to make network nerds drool. You'll also find useful information about updates and troubleshooting tips. The address for the Symantec site is www.symantec.com/techsupp/pca.

Symantec does not provide a direct link to pcAnywhere Version 9.0 support pages. The address provided above is as close as it gets!

Last resort — pay for the answer

Not surprisingly, paid technical support is last on my list. True — you do get 90 days free technical support from the date of your first pcAnywhere call. But you don't want the meter to start running on that 90-day period any sooner than you have to! But when all else fails, you can reach pcAnywhere technical support at 541-465-8565.

The 90-day period begins with the date of your first call, so maximize the benefit by waiting as long as possible to make that first call.

Chapter 3

The Nuts and Bolts of Remote Access

*R*emote access is one of those power phrases, kind of like *infrastructure* or *tax shelter*. Remote access is the means by which you can gain access to an internal network while you're on the move. If you know how to get remote access, you not only can turn on your own computer and talk to it, you can talk to everyone else's — at least theoretically. You're the guy (or gal) who knows what stuff to plug into an unassuming stand-alone computer and make it talk to the world. You become someone who possesses expertise that leaves your coworkers awestruck.

Remote access is an intriguing concept, and the process of making a connection is easy to master. All it takes is the right equipment: modems, cables, and phone lines. Each of these pieces of hardware is known as a *connection device*. In this chapter, I discuss the three different ways computers can talk to each other and how to configure your PC to use the connection device unique to each method.

Connecting Three Ways

You can use any one of the following connection devices to convert a reclusive stand-alone PC to a gregarious machine capable of communicating with other computers:

> ✔ **Modem:** Enables you to dial up other computer buddies over telephone lines or to gain access to the World Wide Web.
>
> ✔ **Cable:** Enables you to make a direct, physical connection to another computer (such as a laptop).
>
> ✔ **Network adapter card:** Enables you to talk to other computers within a network. A network adapter card is actually a circuit board in a PC that looks like a card with wires on it. The PC communicates with other computers on the network through a cable, which attaches to the network adapter card.

Before you can make a connection to another computer, you must tell pcAnywhere which of these three connection devices you want to use.

The rest of this chapter tells you what you need to know to configure a connection device that your computer can use for remote access.

Meeting Your Modem

Computers communicate through modems when they're too far apart to be joined by a standard computer cable. A *modem* is a piece of equipment that makes it possible for a computer to communicate over a telephone line.

How your modem works

If you want your computer to communicate with another computer, you cannot simply ask your computer to dial the phone. The glitch here is that computers communicate by emitting digital electronic signals, whereas telephone lines can transmit only analog (sound) signals.

A modem converts a computer's digital signals into analog pulses that are transmitted over phone lines. A computer's processes of converting digital signals to analog and back again are called *mo*dulation and *dem*odulation; hence, the acronym *modem*.

A modem can be an external unit that sits on your desktop or an internal unit installed inside your machine. The speed at which a modem communicates is measured in bits per second. For example, a 56-kilobit modem transmits data at 56 kilobits per second (Kbps). (A kilobit is equivalent to 1,024 bits.)

Modem interfaces

pcAnywhere accepts several types of modems. Modems use a common set of design conventions called an *interface*, which governs how a hardware device connects to and runs with your computer.

Windows uses the Telephony Applications Programming Interface (TAPI). TAPI automatically detects and configures communication hardware that you hook up to your PC. TAPI is a great time-saving feature that also ensures the accuracy of your modem installation settings by eliminating a lot of the manual configuration that's subject to human error. TAPI is available on Windows 95 and later versions and on Windows NT 4.0. Modems with TAPI are installed in most computers sold these days.

If you're using an ISDN (Integrated Services Digital Network) line (as dis-cussed in the following sidebar "Faster! Faster! ISDN that data now!"), you use an ISDN adapter. An ISDN adapter operates like a modem, but it's designed to work over high-speed ISDN lines that can transmit at speeds of 64 Kbps or 128 Kbps, as opposed to standard telephone lines that transmit at 53 Kbps to 54 Kbps. The telephone company must install an ISDN line at both the send-ing and receiving sites.

If you routinely transfer large files, such as files containing graphics or accounting data over your phone lines, it may be worth your while to con-sider installing a high-speed ISDN line. Check out the sidebar, "Faster! Faster! ISDN that data now!" to find out more about high-speed lines.

Configuring a modem connection

pcAnywhere automatically adds the modem shown in your Windows 95, 98, or NT 4.0 Control Panel. To see what modem you have, consult the documen-tation that came with your computer or follow these steps:

1. **Click the Start button and choose Settings⇨Control Panel.**

2. **Double-click the Modems icon in the Control Panel window.**

   The Modems Properties dialog box appears. If there is more than one tab in the dialog box, click the General tab. The modems configured on your computer are listed, as shown in Figure 3-1. (There may be several.)

3. **Make a note of the modem(s) installed in your computer.**

   The computer shown in Figure 3-1 is set up to use two different modems — a Standard modem or a U.S. Robotics modem.

4. **Click OK or Close (depending on your operating system) to exit the Modems Properties dialog box.**

5. **Click the Close box (X) in the upper-right corner to close the Control Panel window.**

Faster! Faster! ISDN that data now!

Alas, even the most expensive, sophisticated modem can transmit data only as fast as the telephone lines allow. Standard telephone lines transmit data at a rate of 53 to 54 Kbps. Most modems are capable of transmitting data at a rate of 56 Kbps.

Often, a residential telephone line cannot achieve the maximum modem speed. The quality of the line, other traffic, or problems with the consistency and reliability of the connection on that particular day can compromise data transmission rates. (I talk more about telephone line problems in Chapter 10.) And even if the line is transmitting data at the 56-Kbps rate, users who download massive files containing such things as accounting data, large spreadsheets, and graphics will find the connection maddeningly slow.

The answer? Consider installing ISDN service that offers voice, video, and data on lines that run at 64 Kbps. This service is now widely available in the United States and other countries.

One of the original goals of the ISDN technology developers was to link homes and businesses over existing copper telephone lines that currently transmit analog signals. The objective now is to convert those old analog lines to speedy new digital ones. This technology is now being implemented by commercial developers worldwide.

ISDN is a "dial-up" connection, which means that it's cheaper than private leased lines such as T1 service. It is *not* designed to provide you with a 24-hour-a-day uninterrupted connection, as you would have with a costly private leased line.

If you subscribe to the service through your local carrier, you'll be asked to specify whether you want Basic Rate or Primary Rate ISDN. Basic Rate ISDN is capable of transmitting data at a total rate of 128 Kbps by using a process called *channel bonding*, which combines two or more 64-Kbps lines. This speed is sufficient for most small businesses and telecommuters. Primary Rate ISDN provides extremely high (and costly) data transmission by bonding six channels at a time. It can be used for purposes such as high-quality video conferencing at transmission rates of 384 Kbps.

In order to connect your personal computer, you need an ISDN terminal adapter. The terminal adapter is referred to by pcAnywhere as a modem. But, technically, it's not a modem. The ISDN adapter provides a digital-to-digital connection, not a conversion to analog tones.

ISDN lines cost about $120 to install and $30 a month to subscribe to Basic Rate ISDN service. You also have to pay usage charges, which vary, depending on the time of day and whether the line is for a home or business — the usage charges for a business are higher. You can expect your charges to range anywhere from $80 to $800 a month, depending on the transmission rate and whether the line is for home or business. The ISDN "modems" (which are really adapters) cost between $200 and $400.

Figure 3-1:
Open the
Windows
Control
Panel to
figure out
what type of
modem is
installed in
your com-
puter.

To configure pcAnywhere connection information for your installed modem, follow these steps:

1. **Open pcAnywhere by double-clicking the icon on your desktop.**

2. **Click either the Be A Host PC button or the Remote Control button on the Action bar (depending on whether you're configuring a modem on a computer that is to be used as a host or as a remote).**

3. **Choose File⇨New.**

    Either the New Host Properties dialog box (if you clicked the Be A Host PC button) or the New Host to Call Properties dialog box (if you clicked the Remote Control button) appears, as shown in Figure 3-2.

4. **Click the Connection Info tab if it isn't already open.**

5. **From the Device List, click to select the type of modem installed on your computer.**

6. **Click the Details button.**

    The Modem Properties dialog box appears, as shown in Figure 3-3.

7. **Click the General tab if it isn't already open.**

8. **Click the arrow in the Maximum Speed box and choose a maximum speed for your modem from the drop-down list.**

    The drop-down list offers you a choice of several speeds ranging from 110,000 to 115,200 bps.

Most newer modems installed in computers today can handle speeds of 56 Kbps and higher. However, phone lines achieve a maximum rate of 53 to 54 Kbps. Symantec recommends that you set your modem speed at 38,400 bps to avoid the lost connections or corrupted data that can result from a modem speed that is set higher than telephone lines allow. (A kilobit is equivalent to 1,024 bits.)

9. **Click OK to exit the Modem Properties dialog box; then click OK again to exit the New Host Properties dialog box.**

Modems are *backward compatible*. This means that if a fast modem is communicating with a slow modem, the fast modem slows down its transmission of data to accommodate the slower modem's transmission capabilities.

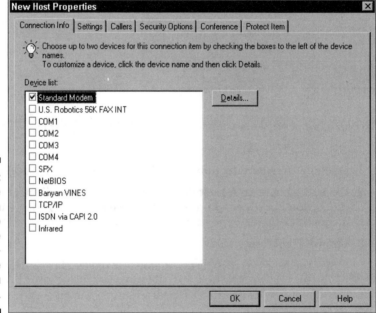

Figure 3-2:
Use the Connection Info tab to configure the connection device that you want to use.

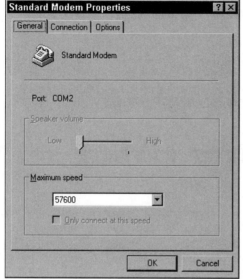

Figure 3-3:
Set your
modem
speed by
using the
Modem
Properties
dialog box
depicted
here.

Connecting Neighboring Computers

If your computers are close together, connecting them directly by using a
cable may be more convenient than a modem. The following sections tell you
more about cables and when you might want to use them.

Hey, laptop lovers!

If you want to use pcAnywhere to coordinate the files on your laptop and
desktop PC, connecting the computers with a cable certainly makes more
sense than dialing up. Plugging your laptop into your home or work computer by using a cable enables you to do the following:

- Browse folders on both your laptop and desktop PC from either
  computer.
- Select folders for transfer files from one computer to the other.
- Synchronize or clone folders so that the changes you made to your sales
  presentation on your laptop during your son's soccer game show up in
  the version of the presentation on your office computer.

What are cables made of?

A cable is a set of wires enclosed in a protective tube. The wires are organized to correspond to 9- or 25-pin adapters located at each end of the cable. These adapters plug into *ports*. Ports are holes in the back of a computer that enable you to plug in peripheral devices, such as printers and modems. (I discuss ports in more detail shortly.)

How does data move through those skinny things?

Cables transfer data in two ways: *serial* and *parallel* transfer. In general, a parallel data transfer is faster than serial data transfer.

Modems and a few types of printers use serial data transfer. Serial data transfer involves transferring data between computers, one bit at a time. Transfer speeds of 110,000 to 115,000 bits per second (bps) are possible through a PC serial port.

Parallel data transfer moves eight or more bits of data, all at once, and requires at least eight wires. Transfer speeds of 12,000 to 92,000 bps (or even faster) are possible. Many printers use parallel data transfer, and pcAnywhere includes a cable for parallel data transfer.

 A cable that directly connects two computers is called a *null modem* cable. The makers of pcAnywhere thoughtfully included with your software a free cable that you can use as a null modem cable. This cable is a special type of parallel cable designed for data transfer between two computers.

This computer is full of holes!

As I mentioned earlier, those little metal holes on the back of your computer are called *ports*. Ports are where you plug in peripheral devices such as printers and modems. A printer uses an LPT port, whereas a modem uses a COM port. Computers can connect to each other directly by using either an LPT or a COM port, depending on whether they're transferring data serially or by a parallel connection.

Parallel connections require LPT ports. LPT is a sloppy acronym for *line printer*. Most computers have three of these ports, aptly named LPT1, LPT2, and LPT3.

Your computer uses COM (originally an abbreviation for *communication*) ports to make serial connections: either between two computers using a null modem cable, or through a modem to a network and on to the rest of the world. Most computers have about four COM ports, labeled COM1 through COM4. The internal modem on your computer usually is connected to COM2.

Configuring a cable connection

A parallel connection between two computers is a lot faster than serial data transfer. You want to use a parallel connection whenever you have the opportunity. Unfortunately, not all computers and operating systems support parallel data transfer. For example, Windows NT does not support parallel data transfer between two computers using a null modem cable.

Checking for available ports

You can easily identify the communications ports on your computer that are available to connect with another computer. Your internal modem probably uses COM1 or COM2. Your printer probably uses LPT1 or LPT2. You can check to see which other ports are available.

If you're using Windows 95 or 98 on your computer, follow these steps to identify the available COM and LPT ports:

1. **Choose Start⇨Settings⇨Control Panel.**

2. **Double-click the System icon.**

   The System Properties dialog box appears.

3. **Click the Device Manager tab and scroll to the Ports icon.**

4. **Click the Ports icon to see the list of ports currently in use.**

   What appears on your screen depends on how your system is set up. For example, after you click the Ports icon, you may (or may not) see subsequent options for different types of ports, such as communication ports, printer ports, and maybe even something labeled *generic* ports. You want to select the communication ports option to display a list of COM ports and the attached devices (such as your modem). If a COM port, for example COM1, is already in use, it's listed with a device next to it. The unlisted ports should be available.

5. **Make a note of the COM ports currently in use.**

6. **Click the Cancel button to exit the System Properties dialog box; then click the Close box (X) to exit the Control Panel window.**

If you're using Windows NT on your computer, you don't need to know how to find the available LPT ports because NT doesn't support data transfer using these ports (parallel data transfer).

For a computer running Windows NT, follow these steps to identify the available COM ports:

1. **Choose Start⇨Settings⇨Control Panel.**

2. **To identify the available COM ports, double-click the Ports icon.**

   The Ports dialog box appears, and the ports currently in use are listed. Any port not listed should be available.

3. **Make a note of the COM ports currently in use.**

4. **Click the Cancel button to exit the Ports dialog box; then click the Close (X) box on the Control Panel window.**

Using LPT1 through LPT4 parallel connections

A parallel connection between two computers is preferable to a serial connection because parallel data transmission is faster. Unfortunately, Windows NT doesn't support parallel connections. So if you're using NT, skip to the next section to find out how to configure a COM port.

Check out the pcAnywhere Administrator Guide on your pcAnywhere installation CD for more help configuring Windows NT connections. (In Chapter 2, I tell you how to access this manual on the CD.)

To select a parallel data connection for the LPT ports on two Windows 95 and/or 98 computers, follow these steps:

1. **From the main pcAnywhere screen, choose File⇨New.**

2. **Scroll to the LPT port that you want to use for the direct cable connection and select it.**

3. **Click OK.**

Using COM1 through COM4 serial connections

Ports COM1 through COM4 are designed for direct serial connections that use a null modem cable. To select a COM port for a direct computer connection, follow these steps:

1. **From the main pcAnywhere screen, choose File⇨New.**

2. **Scroll to the COM port that you want to use for the direct cable connection and select it.**

   You must use the same COM port setting on both computers.

3. **Click the Details button.**

   A COM port dialog box appears, as shown in Figure 3-4.

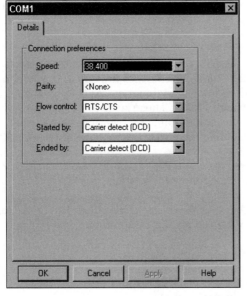

Figure 3-4:
The Details
tab shows
connection
preference
information
that you
need to
know to
complete
the configu-
ration.

4. **Click the arrow in the Speed box; from the drop-down list, choose a transmission speed for communicating with another computer.**

   Most machines can handle parallel data transmission speeds of 38,400 and higher. Select this speed to start, but decrease it if you're experiencing lost connections or garbled data.

5. **Make a note of the Parity (error-checking) setting.**

   The option selected from this drop-down list must match the information in the corresponding drop-down list of the computer with which you are communicating. Transmission speed is faster when no error-checking method is used.

6. **Make a note of the protocol listed in the Flow Control drop-down list.**

   The Parity option must be the same on the two computers you're connecting. The RTS/CTS protocol is most commonly used.

7. **Click OK to exit the COM dialog box, and click OK again to close the Properties dialog box.**

Connecting over a Network

On a network, workstation computers connect to a server computer and access its files and hardware. A *server* is a computer that shares its files or hardware devices with other computers on the network. A *workstation* is any computer that is not a server.

pcAnywhere enables you to use any computer on a network to control another computer, as opposed to just accessing files or a hardware device, such as a printer.

pcAnywhere uses the same network hardware devices that workstations use to access the server. These hardware devices are able to transfer and interpret data on the network as long as each computer is following certain rules and standards for data transmission. These rules are called *protocols*. Configuring your computer to communicate over a network using pcAnywhere involves selecting the correct protocol and tweaking it a bit.

For example, to configure a computer to communicate on a network that uses the common TCP/IP protocol, follow these steps:

1. **From the main pcAnywhere screen, click either the Be A Host PC or the Remote Control button on the Action bar.**

2. **Choose File⇨New.**

   Either the New Host Properties dialog box (if you clicked the Be A Host PC button) or the New Host to Call Properties dialog box (if you clicked the Remote Control button) appears.

3. **Select the network protocol your network uses to communicate (see Figure 3-5).**

   You must consult your network administrator to determine the network protocol.

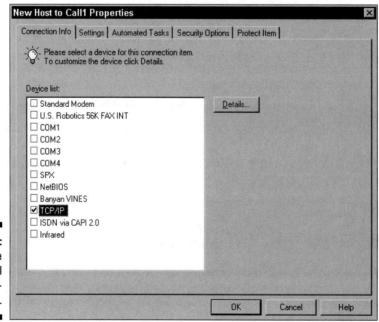

Figure 3-5:
Select the protocol your network uses.

4. **If you clicked the Be a Host PC button in Step 1, you can now skip to Step 6. If you clicked the Remote Control button, click the _D_etails button to display a dialog box for the protocol.**

5. **Click the Dial-Up Networking tab if that page isn't already open.**

6. **Choose the _C_onnect to a pcAnywhere Host Using a Local Area Network option (see Figure 3-6).**

   All the other options, except the Connect to a pcAnywhere Host Using Dial-Up Networking are grayed out because you don't need to specify this information if you're connecting to a PC on a network.

7. **Click OK to save this setting and exit the TCP/IP dialog box; then click OK again to exit the Properties dialog box.**

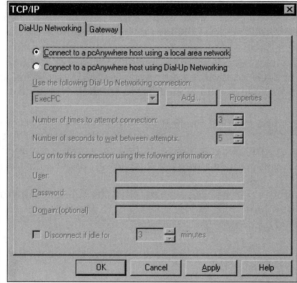

Figure 3-6:
The Dial-Up
Networking
page for the
chosen
protocol —
in this case,
TCP/IP.

Dial-Up Networking Connections

pcAnywhere enables you to access your network from a remote location. There are two ways to get access: *remote networking* and *remote control*. (I discuss these features in depth in Chapter 5, but it's helpful to have some introduction here so that you can take a quick look at how their devices are configured.

Configuring a remote networking device

Remote networking enables you to call from your home PC or your laptop from any remote location and log on to your office network using a modem and a telephone line. The remote PC works as if it's cable-connected to the network, giving you access to any file or application that you have permission to use.

All operations are performed on the PC connected to the network using commands generated on the computer that's off the network. This can be rather slow. Everything takes longer because each command has to travel over phone lines to be executed on the network.

pcAnywhere often uses a *remote control* connection rather than a remote networking connection. Instead of connecting to the network and acting like a PC on the network — as is the case with remote networking — remote control enables a remote PC to actually take control of a computer that is physically part of the network. With remote control, fewer commands have to travel across the telephone lines. Remote control is faster and more efficient. (The differences between remote control and remote networking are discussed later in this chapter and in even more detail in Chapter 5.)

To establish a remote networking connection, you must first provide pcAnywhere with information about the dial-up networking hardware device that you're going to use. To establish a dial-up networking connection using pcAnywhere and a specific hardware device, follow these steps:

1. **From the main pcAnywhere screen, click the Remote Control button on the Action bar.**

2. **Choose File⇨New.**

   The New Host to Call Properties dialog box appears, with the Connection Info page on top.

3. **Select the Network protocol that you want to use from the Connection Info page.**

4. **Click the Details button.**

   A dialog box for the protocol appears.

5. **Select the Connect to a pcAnywhere Host Using Dial-Up Networking option (see Figure 3-7).**

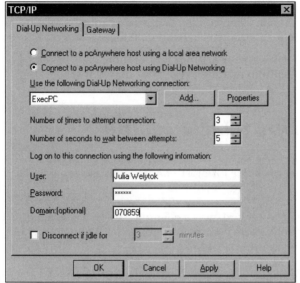

Figure 3-7:
To configure
a remote
networking
connection.

6. **From the Use the Following Dial-Up Networking Connection drop-down box, select the name of your Internet Service Provider (ISP).**

   Your current ISP appears by default. If you have more than one ISP, select the one that you want to use for the connection.

7. **(Optional) pcAnywhere, by default, attempts to connect three times, and waits five seconds between connection attempts. To change this default number, enter a number in the Number of Times to Attempt Connection and the Number of Seconds to Wait Between Attempts boxes.**

8. **(Optional) Click to place a check mark in the Disconnect if Idle for box and enter the number of minutes you want pcAnywhere to wait before disconnecting an idle connection.**

   An idle connection is one during which no data is being transferred to or from either computer.

9. **In the User text box, type the login name assigned to you so that you can access the network.**

10. **In the Password text box, type your assigned network password.**

11. **(Optional) In the Domain text box, type the name of the domain to which you are dialing.**

    A *domain* is a group of computers on a network. Your network may have a single domain, or it may be divided into multiple domains (for example, the sales domain, the management domain, and so on). You only need to specify a domain if your network has multiple domains. If you're on a multiple domain network, you're probably already used to entering this information when you log in. If you're not sure what to enter in this text box, check with your network administrator.

12. **Click OK to save your settings and exit the TCP/IP dialog box; then click OK again to exit the Properties dialog box.**

Introducing remote control

Remote control is a concept central to the use of pcAnywhere. It's the connection method of choice for most pcAnywhere users, as opposed to traditional remote networking.

Traditional remote networking, as covered earlier in this chapter, has its fans and its place. But remote control, covered extensively throughout the remainder of this book, is generally faster.

If you're performing a spreadsheet calculation, for example, it's faster if you have remote control of the host. From your remote PC, you can enter your commands directly onto the host computer and have all the calculations performed on the host while you view (from wherever you are) the host's screen from the comfort of your remote computer. With remote networking, however, you must enter the commands from where you're located, have each command travel to the network, and wait for the result of each calculation to travel back to you. You keep sending data back and forth, instead of having a computer on the network do all the work locally.

In Chapter 5, I talk more about the differences between remote networking and remote control. In Chapter 6, I tell you everything you need to know to start a remote control session.

Part II
Moving Files over Phone Lines

The 5th Wave   By Rich Tennant

"Oh sure, it's nice working at home, except my boss drives by every morning and blasts his horn to make sure I'm awake."

In this part . . .

A pcAnywhere remote control session is a major social event with an exclusive guest list. The invitees include the host computer, the remote computer, and callers permitted to access them. You meet and configure them all in Part II.

This part shows you how to connect to a distant computer and access whatever you need from its drives and directories in a matter of minutes. You can make files fly through your connecting cables and phone lines.

Chapter 4

The Gracious Host

To understand the role of the host computer, think of a pcAnywhere remote communications session as a party — a party where people get together to share some files and applications. The host computer greets the guests as they dial in, confirms that they've actually been invited to attend, and provides the libations — in this case data, instead of drinks.

In this chapter, you find out that planning the party involves setting the correct options on the host computer. And once the party's rolling, I discuss host-management tools that can help you keep remote users mingling smoothly.

Obligations of the Host Computer

A *host* PC is a computer that remote users dial into to access files and other resources. For example, you're working at home for the day, you get hungry, and you want to review the file of carryout lunch menus that you downloaded from the Internet and keep on your office computer. Maybe you also need a client file or two to work on between lunch and dinner. You dial-up the computer located in your office from the one in your home and transfer the files you need. The computer that contains the files you need, along with other resources, is referred to as the host computer. Your home PC is considered the *remote* computer.

A pcAnywhere *host* computer is a PC configured so that a remote PC can dial into it and access its files. A *remote* PC, on the other hand, is a computer configured to access a host computer so that the remote caller can access the files and programs located on the host.

Host? Remote? Who's Who?

Throughout the first six chapters of this book, I make some important assumptions about you and your computers. I assume that

- ✔ The host computer, which contains the files and programs that you need to access, is located in your office or your primary work place.

- ✔ You want to be able to access the host computer from someplace other than your office or primary work place (that is, from a *remote location*).

- ✔ You are the person who is configuring both the host and remote computers so that they can communicate with each other.

Like all assumptions, these may not apply to you precisely. For example you may be a network administrator or a help desk operator. If so, Chapters 8 through 10 are written just for you.

Getting better acquainted with your host

Many of the options that affect a pcAnywhere remote computing session are configured on the host computer. For example, you can set your host computer to initiate a computing session with a remote computer at a designated time. You can also configure the host computer to specify one or more hardware components — such as a modem — from which connections are accepted. The options that you establish on the host also determine which files remote users are allowed to access and what security hurdles they must jump through to get to those files.

To set up a computer as a host PC and enable remote users to dial into it, you must do the following three things:

- ✔ Designate the computer as a host PC.

- ✔ Create a file containing all the information the host needs before it allows a remote computer to connect to it.

- ✔ Set your host PC either to wait for a call from a remote PC, or to call a remote computer itself.

Introduction to Connection Items

A *connection item* (or simply, *item*) is a special type of file — maintained on either a host or remote computer — that contains the information pcAnywhere needs to begin a communication session. This information includes the type of hardware used, security information, phone numbers, and network addresses. You must configure connection items on both the host and remote computers. Each connection item is represented by its own icon on the pcAnywhere desktop.

Figure 4-1 shows host connection items, and Figure 4-2 shows a remote connection item. (In Chapter 5, I tell you how to configure remote connection items.)

Figure 4-1:
This screen displays host connection items.

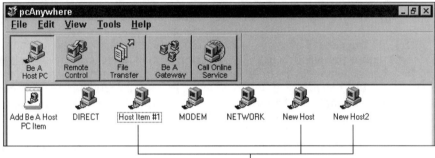

Host connection items

Figure 4-2:
This screen displays a remote connection item.

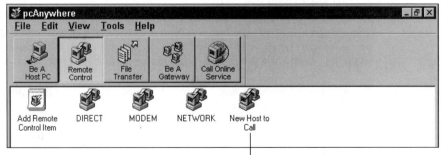

Remote connection item

Host connection items

A host connection item contains the following information:

- ✔ The type of hardware connection device used for each remote computing session. A *device* is any piece of hardware used to make the connection between the host and remote, such as cables or a modem.

- ✔ Rights that a caller on the remote computer may exercise on the host computer after connecting to it. (A *caller* is a person using a remote computer to call into the host PC.)

- ✔ Security features, including a password to protect the host connection item from unauthorized access.

Multiple host connection items

You can set up more than one connection item on the host computer. Each host connection item is assigned a unique name and may specify a different hardware device to be used, different security features, and different callers who can access it. Remote callers identify a particular host connection item that contains the settings they need to perform activities on the host when they make a connection.

In a situation where a database is located on a host computer, several remote callers may be accessing that host. For example, several outside sales reps may call into a common host computer to access pricing files, sales forms, and current customer profiles. Each caller may have rights to access and change different files. (I talk about permissions and security in Chapter 11.) Because of these various access rights, each sales rep may access a different connection item on the host.

You can create a host connection item file manually, or you can expedite the process by using the wizard provided for this purpose. I recommend the wizard, at least the first time you set up a connection item.

To use the connection wizard to set up a new connection item and configure your PC to be a host computer, follow these steps:

1. **Open pcAnywhere; on the main pcAnywhere desktop (see Figure 4-3), click the Be A Host PC button on the Action bar.**

2. **Double-click the Add Be A Host PC Item icon to open the wizard.**

   The Be A Host PC Wizard opens, and a dialog box asking you to select a name for the connection item appears, as shown in Figure 4-4.

Click here

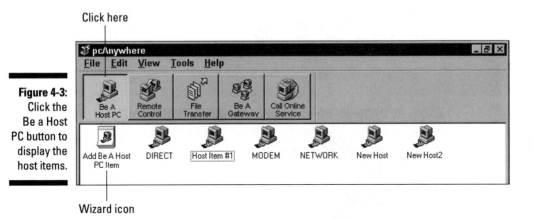

Figure 4-3:
Click the
Be a Host
PC button to
display the
host items.

Wizard icon

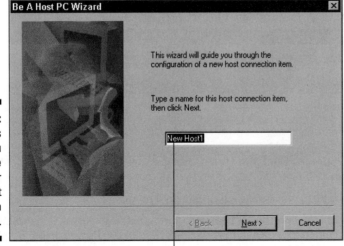

Figure 4-4:
On this
screen, you
designate
a name for
the host
connection
item.

Type the host connection item name here

3. **In the text box, type a name for the connection item file that you're setting up on the host computer.**

   The name New Host1 appears by default in the box. Each subsequent connection item you create using the default name is numbered consecutively (New Host2, New Host3, and so on).

4. **Click Next.**

The screen shown in Figure 4-5 appears and asks what connection device the host connection item will use. You can click the drop-down arrow on the right side of the box to access a list displaying your internal modem and all available COM ports. Most computers have four COM ports. (See Chapter 3 if you need a refresher on ports.)

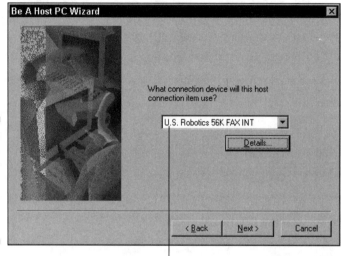

Figure 4-5:
Identify the modem or connection port remote users can connect to.

Select the hardware device or COM port from here

5. **(Optional) Click the Details button to access the dialog box shown in Figure 4-6.**

   The Properties page for an internal modem appears.

   This step is optional because in most situations the default settings specified by pcAnywhere are just fine. In the Properties dialog box, you can adjust the modem transmission options, such as speed and modem speaker volume.

   The default settings for your hardware port and modem are probably just fine. But if you need to fiddle with them, check out the "Messin' with Mr. Modem!" sidebar later in this chapter. The sidebar also provides examples of some situations in which you might want to change some of the settings.

6. **Click Next, and select one of the two security options shown in Figure 4-7.**

Select Allow Any Caller to Access This Host PC if you don't yet know which callers you will let access the host computer. You must be able to identify these specific callers before you can use pcAnywhere security. You can enable pcAnywhere security later, after you figure out who, exactly, you will give access to. (Chapter 11 tells you how to enable pcAnywhere security.)

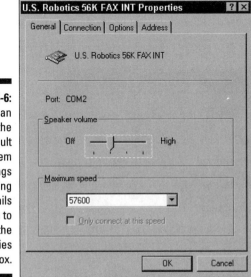

Figure 4-6:
You can modify the default modem settings by clicking the Details button to access the Properties dialog box.

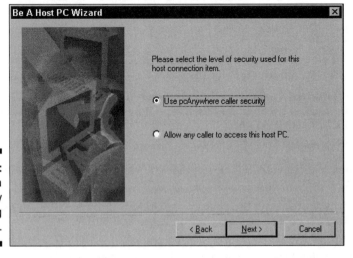

Figure 4-7:
Select a security option using this screen.

7. **If you selected Allow Any Caller to Access This Host PC in Step 6, skip to Step 10. Alternatively, if you selected the Use pcAnywhere Caller Security option, click Next.**

The screen shown in Figure 4-8 appears.

8. **In the Type a Name for This Caller text box, type the name of a caller to whom you are giving access to the host PC or keep the default name.**

The default name is New Caller. Each additional caller you add using the default name is numbered consecutively (New Caller1, New Caller2, and so on).

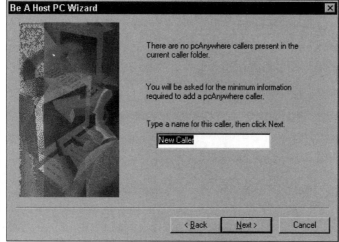

Figure 4-8:
Type a
caller's
name or use
the default
name.

9. **Click Next.**

The screen shown in Figure 4-9 appears, asking you to provide login and password information for the caller.

10. **Type a login name. If you want to use a password (optional), type it in the second text box and then type it again to confirm it in the Confirm the Password text box.**

11. **Click Next.**

A screen appears telling you that you've successfully completed the Be A Host PC wizard.

12. **Click to de-select the check box labeled Automatically Launch This Host Upon Wizard Completion; then click Finish.**

This check box lets you specify whether you want to start the new host immediately after you complete the wizard. Because you have more work to do (such as configuring remote and caller items) before you can begin a remote communication session, you don't want to launch the host just yet.

Messin' with Mr. Modem!

The Details button on the second screen of the Be A Host PC Wizard offers you the option of customizing your COM port or modem settings. After you choose the appropriate port or device from the drop-down list on this screen, click the Details button. A dialog box for the selected connection device appears, enabling you to configure options for the device. The options available for you to configure using the dialog box vary slightly, depending on whether you specified an internal modem or the COM port to which an external modem is attached.

You may need to change some of the options to get your modem to work properly. For example, perhaps you notice an excessive number of lost connections, or you detect errors in the data, with some of it coming through as gibberish. If you're experiencing these problems, it may be that pcAnywhere has specified some defaults that don't work with your particular hardware device.

If you're having problems with your port or device, you may be able to correct the problem by checking the settings for your device. To do so, right-click the icon for the connection item that uses the hardware device that you want to check and select Properties from the pop-up menu. The Connection Info tab appears on top, and you can access the settings for the hardware device by clicking the Details button. When you click the Details button, a dialog box for the connection device appears, displaying some (but not all) of the following settings:

- **Speed:** Indicates how fast data is transferred over your modem and phone lines. Most modems in use today support a transmission rate of 57,600 bps, which may be faster than the phone lines allow. If your modem speed is set faster than your telephone line allows, this may actually slow

your connection because the data is unreliable, which triggers error-checking procedures that slow down transmission. Or you may experience lost connections or receive data containing transmission errors.

If you're having trouble with lost connections, unreliable data, or very slow connections on a standard telephone line, try setting the modem speed to 38,400. This speed allows for the slower transmission rate of the phone line.

- **Parity and Stop Bits:** This option appears when you click the Connection tab of the Properties dialog box for a modem, or the Details tab for a COM port. These terms refer to a method of checking for errors in transmitted information which uses a mathematical calculation that compares and marks data bits. The parity-checking method used by your modem may use odd bits, even bits, or marked bits. This stuff is programmed deep within your modem software, and the only way that you can tell which method your modem uses is by reading the manufacturer's instructions.

- **Flow Control:** This option is available if you've selected a COM port. It regulates the flow of transmission from the modem. Like parity checking, flow control is programmed and deeply buried in the modem software. You have to peruse your modem manual to find out the flow control details for your particular modem.

- **Started By** and **Ended By:** These options tell pcAnywhere the signal by which your particular modem accepts communications and then terminates them. This, too, is something you'll need to find in the modem manufacturer's instructions.

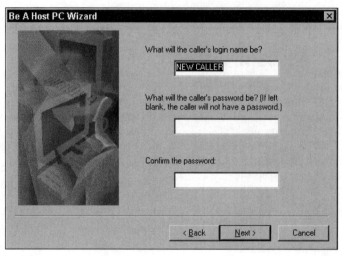

Figure 4-9:
Type a login
name and
optional
password
using this
screen.

After you have whizzed through the wizard, the pcAnywhere desktop reappears with a brand-spanking-new icon bearing the name of the connection item file you just created. You can view this new item, along with all other existing host connection items, by clicking the Be A Host PC button on the Action bar.

Modifying Host Connection Item Properties

Connection items contain the "rule books" that govern how remote users connect to the host computer. The connection item properties lay down the law as to what connection devices are used, what access to files is granted, which security parameters are set, and so on. You can assign different users — connecting to the same host — to different connection item files.

You can modify a connection item's properties from the Properties dialog box for that connection item. To access the Properties dialog box for a connection item, follow these steps:

1. **From the main pcAnywhere desktop, click the Be A Host PC button on the Action bar.**

   All existing host connection items appear on the pcAnywhere desktop.

2. **Right-click the host connection item for which you want to modify the properties and choose Properties from the pop-up menu.**

Alternatively, you can select the connection item and choose File➪Properties.

The Properties dialog box for the host connection item appears, as shown in Figure 4-10.

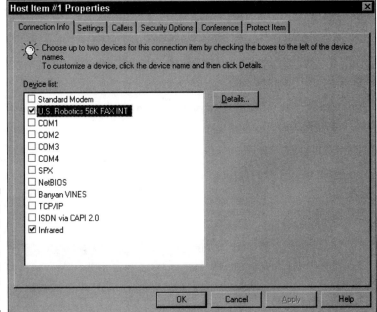

Figure 4-10:
Each
connection
item has
its own
Properties
dialog box.

The host connection item Properties dialog box contains the following tabs:

✔ **Connection Info:** Use the options on this tab to select one or more hardware devices for each session. Hardware connection devices include printers, modems, and scanners.

✔ **Settings:** Use this tab to specify *how* a remote control communication session is conducted. For example, does the host or remote user have keyboard and mouse control during the session? Does the host initiate the session or wait for a call from the remote user? Settings are covered in detail in the next section in this chapter.

✔ **Callers:** Use this tab to determine what rights remote users have on the host after connecting, such as which files they can access and which files are strictly off limits.

✔ **Security Options:** Use these options to prevent unauthorized access to the host (by disgruntled former employees, for example).

✔ **Conference:** Use this option to enable multiple remote PCs to dial in and connect to the remote. The first PC to connect controls the host, and the other PCs are able to view all operations being performed on the host PC.

✔ **Protect Item:** Use this tab to manage users' access to connection items. Each connection item is protected by a password to ensure that remote users are logging into the specific connection item to which they have been granted access. By password protecting your connection items, an employee can't gain access to confidential personnel or company information by dialing in using different connection item that provides greater access.

Settings for a Perfect Session

The Settings tab in the host connection item Properties dialog box, as shown in Figure 4-11, governs much of what happens during a communication session. For example, can a remote PC begin a session, or must it wait for a call from the host? Who gets to use the mouse? What appears on the host's screen during a session?

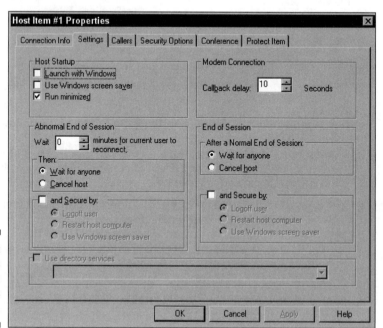

Figure 4-11:
The Settings page of the Properties dialog box.

After you configure the settings on the Settings page, they apply to every session that uses that connection item. Most of the default settings on this tab are fine for your normal work activities. From time to time, however, you may want to adjust some of them.

Host startup settings

The Host Startup options (located in the upper-left corner of the Settings tab) determine when the host computer loads the pcAnywhere software. The following list describes the Host Startup options in detail:

- ✔ **Launch With Windows:** If you check this box, pcAnywhere is started automatically whenever you start your Windows operating system. This means that remote users with dial-in permission have automatic access to the host PC whenever it's turned on. This option is not available if remote users connect to the host through a gateway. (I talk about gateways in Chapter 12.)

- ✔ **Use Windows Screen Saver:** This option is only available with Windows 95 and 98. If you enable this option, it starts the Windows screen saver whenever the host is waiting for a call. The person sitting at the host must enter the password for the connection item (if any) to get past the screen saver. This ensures that someone doesn't sit down at your computer while you're away from your desk and cancel the host while you're waiting for a call.

- ✔ **Run Minimized:** This check box causes the pcAnywhere icon to appear on the host screen as an itty, bitty icon. If this box is left unchecked, pcAnywhere displays a large, ungainly status box that leaves you less room to work in other applications and tasks.

If you're using Windows NT, the Host Startup section of the Settings page looks like Figure 4-12. This section contains the following additional options:

- ✔ **Lock NT Workstation:** This option enables you to lock the keyboard on the host computer during a remote communication session.

- ✔ **Run as a Service:** This option is selected by default; it must be enabled before a host running Windows NT can launch the pcAnywhere program.

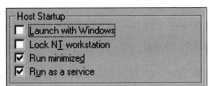

Figure 4-12:
The Host
Startup
options on a
Windows
NT Settings
page.

Settings for abnormally ended sessions (how rude!)

What if you're happily working along at home on your remote computer, connected to the host PC at your office, and you are unexpectedly disconnected from a session by a power failure (or by your toddler pulling the plug out of the wall)? You can specify the circumstances under which a remote caller (in this case, *you*) may reconnect to the host — if at all. To make this designation, right-click the host connection item, select Properties from the pop-up menu, and click the Settings tab. The Abnormal End of Session section offers you the following options:

- ✔ **Wait __ Minutes for Current User to Reconnect:** You can insert the number of minutes that the remote caller (*you*, in the scenario just described) has to wait before reconnecting.

- ✔ **Wait for Anyone:** If you select this option, the host waits for and immediately accepts another call after an abnormal disconnect.

- ✔ **Cancel Host:** If you choose this option, the remote caller can't reconnect at all after a connection is abnormally terminated. This is intended as a security measure.

Hello . . . Who's Remotely Calling?

Think of the Callers tab in the host connection item Properties dialog box as a discriminating doorman with a guest list. Callers who aren't on the list — including you — can't get through the door to visit the host.

The Callers tab lets you set the options on the host that determine who gets to connect to it. These options also determine what control callers (including you) can exercise after they establish the connection.

The options you configure on the Callers tab determine the following:

- ✔ Whether you and other callers can connect to the host PC
- ✔ The times in which callers can connect to the host PC
- ✔ What files you and other callers can access when you do connect

Avoiding excess access

You can grant full access rights to all callers, or you can specify the rights for each caller. For example, you may want full access to dial into the host yourself, but you might not want employees or strangers to have the same freedom.

As I discussed earlier in this chapter (in the steps for using the Be A Host PC Wizard), you can choose from two access options:

 ✔ Use pcAnywhere Caller Security

 ✔ Allow Any Caller to Access This Host PC

During the wizard set up, I told you to choose Allow Any Caller to Access This Host PC because you probably had not yet identified specific callers to whom you want to give access. If you don't change this setting, however, anyone (yes, anyone!) can dial into your host computer if they have the phone number.

The following sections tell you how to specify callers (including yourself) who are allowed to access the host. (In Chapter 11, I talk about how you can enable Windows security options and limit callers' access to files on the host.)

Adding callers to the guest list

To set up a new caller with appropriate privileges on the host PC, follow these steps:

1. **Click the Be A Host PC button on the Action bar.**

   All existing host icons appear on your desktop.

2. **Right-click the icon for any connection item and choose Properties from the pop-up menu.**

   The Properties dialog box for that connection item appears.

3. **Click the Callers tab.**

   The Callers page appears, as shown in Figure 4-13.

4. **Select the Use pcAnywhere Authentication with pcAnywhere Privileges option.**

   The portion of the screen in which the caller item icons appear changes from gray to white.

5. **Double-click the Add Caller icon to start the New Caller Wizard.**

   The first screen of the New Caller Wizard appears, as shown in Figure 4-14.

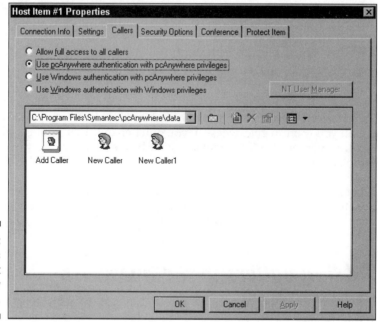

Figure 4-13:
You use this
page to set
up a new
caller item.

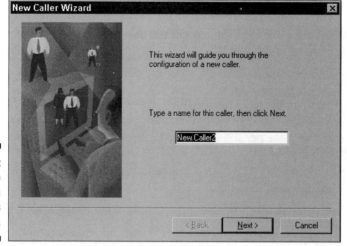

Figure 4-14:
Give the
new caller a
name in this
box.

6. **Type a name for the new caller in the text box that appears or use the
default name; then click Next.**

The default name is New Caller followed by a number. If you add additional callers using the default name, they'll be numbered consecutively
(New Caller1, New Caller2, and so on).

7. **Type a login name for the new caller to use when logging into the host after connecting.**

   This can be the same name that you entered in Step 6.

8. **Type a password for the caller to use after connecting to the host. Then type it once again to confirm it.**

9. **Click Finish.**

Voilà! An icon showing the name of the lucky caller you added appears on the Callers page of the Properties dialog box.

Modifying caller privileges

When you add a new caller by using the New Caller Wizard discussed in the previous section, the default privileges automatically apply. However, you can bestow selective privileges on each caller, depending on how much you trust them not to mess around with host files.

To modify the properties for an individual caller, right-click the icon for that caller and select Properties from the pop-up menu that appears. The Properties dialog box for that particular caller appears, as shown in Figure 4-15. Click the Identification tab and type the caller's login name and password.

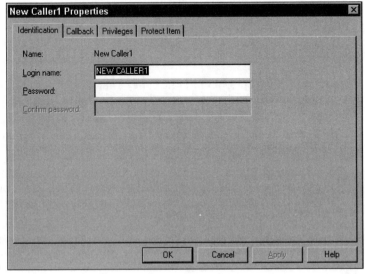

Figure 4-15:
Specify a
login name
and
password
for the
caller.

Next, click the Callback tab. If you select the Callback the Remote User check box (see Figure 4-16), the host automatically disconnects the remote user and calls it back immediately. In other words, the remote user isn't allowed to directly access the host files simply by dialing in. This ensures that remote users are accessing the host from identifiable and legitimate locations.

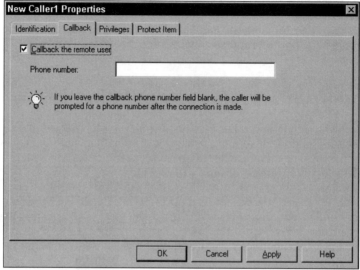

Figure 4-16:
On this screen, you can direct the host to disconnect remote users and then call them back.

The Privileges tab, shown in Figure 4-17, contains some weird terminology. Here is a brief translation of some of the more peculiar pcAnywhere lingo used on this tab:

- ✔ **Superuser:** This option offers the caller unlimited access to the host computer; the caller is automatically granted full privileges.

  The Superuser option is an appropriate choice if you're a sole proprietor with few or no employees. As the business owner, you want full access to all data on the host computer.

- ✔ **Allow Caller to Blank Screen:** This option enables the remote caller to blank the screen on the host PC during a session. This is for privacy. If the host PC is unattended, office staff can't view activities on the host PC during the remote computing session.

- ✔ **Allow Caller to Cancel Host:** This option enables the remote caller to prohibit further connections to the host after the remote computing session. The advantage of this feature is that if you suspect a security breach, you can immediately cut off *everyone's* access to the host.

- ✔ **Allow Caller to Restart Host:** This option enables the remote user to restart the host PC remotely. (I mention this option in Chapter 7 in the discussion of the online toolbar buttons.)

✔ **Allow Caller to Upload Files:** This option determines whether a remote user can send files to the host PC or modify the host drive in any way.

✔ **Allow Caller to Download Files:** This option determines whether a remote user can download files from the host PC. It's analogous to "read-only" access.

✔ **Allow Use of Ctrl +Break:** If this keystroke combination is enabled, the remote user can halt certain applications running on the host PC.

✔ **Limit Time Allowed per Session:** This option automatically disconnects the caller after the allotted time for the session.

✔ **Caller Subject to Inactivity Timeout:** This option — useful for forgetful people — disconnects the remote PC from the host PC if the connection is inactive for a specified amount of time.

✔ **Set Drive Access:** This button enables you to deny remote users access to network drives or provide read-only access to drives containing data that you can't afford to have accidentally deleted.

✔ **Command to Execute After Connect:** This option enables you to specify a program, such as Microsoft Office or QuickBooks, that you want started as soon as the remote user logs on. This is strictly a convenience feature for the remote user.

Figure 4-17:
The Privileges tab contains several specialized caller options.

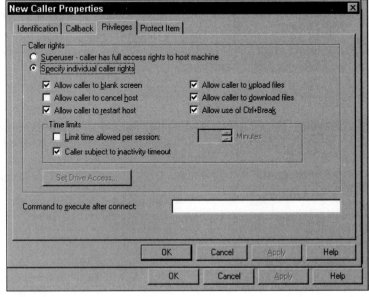

Modifying the Add Caller Template

A pcAnywhere *template* is analogous to a template in Microsoft Word or any other Windows application that uses templates. It's a feature that governs the default settings for something you create using the software, such as a document or file. The Add Caller template is a template used by pcAnywhere to specify the default settings each time you create a new caller item. By changing the settings on the Add Caller Template, you change the default settings for every new caller item you subsequently create.

To modify the Add Caller template, follow these steps:

1. **Click the Be A Host PC button on the Action bar.**

   The Add Be A Host PC Item icon, along with icons for all existing host connection items, appears on your desktop.

2. **Right-click the Add Be A Host PC Item icon and choose Properties from the pop-up menu.**

   The Properties dialog box for the Be A Host PC Wizard appears.

3. **Click the Callers Tab.**

   The Callers page appears.

4. **Click to select the Use pcAnywhere Authentication for pcAnywhere Privileges option that appears at the top of the screen, as shown in Figure 4-18.**

   The bottom half of the screen changes from gray to white, and you can access the icons in the window.

5. **Right-click the Add Caller icon and choose Properties from the pop-up menu.**

6. **Click the Privileges tab, and change any of the options you see on this tab. These settings will become the default settings for any new caller item you create in the future (refer to Figure 4-17).**

   The changes you make on this tab become the default settings for new callers you add later.

Select this option

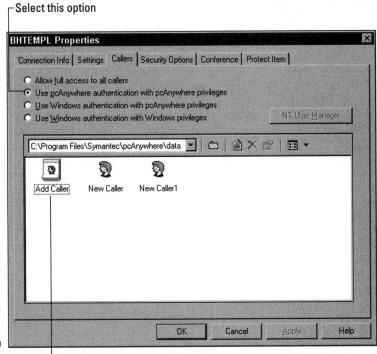

Figure 4-18:
The Callers
tab of the
Add Be A
Host PC
Wizard
Properties
dialog box.

Right-click here

Chapter 5

The Perfect Guest

*T*he previous chapter left a gracious host computer anxiously awaiting a call from a "guest" remote computer. The host PC was properly configured to accept an incoming call from a remote PC to begin a communication session.

In this chapter, I tell you everything you need to do to configure your remote computer to call the host computer. It's important to understand that during the communication session, the remote computer takes control of the host computer. This means that if you're at home in your comfy chair with your remote laptop PC, you can perform applications on the host PC in your office as if you were sitting at your office desk. But first you need to configure that remote laptop to do the job by using the information in this chapter.

Using the Remote Control Wizard

Either the host PC or remote PC can initiate a connection. (I tell you how to start a session in Chapter 6.) But first you must ensure that the remote computer is capable of connecting.

The Remote Control Wizard helps you configure your remote PC in a matter of minutes. To use the wizard, you need the phone number of the host PC (if you're connecting by modem) or its network name. The wizard supplies the rest of the information using default settings, which you can modify if necessary.

Types of configurations

You must configure the remote computer to perform one of the following two tasks:

- ✔ **Dial into the host computer by using a remote connection item on the remote machine.** A *remote connection item* is a file that contains the dialing instructions and other information that the remote PC uses to dial the host PC. (Alternatively, a host connection item contains dialing information that the host needs if it ever calls the remote.)

- ✔ **Receive a call from the host computer.** In order for this option to work, you must set up the remote PC to use the connection device specified on the host PC. A *connection device* is the type of modem, cable, network connection device, or other hardware used to make the actual connection. The settings for this hardware must match on the host and remote PCs.

Sometimes pcAnywhere is incorrectly referred to as a *remote networking* program. This is incorrect. pcAnywhere actually initiates a *remote control* session between the host PC and remote PC, as explained in the sidebar "Remote networking versus remote control," later in this chapter. Remote control is a much faster process that allows the remote computer to perform applications on the host computer. As far as pcAnywhere is concerned, traditional remote networking is a dinosaur.

Setting up a remote connection item

For a remote PC to dial a host PC, you must set up a connection item. And you can set up multiple remote connection items, each connecting to a different host computer or using a different connection device or phone number. That way, you're prepared for many different situations.

You use the Remote Control Wizard to establish each connection item. It's a zippy little wizard that takes 90 seconds to complete. This section tells you what preliminary information you need to gather before you begin the wizard and how to access the wizard.

Preliminary information

Before you begin the wizard, you need to determine the following:

- ✔ What hardware device the connection item on the remote computer uses (for example, a modem, cable, or network connection). If you need more information about connection items, see Chapter 3.

- ✔ What phone number the host computer uses or what network address has been assigned to the host by the network administrator.

Remote networking versus remote control

Remote networking and *remote control* are two different types of connections. pcAnywhere generally uses remote control because it's the faster connection. You can use remote control to access a computer on a network or a stand-alone computer that's not attached to a network. You use remote networking only to access a server on a network.

The choice between remote control and remote networking is only an issue when you're figuring out the best way to access a server on a network. If you're not accessing a computer on a network, remote control is your only connection option.

Remote networking enables you to dial into a network to access a *server* (a network computer that shares data, applications, and hardware devices). With remote networking, you operate your distant computer as if it were attached to the network. This is a rather slow process because each command you execute on the remote computer has to travel across the phone lines to the server computer to access

data, applications, or a device (such as a printer). Then the data or the confirmation that your command has been executed must travel back across the phone lines. If you're working with a large, complicated Excel spreadsheet, for example, and accessing the Excel application from the server, remote networking can be a nightmare.

By contrast, with remote control, you actually *take control* of a host computer that's physically attached to the network. You execute commands on the host computer as if you were sitting in front of it. Commands and data go back and forth between the server and the host. You can watch what's happening on the host because it's displayed on the screen of your remote PC. Only the images on your remote computer screen and your keystrokes to communicate with the host are traveling over the phone lines. Because the commands and data from the application you're running (such as Excel calculations) aren't traveling back and forth over the phone lines, remote control is the speedier way to connect.

Accessing the Remote Control Wizard

You can use the handy Remote Control Wizard to walk you through adding a remote control item. To open the Remote Control Wizard, follow these steps:

1. **Click the Remote Control button on the Action bar.**

   A screen showing the Add Remote Control Item icon and any previously set remote control connection items appears. (You can have multiple remote control items that connect to different host computers or that use different connection devices or phone numbers.)

2. **Double-click the Add Remote Control Item icon to start the Remote Control Wizard (see Figure 5-1).**

   The first dialog box of the Remote Control Wizard appears, as shown in Figure 5-2.

Figure 5-1:
Start the
Remote
Control
Wizard by
double-
clicking the
Add Remote
Control Item
icon.

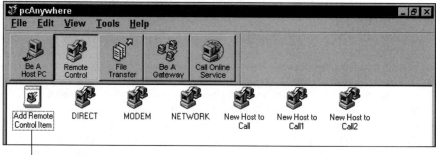

Double-click to start wizard

Figure 5-2:
In this box,
type a name
for the
remote
control
connection
item.

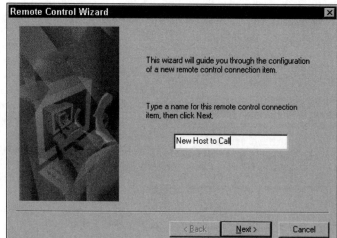

3. **Type a name for the remote control connection item, as shown in Figure 5-2, or leave the default name that already appears in the text box.**

   The default name is New Host to Call. If you add future remote control items using the default name, they'll be numbered consecutively (New Host to Call1, New Host to Call2, and so on).

4. **Click Next.**

   The screen shown in Figure 5-3 appears.

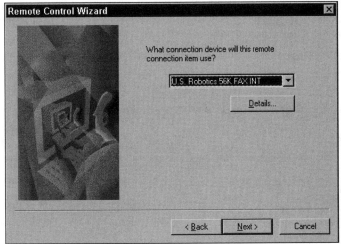

Figure 5-3:
Specify the
connection
hardware
device using
the drop-
down menu.

5. **Select a connection device from the drop-down menu.**

   A connection device is a modem, cable, or other form of hardware used
   to establish the connection. (See Chapters 3 and 4 if you need a
   refresher on connection devices.) If you're using an external modem,
   select the COM port that you want it to use. (COM ports are discussed in
   Chapter 3.)

   pcAnywhere searches for any internal modem used on your computer
   and enters it in the field as a default.

6. **Click Next.**

   The screen shown in Figure 5-4 appears.

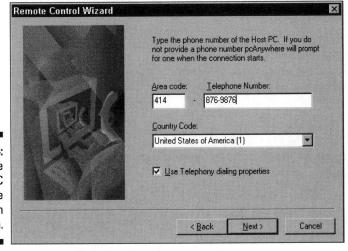

Figure 5-4:
Type the
host PC
phone
number on
this screen.

7. **Type the area code and phone number for the host computer in the appropriate boxes; then choose the country from the drop-down list in the Country Code box.**

8. **Click Next.**

   The screen shown in Figure 5-5 appears.

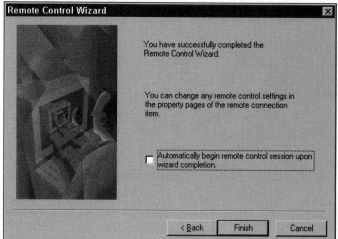

Figure 5-5:
If the check box is selected, pcAnywhere begins dialing when you click Finish.

9. **Deselect the check box labeled Automatically Begin Remote Control Session upon Wizard Completion.**

   If this check box is selected, the remote PC automatically begins dialing the host PC as soon as you finish the wizard. You don't want to start dialing until you've made sure that the host PC is turned on and waiting for a call. (I tell you how to actually start a session in Chapter 6.)

10. **Click Finish**

    The final screen tells you that you successfully completed the wizard. The screen also informs you that you can change any remote control setting in the Properties dialog box of the remote connection item. This option is covered in the next section, "Modifying connection item properties."

Modifying Connection Item Properties

After you set up a connection item, you may find it necessary to modify it (for example, if you get a new modem or if the host computer gets a new phone number). It's usually simpler to modify an existing connection item to reflect the revised information, rather than create a whole new one. This is particularly true if you have multiple connection items, numbered consecutively, and you want to keep your naming convention intact.

Opening the Properties pages for a connection item

Before you can modify a connection item, you first have to access the Properties dialog box for that item.

To open the Properties dialog box for a specific connection item, follow these steps:

1. **Click the Remote Control button on the Action bar.**

   A screen appears showing the Add Remote Control Item icon and any existing remote control connection items.

2. **Right-click the icon for the connection item that you want to modify.**

   A pop-up menu appears, as shown in Figure 5-6.

3. **Select Properties from the pop-up menu.**

   The Properties dialog box appears with the Connection Info page open on top, as shown in Figure 5-7. You can click each tab to open a different page of properties.

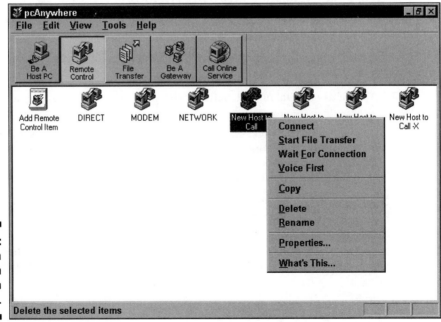

Figure 5-6:
Right-click a connection item to open this menu.

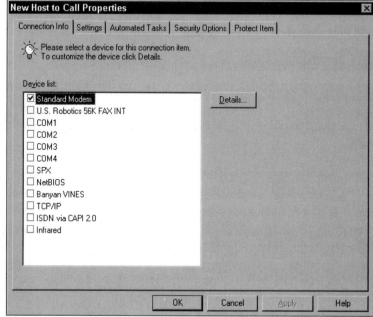

Figure 5-7:
You modify
connection
item proper-
ties by using
the pages in
this dialog
box.

Flipping through the Properties pages

Each connection item Properties dialog box has five Properties pages. You
access each page by clicking one of the following tabs:

- ✓ **Connection Info:** Choose this page if you want to select the hardware
  device used by the connection item.

- ✓ **Settings:** Dialing instructions and login information are found on this
  page.

- ✓ **Automated Tasks:** Use this page to configure pcAnywhere to perform
  automatic functions upon connection, such as running a script or automatically downloading a specified file. (To find out more about scripts,
  take a look at Chapter 14.)

- ✓ **Security Options:** Does your company have a high need for security, or
  are some folks just paranoid? Either way, you can use this page to configure various levels of data encryption.

- ✓ **Protect Item:** Use this page to password protect your remote connection
  item. (Check out Chapter 11 for more information on security.)

Basic connection and login settings

To configure basic connection and log-in information, open the Properties
dialog box for a specific connection item and then use the Connection Info
and Settings tabs.

The Connection Info tab is the default tab that automatically appears on top
each time you open the Properties dialog box for a connection item. On the
Connection Info page, you can click to place a check mark in the box next to a
particular hardware device or port. Then if you click the Details button,
another dialog box opens and offers you additional options and information
about that hardware device or port.

Usually, the default settings for the device or port are adequate. It's a good
idea, however, to take a look at the details dialog box so that you know what
settings can be modified if a conflict arises between the host and remote PCs.
The following figures show you the settings available for various hardware
devices, and the "Details! Details!" sidebar later in this chapter explains how
to modify the settings, when necessary.

Figure 5-8 shows an example of the dialog box that appears when you click
the Details button after selecting an internal modem device.

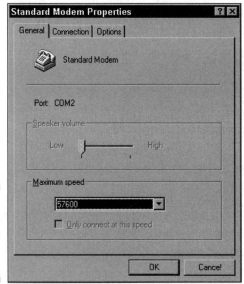

Figure 5-8:
The details
dialog box
for an inter-
nal modem.

Figure 5-9 shows the details dialog box for an external modem device
attached to a COM port.

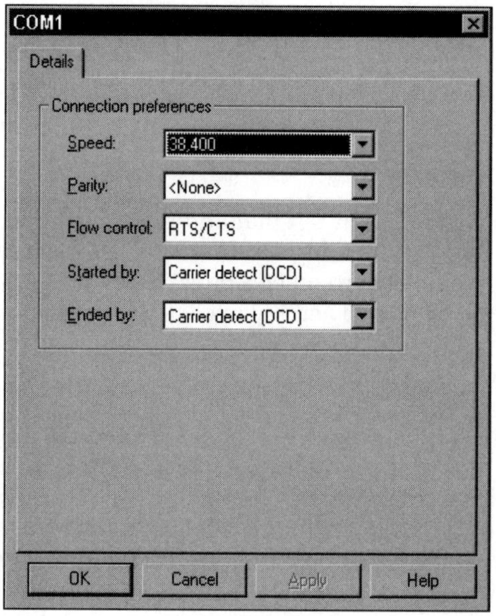

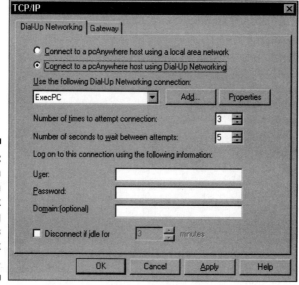

Figure 5-9:
The details
dialog box
for a COM
port.

Figure 5-10 shows you the details dialog box for a TCP/IP network. These settings determine whether the device connects to the host by using a dial-up
connection or over a local area network. You find out more about these settings in the "Details! Details!" sidebar.

Figure 5-10:
You can
configure a
network
device using
a details
dialog box
like this one.

Details! Details!

pcAnywhere does a good job with its default settings. The defaults reflect the features of the most commonly used devices on the market. (In Chapter 4, I explain that a device is the hardware used to connect computers: modems, cables, and so on.) You may never have to modify the default settings if you use reasonably up-to-date equipment, and a current version of the software. But if you work for a company that should consider donating its computers to a museum and taking the tax write-off, you may need to modify some hardware settings before you can work from home.

After you specify a particular connection device, you click the Details button to get to the actual settings for that device. The Details button appears in these two places in pcAnywhere:

- On the second screen of the Remote Control Wizard. You use it in the wizard to specify the type of connection device that you want to use for a new connection item.

- On the Connection Info tab of the Properties dialog box.

After you click the Details button, a dialog box opens with options that pertain specifically to the connection device that you've chosen. You can configure the following options for each type of connection device:

- **Internal modem:** You can specify the volume of the tone you hear upon connecting and the maximum modem speed. The default speed is 115,200. Remember that modems are *backward compatible*. If a fast modem is trying to communicate with a slow one, the faster one automatically adjusts its speed down.

- **COM port device (external modem):** The Details button allows you to set the following:

  - The speed of the modem transmission.

  - The method that the machine uses to check for errors in the transmission of data. (The same method must be used for both the remote and host computers.)

  - The method by which a connection is initiated.

  - The type of modem.

- **Network connection devices:** If you're utilizing a networked computer, use the Details page to specify the following:

  - Whether a device can use a dial-up connection or a connection over a local area network. If you're using a dial-up connection, pcAnywhere searches your operating system for information about your Internet service and assumes that you want to use it for your dial-up connection.

  - The number of attempts to try and connect, and the number of seconds between attempts. (The defaults are set to three and five, respectively.)

  - The username and password information required to access the host PC.

The Details button is a good thing to know about if you're having difficulty establishing a connection. The culprit may be settings on the host and remote computers that don't match, such as the passwords, connection devices, or domain names if a network device is used.

Changing Information about the Host PC

If the host PC's telephone number changes, if the host is moved to a different address on the network, or if you, as the remote user, are assigned to connect to a different host computer, you need to change the host PC connection information configured on the remote connection item. You change the host PC connection information from the Settings tab of the Properties dialog box.

The procedure for changing the host connection information differs slightly, depending on whether you connect to the host PC through a network or dial up the host using a modem.

Modifying host information on a network

To change the host PC connection information when you're connecting through a network, follow these steps:

1. **Click the Remote Control button on the Action bar.**

   A screen appears displaying all the icons for previously created remote control items.

2. **Right-click the icon of the connection item that you want to modify and choose Properties from the pop-up menu.**

   The Properties dialog box for the connection item appears.

3. **Click the Settings tab.**

   The Settings page appears, as shown in Figure 5-11. (As you can see in the title bar of the figure, this remote connection item is named New Host to Call1.)

4. **Type the network address for the host PC in the Network Host PC to Control or IP Address text box.**

   This information is available from your network administrator.

5. **Click to place a check mark in the Automatically Login to Host upon Connection box.**

   Selecting this option instructs pcAnywhere to automatically provide the host PC with your login information upon connecting.

6. **Type your login name and password.**

   If you're connecting to a host PC that uses Windows NT, you also need to enter your domain name.

7. **In the Connection Options section, indicate the number of times that you want pcAnywhere to attempt to establish a connection and how long you want to wait between attempts.**

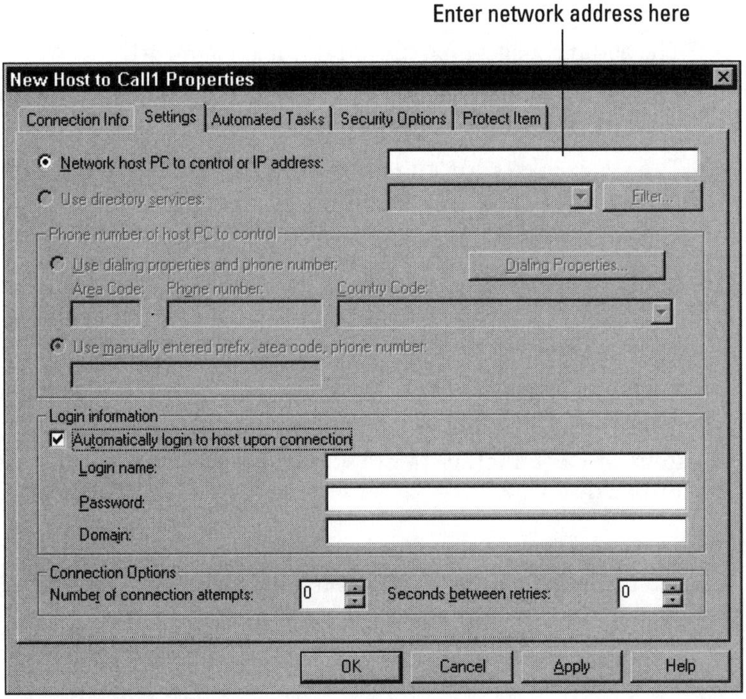

Enter network address here

New Host to Call1 Properties

| Connection Info | Settings | Automated Tasks | Security Options | Protect Item |

○ Network host PC to control or IP address: [   ]

○ Use directory services: [▼] [Filter...]

Phone number of host PC to control
○ Use dialing properties and phone number.   [Dialing Properties...]
Area Code: Phone number: Country Code:
[   ] - [   ]   [▼]

● Use manually entered prefix, area code, phone number.
[   ]

Login information
☑ Automatically login to host upon connection
Login name: [   ]
Password: [   ]
Domain: [   ]

Connection Options
Number of connection attempts: [0 ⇕]   Seconds between retries: [0 ⇕]

[OK] [Cancel] [Apply] [Help]

Figure 5-11:
You modify a network device connection item from the Settings page of the Properties dialog box.

8. Click **Apply** to save the information you entered on this page.

9. Click **OK** to close the Properties dialog box for the remote connection item, or click another tab to view the settings on a different Properties page.

Modifying host information for a modem connection

To change the host PC connection information when you are connecting with a modem, follow these steps:

1. **Click the Remote Control button on the Action bar.**

   A screen appears displaying all the icons for previously created remote control items.

2. **Right-click the icon of the connection item that you want to modify and choose Properties from the pop-up menu.**

   The Properties dialog box for the connection item appears.

3. **Click the Settings tab.**

   The Settings page appears, as shown in Figure 5-12.

4. **Click to place a check mark in the Use Dialing Properties and Phone Number box on the Settings page.**

5. **Type your area code and phone number in the appropriate boxes.**

   Use the drop-down arrow in the Country Code box to select a country code if you are making an international connection.

6. **In the Connection Options section, indicate the number of times that you want pcAnywhere to attempt to establish a connection and how long you want to wait between attempts.**

7. **Click Apply to save the information you entered on this page.**

8. **Click OK to close the Properties dialog box for the remote connection item, or click another tab to view the settings on a different Properties page.**

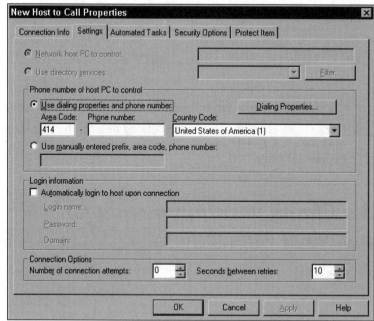

Figure 5-12:
You can
modify a
dial-up
connection
item from
the Settings
page of the
Properties
dialog box.

TCP/IP tidbits

You see the intimidating five-letter TCP/IP acronym scattered throughout various pcAnywhere lists and windows. You may wonder whether it applies to you and whether everyone else using the program knows what it means.

TCP/IP stands for Transmission Control Protocol/Internet Protocol. A *protocol* is a set of rules governing receipt and transmission of data. TCP/IP is actually a protocol *suite*. A suite is a collection of protocols, serving different purposes, that are bundled together in one package for easy installation. Some of the protocols in TCP/IP include e-mail protocols (SMTP), file transfer protocols (FTP), and protocols for naming files (WINS and DNS).

Computers use a number of protocol suites to talk to each other. Some of these protocol suites are used only to talk to computers on the same network.

In contrast, TCP/IP is a *routable* protocol. This means that TCP/IP messages are sent to different networks within an organization or even to multiple networks around the world. The address used to send TCP/IP messages must contain not only the name of the destination computers, but also the name of its network, or *domain*.

TCP/IP is the standard protocol used on the Internet and is becoming *the* standard for global communications. Networks that use TCP/IP are often referred to as TCP/IP networks. Every client and server on a TCP/IP network requires a special numeric TCP/IP address. Numeric names are tough to remember, though. So TCP/IP uses an application to convert the numeric names to an easy-to-remember alphabetic name, such as the user's name. For example, the TCP/IP address 125.657.999.111 might be converted into Workstation1. The DNS and WINS protocols, which are part of the TCP/IP protocol suite, are responsible for translating easily remembered alphabetic names into numeric TCP/IP addresses.

Chapter 6

Starting a Session

• •

In This Chapter
▶ Starting a session from a remote PC
▶ Starting a session from a host PC
▶ Making a host PC call back a remote PC

• •

C ongratulations! You have configured the seemingly endless array of host and remote connection options. Now you have a bunch of lonely computers waiting for the phone to ring so that they can begin a session.

But who is going to call who (or is it whom)? *Which* computer do you want to initiate the communication session, and *how* do you want a session to be initiated?

Lonely Computers: Waiting for the Phone to Ring

pcAnywhere etiquette allows for three different social scenarios between host and remote computers:

- ✔ A remote PC can call a host PC.
- ✔ A host PC can call a remote PC.
- ✔ A host PC can receive a call from a remote PC, disconnect, and call back the remote PC to initiate the session.

Calling a Host PC from a Remote PC

Connecting to a host PC from a remote PC is the most common scenario. For example, you need important files that are on your office computer (the host

PC), but you're at a cabin in the mountains with your laptop computer (the remote PC). You want to dial into the host and access the files you need — and you want the host to accept this important call and respond immediately.

Launching the Host

Before your remote PC can call the host computer, the host must be *launched.* Launching the host means that the pcAnywhere program has been opened on the host computer, and it's eager and ready to receive a call from the remote computer.

You must launch the host prior to calling into it from the remote computer; otherwise, the remote won't be able to establish a connection with the host.

To launch a host and make it accessible to the remote, follow these steps:

1. **Make sure that the host PC is turned on**.

   You can't access a host computer that's not running!

2. **Click the Be A Host PC button on the Action bar.**

   All the existing host connection items appear on your desktop.

3. **Right-click the host connection item that you want to use and choose Launch from the pop-up menu.**

   The pcAnywhere screen disappears from the desktop, and a tiny Host Waiting icon appears on the Windows taskbar at the bottom of the screen (see Figure 6-1). The host is now ready to receive a call from the remote.

The pcAnywhere support number often receives calls from customers saying that they can't launch the host. This is because the tiny Host Waiting icon is so difficult to see on the taskbar. You really have to look carefully! If you can't find the Host Waiting icon — and you know that you're looking in the right place — refer back to Chapter 4 to make sure that you configured your host correctly to receive a call from the remote.

Figure 6-1:
This icon
shows that
the host PC
is ready to
receive a
call.

Host Waiting icon

Taking a look at the Host Waiting icon

The Host Waiting icon provides a pop-up menu, shown in Figure 6-2, when you right-click the icon.

Figure 6-2:
The Host
Waiting
pop-up
menu.

Display Status
Cancel Host
Help

You can select from the following options on the Host Waiting pop-up menu:

- ✔ **Display Status:** Tells you the dialing status of the host and when a connection has been made
- ✔ **Cancel Host:** Makes the host inaccessible to remote callers
- ✔ **Help:** Launches the pcAnywhere Help menu

Make sure that you select a connection item on the host PC that specifies the same hardware connection device as the connection item being used on the remote PC.

Configuring a remote PC to dial up a host PC

The information in the remote control connection item that you're using to dial up a host PC is the key to establishing a remote control session. This information includes the network address or telephone number of the host PC. Chapter 5 covers setting remote control connection items on the remote PC.

Dialing a host PC with a modem

To access a host computer from a remote computer by using a modem, follow these steps:

1. **Click the Remote Control button on the Action bar.**

   The icons for all existing remote control items appear on your desktop.

2. **Right-click the icon for the remote connection item that you want to use and choose Connect from the pop-up menu (see Figure 6-3).**

   You hear a dial tone, and a status box appears telling you that pcAnywhere is connecting (see Figure 6-4). This status box disappears from the screen after the connection is established.

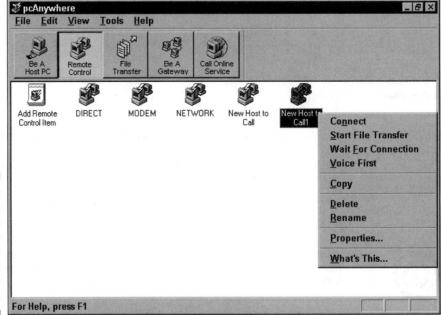

Figure 6-3:
This pop-up menu appears when you right-click a connection item.

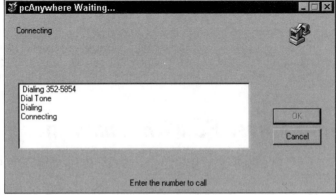

Figure 6-4:
This status box lets you know that pcAnywhere is connecting.

What if you forget what connection item to use? This could happen if you've configured a number of them. The best thing to do in this situation is to right-click each connection item and select Properties from the pop-up menu. The Properties dialog box for the connection item appears, and you can click the various tabs to examine the settings on each page and confirm that they're what you want to use for the remote control session you're about to begin.

Calling a host PC on a network

To connect to a host PC connected to a local area network (for example, your office network) from a remote PC, follow these steps:

1. **Click the Remote Control button on the Action bar.**

   The icons for all existing remote control items appear on your desktop.

2. **Right-click the icon for the remote control connection item that has the settings you want (such as the correct hardware device) and choose Connect from the pop-up menu.**

   You hear a dial tone, and a status box appears telling you that pcAnywhere is *initializing* (connecting to the network), as shown in Figure 6-5. After pcAnywhere has finished connecting, a dialog box with a list of available hosts appears.

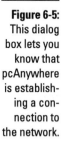

Figure 6-5:
This dialog box lets you know that pcAnywhere is establishing a connection to the network.

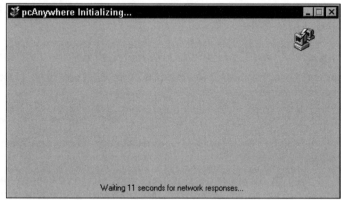

Waiting 11 seconds for network responses...

3. **Select the host to which you want to connect and click OK.**

If you've configured the remote connection item to always dial the same host, you won't see a dialog box with a list of available hosts. But don't worry. It's not necessary to select a host for the session because you already did this when you configured the remote connection item in Chapter 5.

Chapter 4 told you how to configure a host connection item. If you didn't properly configure the host connection item, you won't be able to access it from the remote. If you're having difficulty connecting to the host, refer to the section "Modifying Host Connection Item Properties" in Chapter 4 and check the settings that you configured. Pay special attention to the Connection Info tab (be sure that you've specified the correct hardware device) and the Settings tab (be sure that you've entered the correct phone number).

Waiting for a Voice-First call from a remote PC

One of the features offered by pcAnywhere is an option that lets you contact the host PC, carry on a verbal conversation with an actual person who answers the phone, end the conversation, and then immediately begin a communication session between the host and remote computers. This is known as the *Voice-First* option. You can use Voice-First only if the host computer doesn't have a dedicated modem line. You can call the person sitting at the host PC and let them know that you want to begin a remote communication session. When they hang up the phone, the host and remote PC can begin communicating without you having to terminate and restart the connection.

You can initiate a Voice-First call only from a remote computer; you can't configure a host computer to initiate a Voice-First session. And before you can initiate a Voice-First session, you have to set the host computer to receive a Voice-First connection.

Configuring a host PC to receive a Voice-First call

To configure a host computer to accept a Voice-First call from a remote computer, follow these steps:

1. **On the host computer, click the Be A Host PC button on the Action bar.**

   All the existing host connection items appear on the pcAnywhere desktop.

2. **Right-click the host connection item configured to use the same connection device as the remote PC; then choose <u>V</u>oice First from the pop-up menu.**

   The Host Waiting icon appears at the bottom of the screen to indicate that the host PC is ready to begin the communication session.

Initiating a Voice-First call from a remote PC

To initiate a Voice-First connection from a remote computer, follow these steps:

1. **Click the Remote Control button on the Action bar.**

   Icons for all existing remote control items appear on your pcAnywhere desktop.

2. **Right-click the remote connection item that you want to use for the session and choose Voice First from the pop-up menu (see Figure 6-6).**

   A status box appears, letting you know that pcAnywhere is establishing a Voice-First connection.

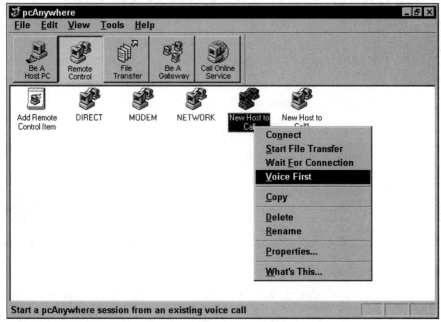

Figure 6-6: Choose the Voice First option if you want to have a conversation before you begin exchanging data.

3. **When the person on the other end of the line picks up the phone (remember the line isn't a dedicated modem line), a connection is established and you can jabber away.**

   While you're chatting, the dialog box shown in Figure 6-7 appears.

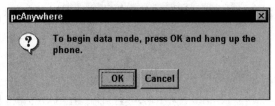

Figure 6-7:
Click OK to
begin trans-
ferring data.

4. **When you finish talking, click OK and hang up the receiver to begin the data transfer portion of the remote control session.**

Having a Host PC Call a Remote PC

For security or convenience reasons, you may not want *any* outside computers to have access to your host PC. You may, however, want the host PC to dial up a remote PC. If you choose this connection method, the remote PC controls the activities on the host PC during the session.

To dial up a remote PC from a host PC, follow these steps:

1. **Click the Be A Host PC button on the Action bar.**

   Icons for all existing host connection items appear on the pcAnywhere desktop.

2. **Right-click the connection item that has the settings that you want to use (including the ones specifying the modem or other connection device) and choose Call Remote from the pop-up menu (see Figure 6-8).**

   Depending on whether you're connecting to the host over a network or via a modem, you will see either a network host list box or a status box (see Figure 6-9).

3. **If you're connecting over a network, select a network host from the network host list box. If you're connecting by modem, type the phone number for the remote PC in the Phone Number field of the pcAnywhere Waiting box.**

4. **Click OK in either the network host list box or the pcAnywhere status box to close the box and initiate the call.**

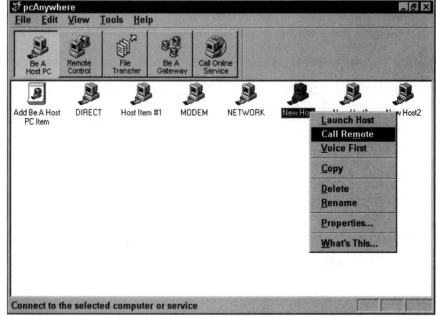

Figure 6-8:
Select Call
Remote
from the
pop-up
menu to
enable a
host PC to
initiate the
call.

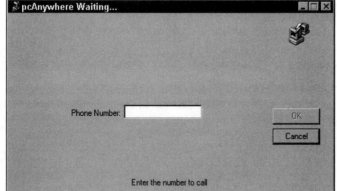

Figure 6-9:
Type the
phone
number for
the remote
PC's modem
in this dialog
box.

Returning the Remote PC's Call

Occasionally, you may want to configure a host computer to wait for a call
from a remote computer, and then have the host computer disconnect and
call back the remote computer. This configuration has two benefits: First,
from a security standpoint, the host PC can ensure that the remote PC is call-

ing from where the remote user is supposed to be. (The host can ensure that the call is coming from a company branch office, for example, and not from the office of your biggest competitor.) Second, if the host is a company-owned machine, you can ensure that the bulk of the telephone charges are billed to the company, rather than to the employee's personal phone line.

To configure a host PC to accept a call from a remote PC, disconnect, and then call back the remote PC, you need to modify the properties of the caller connection item. (In Chapter 4, I explain configuring and setting up a connection item for each caller dialing the host.)

When you first set up a new caller item, pcAnywhere gives the caller a set of default privileges used in accessing the host. To change the default privileges so that the remote caller can access host files only by waiting for a call back, follow these steps:

1. **Click the Be A Host PC button on the Action bar.**

   Icons for all existing host connection items appear on your pcAnywhere desktop.

2. **Right-click the icon of the host connection item that has the settings you want to use (including the modem or other connection device) and choose Properties from the pop-up menu.**

   The Properties dialog box for the host connection item appears.

3. **Click the Callers tab.**

   The Callers page appears, as shown in Figure 6-10.

4. **Click to select the Use pcAnywhere Authentication with pcAnywhere Privileges option.**

5. **Right-click the icon for the caller item that you want the host PC to disconnect from and then call back; then choose Properties from the pop-up menu.**

   The Properties dialog box for the caller item appears.

6. **Click the Callback tab.**

   The Callback page appears, as shown in Figure 6-11.

7. **Click to place a check mark in the Callback the Remote User box.**

8. **In the Phone Number text box, type the phone number of the remote PC.**

   If you leave the callback phone number box blank, you are prompted to enter the callback phone number at the time the connection is made.

9. **Click OK to save the settings you've changed and to close the Callback page.**

10. **Click OK again to close the Properties dialog box.**

After you complete these steps, the next time that the remote PC calls the host PC, the remote PC will be disconnected. The host will then call back the remote PC immediately.

Select this option

Figure 6-10:
The Callers page for the host connection item.

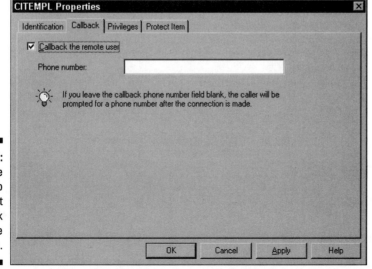

Figure 6-11:
Click the Callback tab and select the Callback the Remote User option.

Chapter 7

Hello, It's Me . . . Your PC

· ·

In This Chapter

▶ Classifying your connection

▶ Navigating the online menu options and toolbars

▶ Adjusting online options

▶ Communicating with other pcAnywhere users

▶ Using the pcAnywhere Clipboard

▶ Finishing a session

· ·

*W*hat a beautiful concept! Two computers meet across space, time, and telephone lines to fulfill their technological destiny. There isn't a network administrator, traveling sales rep, telecommuter, or computer geek alive who doesn't feel a small sense of fulfillment when a successful connection is made.

In this chapter, I help you understand how to manage your session after you make an online connection, discuss how to use the pcAnywhere chat dialog box to communicate with other users, talk about how to spruce up the host PC and remote PC screens by using the Clipboard feature, and, finally, give you some tips on bringing the session to a happy ending.

Reviewing the Types of Connections

You can manage and troubleshoot your communication session more effectively if you know what *type* of pcAnywhere session you've initiated. Here's a brief summary and review of the four types of pcAnywhere communication sessions:

✔ **Remote Control Connection:** A remote PC calls a host PC. The connecting session proceeds in remote control mode with the remote computer controlling the host computer. This is the most common type of connection. Remote control is discussed in detail in the next section.

✔ **Wait for Host Connection:** A host PC calls a remote PC. After the connection is established, the remote PC controls the host PC. The Wait for Host Connection works much like the remote control connection discussed above.

✔ **File Transfer Connection:** A remote PC dials up a host PC and begins the session in file transfer mode, which enables you to browse, compare, delete, and synchronize files on the host and remote PCs. A remote PC has more limited control in this type of session. For example, the remote PC can't perform applications, such as running a word processing program on the host computer, while it's in file transfer mode. I discuss the File Transfer Connection in more detail later in this chapter.

✔ **Voice-First Connection:** The Voice-First connection enables a remote user to dial a host PC, chat on the telephone line to a person on the other end, and, when finished, click OK on the remote PC screen to begin transferring data. (This one still amazes me.)

Managing an Online Session

You may have noticed, after installation, how incredibly austere and uncluttered the pcAnywhere desktop appears. In fact, the Action bar has only four buttons, and on the desktop below it are fewer than a half dozen icons. Additionally, the pcAnywhere menu bar has only a couple dozen options. Is this really everything you need to manage a complex online session?

The answer is *no* — the program designers are holding out on you. Additional online menus appear after a session is started.

Host PC versus remote PC online menus

The online menu is available only after a session has started. The online menu can be a source of confusion because the options on this menu are not identical for the host PC and the remote PC. The remote PC online menu has more options because it controls the host PC during a remote control session. The next section tells you how to access the online menu.

Both the host and remote PCs can execute commands on the host PC during a remote control session.

Making the online menu appear

To access the online menu, follow these steps:

1. **Click the Remote Control button on the Action bar.**

   All existing remote control connection items appear on the pcAnywhere desktop, as shown in Figure 7-1.

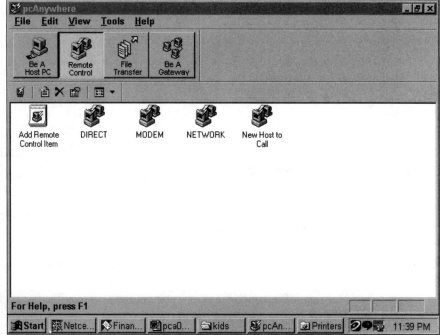

Figure 7-1:
This is how the pcAnywhere desktop looks before you establish a remote control connection.

2. **Select a Remote Control connection item that uses the appropriate modem or network connection device.**

   If you're not sure which remote control connection item to use, right-click one and select Properties from the pop-up menu. The Properties dialog box for the connection item appears. Click the Connection Info tab to see what hardware device the connection item uses.

3. **Right-click the icon and choose Connect from the pop-up menu (see Figure 7-2).**

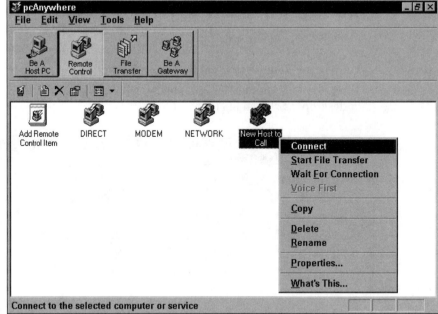

4. **After a connection is established, the online toolbar appears at the top of the Windows desktop (see Figure 7-3).**

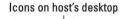

Icons on host's desktop

5. **Click the small pcAnywhere icon in the left corner of the pcAnywhere title bar to open a short menu that gives you access to the online menu.**

   pcAnywhere is the final option on this short menu, as shown in Figure 7-4.

6. **Click the pc<u>A</u>nywhere option.**

   A submenu, referred to as the *online menu*, opens and offers a list of online commands.

Trying the online toolbar

The online toolbar buttons, as shown in Figure 7-5, are always available on your screen during a pcAnywhere session. You can customize the buttons on the toolbar to reflect the online menu options.

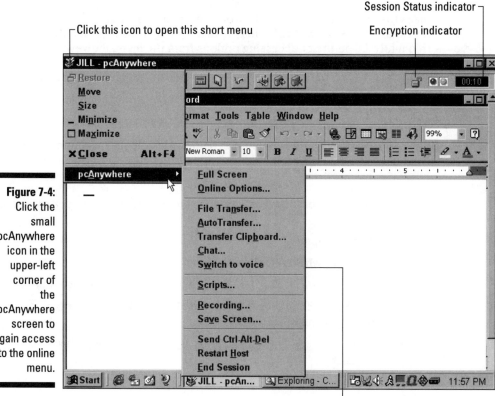

Session Status indicator

Encryption indicator

Click this icon to open this short menu

Figure 7-4: Click the small pcAnywhere icon in the upper-left corner of the pcAnywhere screen to gain access to the online menu.

Online menu

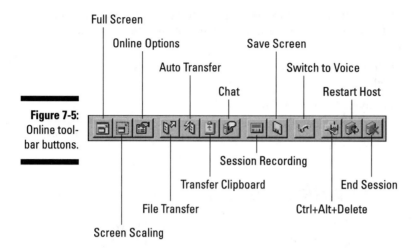

Figure 7-5:
Online tool-
bar buttons.

Full Screen

Online Options

Auto Transfer

Chat

Save Screen

Switch to Voice

Restart Host

Session Recording

Transfer Clipboard

End Session

File Transfer

Ctrl+Alt+Delete

Screen Scaling

The fact that the online toolbar is always displayed and that it's customizable make the online toolbar easier to work with than the online menu. You can, for example, customize the toolbar to display only those options that you use frequently. If you prefer accessing options from the menu, however, you can open it at any time by clicking the pcAnywhere icon and choosing pcAnywhere from the drop-down menu. The online menu offers pretty much the same options available on the online toolbar.

Displaying the online toolbar

The online toolbar appears on your screen by default after a communication session has been initiated. If it doesn't appear, you can make it show itself by following these steps:

1. **Click the small pcAnywhere icon in the left corner of the pcAnywhere title bar.**

   A short menu opens.

2. **Choose pc_Anywhere⇨_Online Options.**

   The Online Options dialog box appears with the General page on top.

3. **Click to place a check mark in the box labeled Remote Control _Toolbar (see Figure 7-6).**

   By default, the Remote Control Status Tray box is already checked.

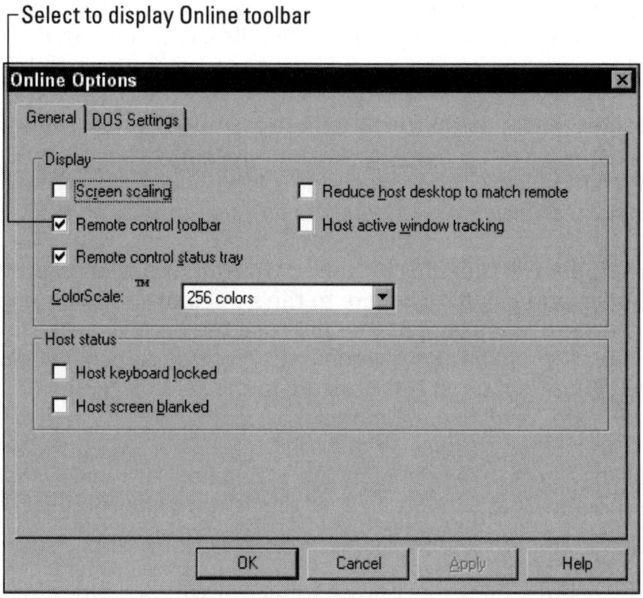

Select to display Online toolbar

Figure 7-6:
The Online
Options
dialog box.

The graphics used for pcAnywhere icons are pretty unimaginative. And until you get used to the relatively indistinguishable pictures on the icons, they all look alike. But you can save time in the long run by taking a few minutes to familiarize yourself with the various online buttons and icons, rather than having to access the menu each time you want to execute an online command.

Ogling the online toolbar buttons

Here's a quick rundown of the online toolbar buttons and their functions. The buttons are listed in order, from left to right, as they appear on the toolbar:

 Full Screen: Click this button to display the full host screen on the remote computer. To reduce the host screen size and leave room to display both the remote online options and the host screen, press Alt+Enter to open the Windows System Key Pressed dialog box. Then you can select Execute Locally and click OK.

 Screen Scaling: Click this button when the host computer is set to use a higher screen resolution than the remote computer. This option scales down the host screen to fit nicely into the remote window.

 Online Options: This is one powerful little button! It lets you change all the session options, such as screen appearance and keyboard handling, for an active session. In fact, this one button enables you to accomplish so much that it has its own section following this one, under the catchy subheading "Modifying Online Options During a Session."

File Transfer: Click this button to display the pcAnywhere File Manager options for transferring and synchronizing files. (I talk about File Manager in Chapter 8.)

 AutoTransfer: Click this button to initiate an AutoTransfer session. AutoTransfer is a feature that lets you automatically transfer and synchronize host and remote files without executing additional commands. (I tell you more about AutoTransfer in Chapter 8.)

 Transfer Clipboard: Click this button to transfer information on the screen of one computer running pcAnywhere to the screen of another computer running pcAnywhere. For example, you may use the pcAnywhere Clipboard to transfer clip art from the host screen to the remote screen. (I talk more about using the Clipboard later in this chapter, in the section "Using the Clipboards to Cut and Paste," and also in Chapter 8.)

 Chat: Click this button to communicate with a host or remote computer by typing text in the Chat window. I cover this feature later in this chapter in the section "Chatting with Other Users."

 Session Recording: Click this button to record your activities for the current session for future playback. Recording allows you to replicate a session or procedure that went well, or analyze one that was a bust.

 Save Screen: Click this button to take a picture (called a *screen shot*) of your current screen to save for future reference.

 Switch to Voice: Click this button to suspend a data transfer session and switch to a voice conversation.

 Send Ctrl+Alt+Del to Host: If your system is running Windows NT, click this button to open the Windows NT task box, which is used for login and for switching tasks.

 Restart Host: Click this button to restart the host computer from the remote computer (if you have permission to do so).

 End Session: Click this button to disconnect the remote computer from the host computer and end the current session.

In addition to the online toolbar, a couple of informative indicator icons grace the far right side of your screen when you're online.

 Encryption indicator: Click this icon to get information about the level of encryption being used. Encryption is a method of scrambling data, which ensures that only the intended user with the necessary software to unscramble it reads the data. (I discuss encryption in more detail in Chapter 11.)

Session Status indicator: This timer shows the length of time that you've been online.

Modifying Online Options During a Session

pcAnywhere uses the term *online options* to refer to settings that affect the appearance of your screen during an online session. Online options are set by default, but you can modify them from the Online Options page of the Properties dialog box.

To modify online options, follow these steps:

1. **Click the small pcAnywhere icon in the left corner of the pcAnywhere title bar.**

   A drop-down menu opens.

2. **Choose pcAnywhere➪Online Options from the menu.**

   The Online Options dialog box appears with the General page on top.

3. **On the General page, choose from the following options:**

   - **Screen Scaling:** Check this box to fit the entire host screen comfortably on the remote screen.

   - **Remote Control Toolbar:** Check this box to make the online toolbar appear.

   - **Remote Control Status Tray:** Check this box to specify whether a status line appears at the bottom of the screen. This status tray displays the terminal type, the current communications port, and technical information about the flow of data. (This information is useful for troubleshooting your connection; if there's a problem you may need to know the information that appears in the status tray.)

   - **ColorScale:** This option enables you to decrease the number of colors that the host PC uses. Fewer colors result in improved session performance.

   - **Reduce Host Desktop to Match Remote:** Check this box to make the host screen resolution automatically match the remote screen resolution. If the resolution on the host screen is higher than the resolution on the remote screen, your connection can be slowed.

- **Host Active Window Tracking:** Check this box to display the active host list box on the remote window. For example, dialog boxes and error messages appearing on the host screen automatically pop up on the remote screen so that the remote user can respond to or cancel them.

- **Host Keyboard Locked:** It's a good idea to disable the host keyboard during the remote control session. Checking this box ensures that an unwitting coworker doesn't sit down at the host computer and accidentally compromise your connection.

- **Host Screen Blanked:** This option employs the same logic as the one above — you don't want an unknowing user sitting down at a host PC while a remote session is in progress. Checking this box has an added privacy advantage — the trespassing coworker is unable to see what's happening on the host computer.

The remote caller can't blank the screen unless they were specifically granted this privilege at the time that the remote caller item was configured. (I talk about configuring the remote caller item in Chapter 5.)

Chatting with Other Users

pcAnywhere has an online function — the Chat window — that features many of the attributes of e-mail. You can exchange written information prior to, or after, transferring files.

The Chat window is a special type of dialog box that allows people sitting at the host and remote computers to exchange written messages. The Chat window appears on both the host and remote screens.

To communicate by using the pcAnywhere Chat window, follow these steps:

1. **Click the small pcAnywhere icon in the left corner of the pcAnywhere title bar.**

   A drop-down menu opens.

2. **Choose pcAnywhere➪Chat from the menu.**

   The pcAnywhere Chat dialog box appears. Alternatively, you can click the Chat button, which looks like a computer with a dialog balloon coming out of it.

3. **Type your message in the lower portion of the dialog box window (see Figure 7-7).**

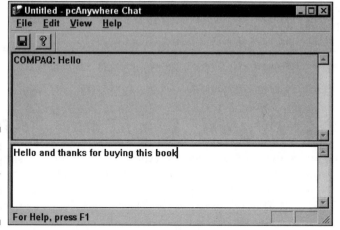

Figure 7-7:
Chat with
other
pcAnywhere
users.

> 4. **Press Enter to send the message. Click the Close box (X) in the upper-right corner to close the Chat window.**

You can save the contents of a Chat "conversation" to a file. Taking this extra step enables you to keep a more complete record of your business communications and transmitted information.

To save your Chat correspondence to a file before exiting the Chat dialog box, follow these steps:

> 1. **From the Chat window, choose File⇨Save As.**
>
>   The Save As dialog box appears, as shown in Figure 7-8.

Figure 7-8:
Save Chat
correspon-
dence by
using this
dialog box.

> 2. **Select the folder or location from the Save As dialog box in which you want to save your communication.**

3. **Type a name for the file in the File Name text box.**

4. **Click the Save button.**

5. **Choose File➪Exit Chat to close the Chat window, or click the X in the upper-right corner of the window.**

Using the Clipboards to Cut and Paste

You can spruce up your Chat screen on the host and remote desktops by using the Clipboards. You use both the Windows and pcAnywhere Clipboards to transfer art and text from one application to another until you have it placed just where you want it to appear on your screen.

Copying from one application to another

This procedure is basically the same for all Windows-based programs. But a little refresher on how a Windows Clipboard works can't hurt. To copy text from one Windows-based application to another (such as pcAnywhere), follow these steps:

1. **After you've established a pcAnywhere remote control connection from the remote computer, select the text or images on either the host or remote screen that you want to duplicate or move.**

2. **Choose Edit➪Copy if you want to duplicate the text or image so that you can place it in another location without removing it from its original location. Choose Edit➪Cut if you want to duplicate the text or image so that you can place it in another location, while also removing it from its original location.**

   Choosing either Copy or Cut places the text or image on the Windows Clipboard.

3. **Go to the pcAnywhere screen where you want the copied or cut material to appear, and move your cursor to the exact spot where you want to place it. Choose Edit➪Paste.**

   The cut or copied material appears in the spot where you placed your cursor.

Copying from the host's Clipboard

pcAnywhere lets you transfer text and graphics from the host computer's Clipboard to the remote computer's Clipboard and vice versa.

To copy text from one pcAnywhere screen to another, follow these steps:

1. **Select the text you want to duplicate or move.**

2. **Click the small pcAnywhere icon in the left corner of the title bar.**

   A short drop-down menu opens.

3. **Choose pcAnywhere⇨Transfer Clipboard from the menu.**

   The Transfer Clipboard dialog box appears, as shown in Figure 7-9.

Figure 7-9:
Use
Transfer
Clipboard to
move text or
graphics
between the
host and a
remote PC.

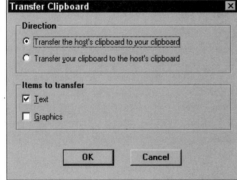

4. **In the Direction section of the Transfer Clipboard dialog box, click to select one of the following options:**

   • Transfer the Host's Clipboard to Your Clipboard

   • Transfer Your Clipboard to the Host's Clipboard

   The wording of these options in the dialog box differs, depending on whether you're working on the host or remote computer.

5. **In the Items to Transfer section, click to select one or both of the following options:**

   • Text

   • Graphics

   If you select the text option only, the text is transferred and any graphics are ignored. If you select the graphics option only, the graphics are transferred and any text is ignored.

6. **Click OK.**

Make sure that you transfer any data from the host or remote Clipboard to either of the two screens before ending a session. Information left on the Clipboard is purged at the end of a session.

Goodbye! Ending a Session

You can end a session from either the host or remote PC.

To end a session from the remote PC, follow these steps:

1. **Click the small pcAnywhere icon in the left corner of the title bar.**

   A short drop-down menu opens.

2. **Choose pcAnywhere⇨End Session from the menu.**

   A dialog box appears, confirming that you want to end the session.

3. **Click Yes.**

To end a session from the host PC, simply click the End Session button on the online toolbar.

Chapter 8

Making Files Fly!

. . . .

In This Chapter

▶ Working with File Manager

▶ Understanding the file transfer process

▶ Discovering the ins and outs of file synchronization and cloning

▶ Copying, deleting, renaming, and comparing files and folders

▶ Using AutoTransfer

. . . .

*F*ile Transfer is one of the most useful functions of pcAnywhere. File Transfer enables you to move files between a host PC and a remote PC during a communication session. It also enables you to sort, synchronize, and compare files on both PCs.

In this chapter, I help you become familiar with File Manager, the pcAnywhere feature that opens the door for file transfer. I also introduce you to some basic file-management features, such as copying, deleting, and renaming files, along with the slightly more advanced features of file synchronization and cloning.

The Friendly File Manager

During a file transfer session, you work in the File Manager window. For some reason, the folks at Symantec didn't call it the File Transfer window — which is really what it is. So you just need to begin thinking "File Manager window" whenever you think about transferring files.

You can access the File Manager window in any of the following ways:

✔ From a remote control session initiated by a remote PC

✔ From a remote control session initiated by a host PC

✔ From a File Transfer–only session initiated from either the host or remote PC

Accessing File Manager from a remote PC

You can access the File Manager window only after you establish a connection between the host and remote PCs. The same is true of the online menu and the online toolbar, which are used to access the File Manager window and manage the File Transfer session. (I discuss the online menu and toolbar in Chapter 7.)

To access the File Manager window from a remote PC, follow these steps:

1. **Click the Remote Control button on the Action bar.**

   All the remote control connection items appear on your desktop.

2. **Right-click a remote control connection item that uses the hardware connection device that you want to use for the remote control session; then choose Connect from the pop-up menu.**

   The remote online menu and toolbar are available after a connection is established. (In Chapter 3, I tell you how to select and configure a hardware connection device, such as a modem, cable, or network connection, depending on your needs and where you are when dialing.)

3. **Click the File Transfer button on the remote online toolbar (see Figure 8-1).**

   A status box briefly appears telling you that File Manager is loading. Then the File Manager window appears on the screen of the remote computer, as shown in Figure 8-2.

   The left side of the screen is called the *remote list box* and displays the drives and files of the remote computer. The right side of the screen is called the *host list box* and displays the drives and files of the host computer. The column of icons down the center is called the *File Manager Action bar.*

Remote online toolbar

Figure 8-1:
Use the File Transfer button to open File Manager on a remote PC.

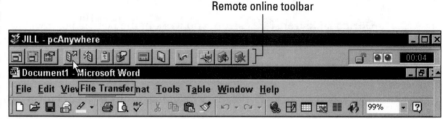

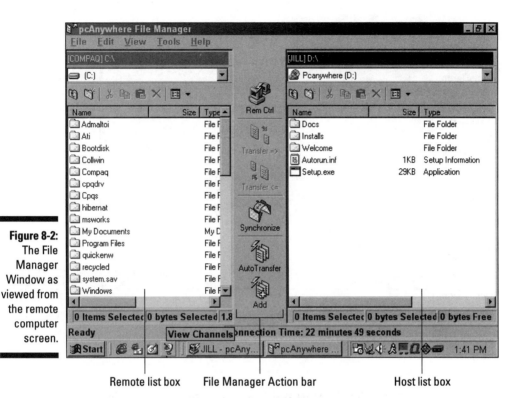

Figure 8-2:
The File
Manager
Window as
viewed from
the remote
computer
screen.

Remote list box   File Manager Action bar   Host list box

Accessing File Manager from a host PC

To open the File Manager window from a host PC, follow these steps:

1. **Click the Be A Host button on the Action bar.**

   All the existing host connection items appear on your screen.

2. **Right-click a host connection item that uses the modem or network connection device that you want to use for this session; then choose Call Remote from the pop-up menu.**

   A status box appears, as shown in Figure 8-3, telling you that pcAnywhere is dialing the remote. The status box abruptly disappears, leaving the Host Waiting icon on the Windows taskbar, as shown in Figure 8-4. The host has successfully made the connection.

   Don't be surprised when pcAnywhere abruptly disappears from your desktop and is replaced by the Host Waiting icon — it's so unobtrusive, you can miss it if you aren't looking for it. This generates many calls to pcAnywhere technical support. People miss the icon on the screen and don't realize that the host has made a successful connection to the remote PC. Check out Chapter 15 for more information.

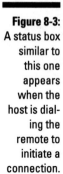

Figure 8-3:
A status box
similar to
this one
appears
when the
host is dial-
ing the
remote to
initiate a
connection.

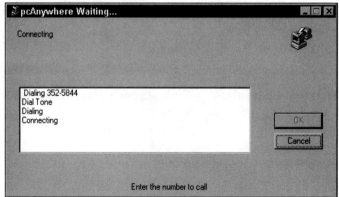

Figure 8-4:
The Host
Waiting icon
is tiny and
easy to
miss.

Host Waiting icon

**3. Right-click the Host Waiting icon on the Windows desktop, and choose
File Transfer⇨Controlled by Host from the pop-up menu (see Figure
8-5).**

A status box appears, telling you that File Manager is loading. The status
box then disappears and the File Manager window appears on the host
screen. The remote user sees a dialog box with a Waiting message.

Figure 8-5:
Right-click-
ing the Host
Waiting icon
opens this
pop-up
menu.

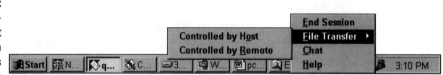

The options on the pop-up menu for the Host Waiting icon may differ,
depending on whether the host has initiated a connection to the remote
or is waiting for a call from the remote.

Getting Familiar with the File Manager Window

After you successfully start a File Transfer session from either the host PC or the remote PC, the File Manager window pops up in the center of your screen. The File Manager window looks similar to the Explorer screen currently used with Windows-based programs. The difference here is that you have the opportunity to explore the contents of *two* computers, instead of just one.

Looking at the list boxes

As I mentioned earlier, the File Manager window is divided into two halves, each displaying active files. The creators of pcAnywhere refer to the host PC and remote PC sections of the window as *list boxes*.

The left list box displays all the drives and files currently available for viewing on the remote computer. (This is the one at which you're probably seated since most pcAnywhere sessions are conducted from a remote computer.) The right list box displays all the drives and files currently available for viewing on the host computer. The center of the screen consists of a column of icons referred to as the File Manager Action bar.

Only one list box — the one you're working in — is active at a time. Click the list box you want to activate so that you can change viewing options, sort, or transfer files.

Selecting files to view

You may notice that each side of the File Manager window includes its own title bar. If you refer back to Figure 8-2, my remote list box shows COMPAQ in the title bar, and my host list box shows JILL in the title bar.

Both list boxes display drives, folders, and files for the computer, just like you would see in the Microsoft Windows Explorer screen. Select the drive that you want to browse by clicking on the arrow in the drop-down list directly below the title bar. After you select a drive, a list of folders and files on that drive appears in the list box. Double-click the icon of any folder to display its contents.

Sorting files

File Manager lets you sort files by using four different criteria:

✔ **Name:** Lists files alphabetically by name

✔ **Type:** Groups files alphabetically by the extension assigned according to their file format (.doc, .jpg., .tif, and so on)

✔ **Size:** Sorts files by size in ascending or descending order

✔ **Date:** Sorts files chronologically

To change the way in which your files are displayed, follow these steps:

1. **Click anywhere within either the remote PC or host PC list box that you want to sort in order to make it active.**

2. **Choose View➪Arrange Icons.**

   A submenu appears listing sorting options, as shown in Figure 8-6.

3. **From the submenu, choose the option that describes the way in which you want to sort your files: by Name, Size, Type, or Date.**

Viewing more information about files

You can select a sorting option that allows you to see specific information about a file. For example, if you choose to sort files by size, the size of each file appears in the list box next to its name. Similarly, if you sort by date or type, you can view that information about each file in addition to the name.

You can also select an option that enables you to simultaneously view size, date, and time information for each file. To view detailed information about each file in the host or remote list box, follow these steps:

1. **Click anywhere in either the host or remote list box, depending on the location of the file for which you want to display detailed information.**

2. **Choose View➪Details to see detailed file information, or choose View➪List to display the name of the file only (to avoid taking up extra room on the screen for information not immediately necessary).**

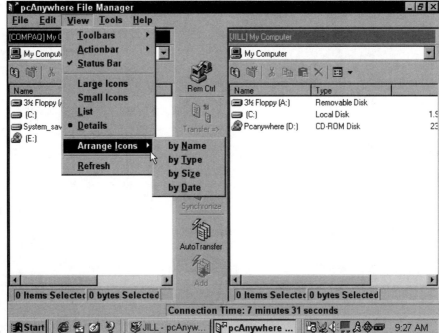

Figure 8-6:
You can choose to sort your files in several different ways.

If you select the Details option, you don't have enough room in the host or remote list box to display the full line of information provided about each file. Move the Action bar to the left or right by holding down the shift key and dragging it with your mouse. This allows you to view the full line of information provided for each file by using the Details view, as shown in Figure 8-7.

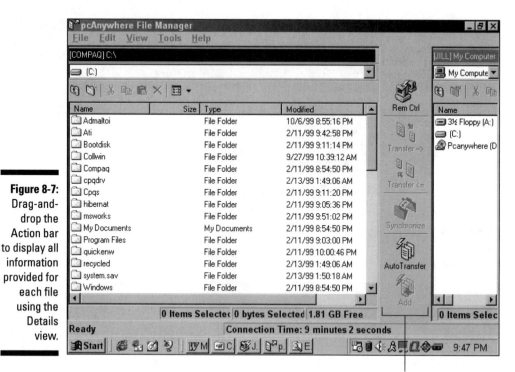

Figure 8-7:
Drag-and-
drop the
Action bar
to display all
information
provided for
each file
using the
Details
view.

Drag and drop this Action bar

Transferring Files

You've arrived at the most important part of this chapter. It's time to make files fly! You can start a file transfer session from either a host PC or a remote PC.

Transferring files from a remote PC

To begin a File Transfer session from a remote PC, follow these steps:

1. **Click the Remote Control button on the pcAnywhere Action bar.**

2. **Right-click a remote control connection item icon that uses the appropriate modem or network connection device; then choose Connect from the pop-up menu.**

   The connection is established, and the online toolbar appears.

3. **Click the File Transfer button on the online toolbar or choose File Transfer from the online menu.**

The File Manager window appears.

Remember that you access the online menu by clicking the pcAnywhere icon in the left corner of the pcAnywhere title bar and choosing pcAnywhere from the menu. This opens a submenu of online commands. (I talk about the pcAnywhere online menus in more detail in Chapter 7.)

4. **In the remote list box, click to select the file or files that you want to send to another computer.**

5. **In the host list box, click the destination drive or file in which you want the transferred files to be located.**

After files for transfer have been selected from the remote list box, and a destination drive or folder is selected from the host list box, the Transfer buttons on the File Manager Action bar are no longer grayed out. There are two such buttons, with arrows pointing in opposite directions.

6. **Click the Transfer button on the File Manager Action bar that has the arrow pointing in the direction of the computer to which you want to transfer the files (from remote to host or from host to remote, as shown in Figure 8-8).**

A pop-up menu appears.

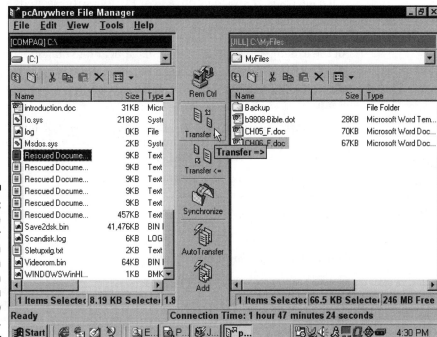

Figure 8-8: Click the Transfer button pointing in the direction in which you want to move files.

   7. **Choose Transfer from the pop-up menu.**

   A message prompts you to confirm whether you want to transfer the files.

   8. **Click OK to confirm the transfer. Choose File⇨Close to exit the File Manager window if you have no other tasks to perform.**

You can send multiple files at one time. To select a group of files that are contiguous (displayed in sequence, one right after the other), click the first one in the group and then press and hold down the Shift key while you click the last filename in the group. If the files are not contiguous, but are scattered around the list, press and hold down the Ctrl key while you click each individual filename. Alternatively, you can drag-and-drop files from one list box into another.

Transferring files from a host PC

You can also start a file transfer from a host PC. When the host computer controls the file transfer session, the File Manager window appears on the host screen.

To begin a file transfer session from a host PC, follow these steps:

   1. **Click the Be A Host button on the Action bar.**

   All the existing host connection items appear on your screen.

   2. **Right-click a host connection item that uses the appropriate modem or network connection device; then choose Call Remote from the pop-up menu.**

   A status box appears telling you that pcAnywhere is dialing the remote computer. The status box then abruptly disappears, leaving the Host Waiting icon on the Windows taskbar.

   The Host Waiting icon is so unobtrusive that you won't see it if you aren't looking for it.

   3. **Right-click the Host Waiting icon.**

   A pop-up menu appears.

   4. **Choose File Transfer⇨Controlled By Host.**

   The File Manager window appears.

   5. **Click to select the file or files that you want to send to another computer.**

6. **Choose File⇨Transfer or drag-and-drop the selected files to the other list box.**

Drag-and-drop files from one list box into another by selecting them, holding down the Shift key, and then with your mouse, dragging the files from one list box to the other.

7. **Click OK to confirm the transfer.**

Synchronizing and Cloning Files

There are a lot of misconceptions about these two processes for coordinating updates to files — and some of these misconceptions can get you into trouble. Cloning files when you mean synchronizing may cause you to lose data. On the other hand, if you synchronize when you darn well should have cloned, you, or folks in your office, may inadvertently end up working on old versions of files that don't include the necessary changes and updates that you made. Before you take action, I suggest that you make sure that you have a solid understanding of the consequences. (Good advice for life in general.)

Synchronizing versus cloning

Synchronizing and cloning are methods of coordinating changes and updates to files between computers. These techniques enable you to work off the latest versions of files regardless of whether recent changes were made at the host or remote computer. Changes to files (including newly created files) are sent from one computer to another so that both computers have current versions. The computer to which new files and modified old files are being sent is called the *source* computer. The computer receiving the updates is referred to as the *destination* computer.

Synchronizing enables pcAnywhere to make duplicates of new or existing files and then ensures that both the host PC and remote PC have copies of the files. Synchronizing doesn't delete files; it creates duplicates and assigns them filenames that are only slightly different from the original names. Synchronizing files is confusing and, if done incorrectly, can cause you to end up working in an obsolete file that doesn't incorporate recent changes.

If you already have synchronized files and you're working at the destination computer, make sure that you're running the most current version of the file.

Cloning files, on the other hand, deletes (yes, deletes!) duplicate files in the destination folders. This is true even if the files flying over from the source folder have older dates and do not incorporate the latest changes. Files coming from the source folder on a cloning mission have instructions to search and destroy. So, if you instruct File Manager to clone files, be sure — and I mean be *very* sure — that the source file contains the most recent changes.

Cloning overwrites data in the destination file even if the source files are older and don't contain the most recent updates. In addition, any items in the destination folder that aren't in the source folder are deleted.

Synchronizing files and folders

To synchronize host PC and remote PC files and folders, follow these steps:

1. **Click the Remote Control button on the Action bar.**

2. **Right-click a remote control connection item that uses the appropriate modem or network connection device; then choose Co_n_nect from the pop-up menu.**

   The connection is established, and the online toolbar appears.

3. **Click the File Transfer button on the online toolbar.**

   The File Manager window appears.

4. **From the remote PC list box, click to select the files or folders that you want to synchronize.**

5. **Click the Synchronize button on the File Manager Action bar.**

   The Synchronize Folder dialog box appears, as shown in Figure 8-9, asking you to confirm whether you want to synchronize all files or only the ones you selected. Select the Include Subfolders check box if you want any files or folders within the previously selected files and folders to also be synchronized.

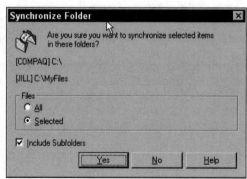

6. **Click Yes to begin the synchronization.**

   After the synchronization is complete, duplicates of the files and folders you selected appear on the destination computer.

Cloning — carefully, please!

Cloning is an option that, if it falls into the wrong hands, can cause untold grief. With a single command, you can delete all up-to-date versions of selected files and folders and replace them with older versions. So, and this may sound obvious, *please* remember one simple rule when performing a pcAnywhere cloning procedure: Always make sure that the source PC contains the most recent versions of the files.

The source PC is the computer that you're transferring files from. It sends files to the destination computer on a search and destroy mission for impostors and eradicates them.

To clone a file or folder, follow these steps:

1. **From either the host or remote PC, click the Remote Control button on the Action bar.**

   All existing remote control connection items appear on the desktop.

2. **Right-click a remote control connection item that uses the appropriate modem or network connection device; then choose Connect from the pop-up menu.**

   After the connection is established, the online toolbar appears.

3. **Click the File Transfer button on the online toolbar.**

   The File Manager window appears.

4. **From either the remote or host PC list box, click to select the files or folders that you want to clone.**

   The files you select become source files, coming from the source computer. They delete and replace other versions of the same file on the destination computer.

5. **Choose File➪Clone.**

   The Clone Folder dialog box appears, as shown in Figure 8-10. The dialog box asks whether you're sure that you want to clone the files and folders that you selected. At the bottom of the box is a warning, similar to the one I stated earlier in this section.

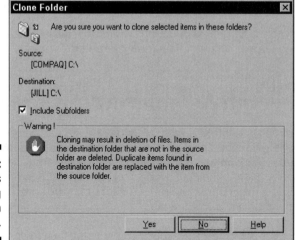

Clone Folder

Are you sure you want to clone selected items in these folders?

Source:
[COMPAQ] C:\

Destination:
[JILL] C:\

☑ Include Subfolders

Warning !

Cloning may result in deletion of files. Items in the destination folder that are not in the source folder are deleted. Duplicate items found in destination folder are replaced with the item from the source folder.

Yes   No   Help

Figure 8-10: Heed this warning when cloning files.

6. **Click Yes to continue the cloning process.**

   Another dialog box appears asking if you're sure that you want to clone the selected files.

7. **Click Yes to complete the cloning process.**

Advanced File Transfer Options

Advanced File Transfer options include Overwrite Preferences, Compression, Crash Recovery and Speed Send. You set these options by using the File Transfer Options dialog box.

To access the File Transfer Options dialog box, follow these steps:

1. **From either the host or remote PC, click the Remote Control button on the Action bar.**

   All existing remote control connection items appear on the desktop.

2. **Right-click a remote control connection item that uses the appropriate modem or network connection device; then choose Connect from the pop-up menu.**

   After the connection is established, the online toolbar appears.

3. **Click the File Transfer button on the online toolbar.**

   The File Manager window appears.

4. **Choose Tools⇨Options.**

   The File Transfer Options dialog box appears, as shown in Figure 8-11.

5. **Click the check boxes of the features you want enabled. (I cover these features in detail later in this chapter.)**

   Click the Include Subfolders in All Operations check box if you want the features that you've enabled to apply to folders and files included in the files that you're transferring.

   You almost always want to click the Include Subfolders in All Operations check box. In fact, I tried to think of a practical example where you wouldn't want to do so, but I couldn't come up with one!

6. **Click OK.**

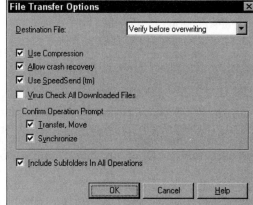

Figure 8-11:
Use the File
Transfer
Options
dialog box
to enable
advanced
file transfer
options.

The advanced file transfer options covered in the following sections can go a long way toward preventing your data from encountering equipment failures, computer viruses, and plain old human error.

Overwrite Preferences

Overwrite Preferences can be a lifesaver (or should I say data saver). The options in this drop-down box enable you to choose whether verification must occur before a file is overwritten during the transfer process. You choose an overwrite preference from the Destination File drop-down box in the File Transfer Options dialog box. Here are the overwrite options that you can choose from:

- ✔ **Verify Before Overwriting:** This is the careful choice. It slows things up a bit to verify each file before it's overwritten — but it's better to be safe than sorry.

- ✔ **Overwrite Automatically:** Choose this option if you're transferring or synchronizing large numbers of files (or running an AutoTransfer as discussed in the next section). When large numbers of files are involved, you may find it too time consuming to confirm your intention to overwrite each one.

- ✔ **Overwrite Older Files Only:** This is the compromise option, intended to prevent you from accidentally overwriting the most recently changed version of a file.

Compression

If you want to speed up transmission of your files, you can enable the pcAnywhere Compression feature. The Compression feature applies a special format to your data that makes it take up less space, thereby increasing the speed at which it is transferred between two computers.

Enabling file compression by using pcAnywhere won't improve transmission speed for files that have already been compressed by another utility, such as WinZip. All the repeating patterns and extra spaces in the data that the Compression feature eliminates — in order to save space — have already been ferreted out by the other utility. The pcAnywhere Compression feature can't further compress data that has already been compressed.

You get better results enabling compression when you're transferring text files than when you're transferring graphics files. Text files can be reduced by about 60% with compression. In other words, they take up only 40% of the space that they did before compression. In contrast, graphics files can only be reduced in size by about 10%.

You enable data compression by selecting the Use Compression check box in the File Transfer Options dialog box.

Crash Recovery

The Crash Recovery feature can save you time, even if it doesn't literally "recover" anything. If a file transfer session is interrupted (by a power failure or because someone needs to carry out another operation on the host computer, for example), crash recovery enables the file transfer to continue from the exact point at which it was interrupted. To enable the crash recovery feature, you select the Allow Crash Recovery check box in the File Transfer Options dialog box.

Be sure to enable crash recovery when you're transferring a very large file or a large number of individual files. If your session is abnormally terminated, the file transfer operation can pick up where it left off without having to start from the beginning when the connection is resumed.

SpeedSend

The SpeedSend feature enables pcAnywhere to compare versions of a file on the source computer with the version of the same file on the destination computer. Only the information that is different is actually transferred, as opposed to the entire file being transferred. To enable SpeedSend, select the Use SpeedSend check box in the File Transfer Options dialog box.

Virus Check All Downloaded Files

Why enable this option? If you have to ask, you probably don't read the papers. This little feature goes a long way toward inoculating your system. Symantec is the developer of cutting-edge antivirus software, so it stands to reason that this is a well-designed feature.

Confirm Operation Prompt

The Confirm Operation Prompt options cause extra dialog boxes to appear warning you of the dire consequences and lost data that can occur if you're too nonchalant when transferring, moving, and synchronizing files. Personally, I feel better seeing these warning prompts. The extra two seconds it takes to confirm that I want to continue with the operation is time well spent in my humble opinion.

Other File Management Features You Need to Know About

When you're working in File Manager, you have control over both the host PC files and folders and the remote PC files and folders. You can even view the files and folders on both computers simultaneously. This control, combined with the file management tools described in this section, enables you to efficiently organize, store, and access data on both computers.

Creating a new folder

When you're transferring files or folders from one computer to another, it's sometimes convenient to create a new folder in which you can segregate and store the transferred files. For example, you may want to create a folder on the host labeled Files Transferred from Remote. This helps you store transferred files that don't fit in an existing folder.

To create a new folder during on online session, follow these steps:

1. **From either the host or remote PC, click the Remote Control button on the Action bar.**

   All existing remote control connection items appear on the desktop.

2. **Right-click a remote control connection item that uses the appropriate modem or network connection device; then choose Connect from the pop-up menu.**

   After the connection is established, the online toolbar appears.

3. **Click the File Transfer button on the online toolbar.**

   The File Manager window appears.

4. **From either the host PC or remote PC list box, click to select the drive on which you want to create the new folder.**

   You choose this drive from the drop-down list box directly beneath the list box's title bar.

5. **Choose File⇨New Folder.**

   A folder icon appears with the default name New Folder, and the folder name remains highlighted.

6. **Type a distinctive name, such as** Files Transferred from Remote, **over the highlighted text; press Enter when you have finished typing.**

   A new folder, labeled with the name you designated, now appears in the remote PC or host PC list box.

Deleting, renaming, and copying files and folders

You can delete, rename, and copy files and folders on either the host PC or remote PC, regardless of which computer you're sitting in front of.

Deleting a file or folder

To delete a file or folder, follow these steps:

1. **With a connection already established, click the File Transfer button on the online toolbar.**

   The File Manager window opens.

2. **From either the host PC or remote PC list box, click to select the file or folder that you want to delete.**

3. **Press the Delete key.**

   A dialog box appears asking you to confirm that you want to delete the file or folder.

4. **Click Yes.**

   The file or folder you selected disappears without a trace.

Renaming a file or folder

To rename an existing file or folder on either the host PC or remote PC, follow these steps:

1. **With a connection already established, click the File Transfer button on the online toolbar.**

   The File Manager window opens.

2. **From either the host PC or remote PC list box, right-click the file or folder that you want to rename and choose Rename from the pop-up menu.**

   The name of the file or folder is selected, as shown in Figure 8-12.

3. **Over the existing highlighted text, type a new name for the file or folder and press Enter when you are finished.**

Copying a file or folders

To copy a file or folder to either the host PC or remote PC, follow these steps:

1. **With a connection already established, click the File Transfer button on the online toolbar.**

   The File Manager window opens.

2. **From either the remote PC or host PC list box, click to select the file or folder that you want to copy.**

3. **Choose Edit⇨Copy from the File Manager menu bar (see Figure 8-13).**

   This copies the selected file or folder to the pcAnywhere Clipboard.

4. **Select the folder on the host PC or remote PC that you want to copy the file or folder to.**

5. **Choose Edit⇨Paste to copy the file or folder from the Clipboard to the destination folder that you identified in Step 4.**

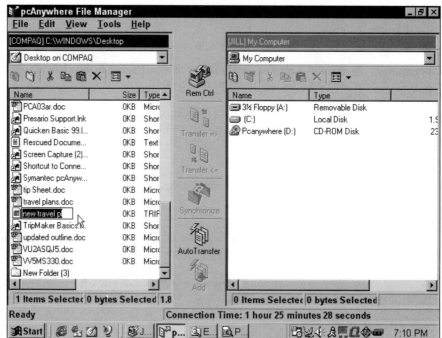

Figure 8-12:
Rename a
file by typing
over the
highlighted
name.

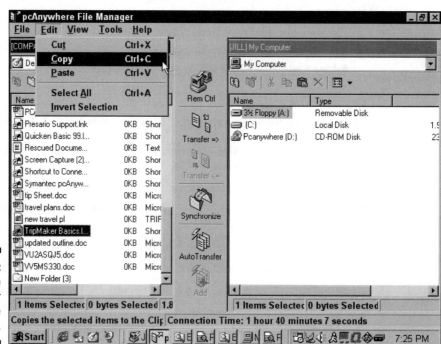

Figure 8-13:
Copy a file
or folder
using the
Edit menu.

The Begin File Transfer dialog box appears, as shown in Figure 8-14, asking whether you're sure that you want to transfer the selected file or folder. Don't be confused — a cut-and-paste operation accomplishes the same result as a file transfer operation. That's why you see the file transfer dialog box in the midst of your cutting and pasting.

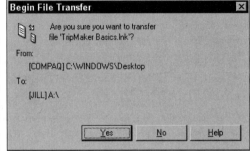

Figure 8-14:
Copying and
pasting files
is similar to
transferring
them.

6. **Click Yes to proceed with pasting the file or folder.**

   The File Status box appears, telling you that a file transfer operation is taking place. Again don't be confused. Just remember that a cut-and-paste operation has the same result as a file transfer.

Comparing folders

pcAnywhere includes a useful feature for comparing folders on the remote computer and host computer, and letting you know whether they contain the same files. Any files that are different or missing are highlighted. This feature is particularly helpful if you're about to synchronize or clone files.

To use the Compare Folders feature, follow these steps:

1. **With a connection already established, click File Transfer from the online toolbar.**

   The File Manager window opens.

2. **Click to select in both the host and remote list boxes the folders that you want to compare.**

3. **Choose File⇨Compare Folders.**

   pcAnywhere compares the two folders and highlights in the File Manager window the files that are different. A message box appears that explains this, as shown in Figure 8-15.

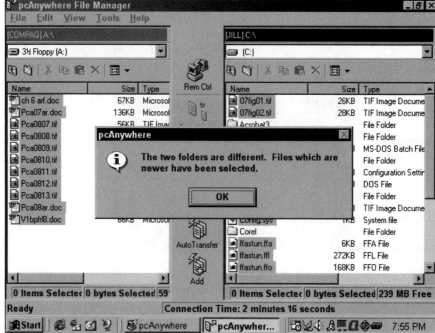

Figure 8-15:
As this mes-
sage box
states, files
that are
different are
highlighted.

4. **Click OK to exit the message box.**

It's a good idea to use the Compare Folders feature before running a cloning
or synchronization procedure to ensure that you know what files will be
affected by the operation.

Using AutoTransfer

AutoTransfer is a fast way to transfer and synchronize lots of files using something called a *script*. A script is a mini program of commands and directions
that specify the destination drive or folder for the files and folders you transfer. (In Chapter 5, I explain how to configure AutoTransfer from the remote
computer. In Chapter 14, I tell you more about writing and running scripts
and how to access the pcAnywhere Script Guide on the installation CD.) After
a script has been written for your system, you can run it using the steps
described in this section.

To run an AutoTransfer operation, follow these steps:

1. **Make sure that an AutoTransfer script exists on your system to automate the transfer of files.**

Check with your network administrator, or take a look at Chapter 14 for more details on locating or creating an AutoTransfer script on your system. The script specifies the destination folders to which files are to be transferred using the AutoTransfer procedure.

2. **After you've established a connection, select the files or folders that you want to transfer using the AutoTransfer operation and the previously created script, and click the Add button on the pcAnywhere File Manager Action bar (see Figure 8-16).**

Clicking the Add button transfers the selected files to the pcAnywhere Add to AutoTransfer dialog box, as shown in Figure 8-17. This dialog box appears on your screen automatically after you click the Add button.

3. **Click the OK button to close the dialog box.**

4. **Click the AutoTransfer button on the pcAnywhere File Manager Action bar.**

The selected files are transferred to the destination specified by the script.

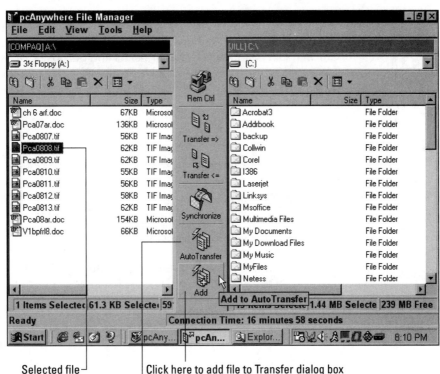

Figure 8-16:
Use the Action bar buttons for an AutoTransfer.

Selected file

Click here to add file to Transfer dialog box

Click here to begin AutoTransfer

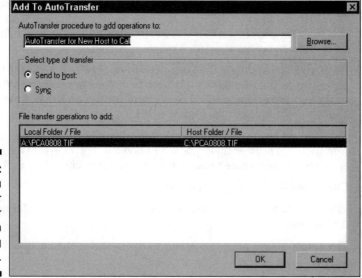

Figure 8-17:
The files you
select for
AutoTransfer
appear in
this dialog
box.

Don't want to take the time to learn how to write a script? Ask your network administrator if a pcAnywhere AutoTransfer script already exists that you can use or that can be modified for your needs and purposes. Network administrators often write scripts to help them back up files on the network, and your administrator may be willing to help you modify an existing one so that you can expedite file transfer operations.

Finding Your Way out of File Manager

If you initially opened File Manager from either the host PC or remote PC online menus, you can exit the File Manager window and return to a remote control session without ending the connection. Choose File⇨Close to exit File Manager and continue with your session.

However, if you initiated a File Transfer–only session by clicking the Remote Control button on the Action bar, closing File Manager ends your session.

Chapter 9

Knock! Knock!
Who's Remotely Calling?

● ●

In This Chapter

▶ Dialing the host from exotic locales

▶ Making the Button bar and toolbar work for you

▶ Printing from remote locations

● ●

*A*fter you've mastered the basics of starting and managing a pcAnywhere remote control session, you're ready to take your laptop to any far corner of the world that has telephone service. This chapter tells you how you can liberate yourself from the constraints of working at home or in an office. It tells you how to configure your computer to automatically dial your office PC from faraway places (or nearby suburbs).

You find out how to fine-tune the picture you see on the remote screen during your session, and how to customize the Button bar with the settings you use most. This chapter also covers printing a document remotely, even if you're living in a suburb in the United States but dialing the host in Outer Mongolia.

Dialing in from Faraway Places

If you want to dial in to your office PC from an Aspen ski condo, a lakefront cottage, or even a Jamaican villa, you can do it with pcAnywhere. You just need to configure the correct connection items on the host and remote PCs before you board the plane.

Review your connection items before you pack

There are three main types of connection item files: remote, host, and caller. Each connection item file is represented as an icon on the pcAnywhere desktop.

A remote connection item contains dialing, security, and hardware information required to enable a remote PC to call a host PC. The host connection item contains hardware and security information required to enable the host PC to accept a call from a remote PC. Caller connection items contain information about callers authorized to connect to the host, such as their login name and password.

The remote connection item usually needs to be reconfigured when you dial in from a new place. The host and caller items generally remain unchanged. For more information on connection items, take a look at Chapters 4 and 5.

Multiple connection items for callers on the go

If you're always on the go, you may need to configure multiple connection items. For example, if you're in a hotel, you may have to dial "9" to place an outside call. You need to tell pcAnywhere what country and area code you're dialing from. You also must specify the procedure to be followed if you're dialing from outside your own area code. Chapter 5 tells you how to create a new connection item for each port of call.

Modifying a single remote connection item

If you're calling from a new place — say your summer cottage — but you only dial in from one or two locations, you may find it simpler to modify your existing remote connection item rather than create a new one.

To modify an existing remote connection item, follow these steps:

1. **Click the Remote Control button on the pcAnywhere Action bar.**

   All existing remote control connection items appear on your desktop.

2. **Right-click the connection item that you want to modify, and select Properties from the pop-up menu.**

   The Properties dialog box for the connection item opens with the Connection Info page on top.

3. **Select the type of connection device that you're using or the port number (COM1, for example) where your external device is attached, as shown in Figure 9-1.**

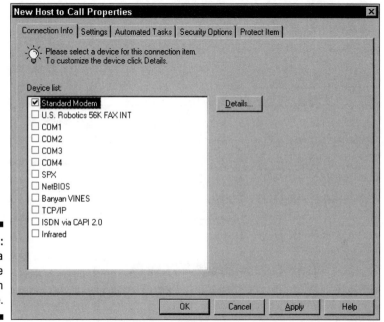

Figure 9-1:
Select a
hardware
connection
device.

4. **Click Apply to save the change (if any) that you've made to the Connection Info page.**

5. **Click the Settings tab.**

   The Settings page appears, as shown in Figure 9-2.

6. **Select the Use Dialing Properties and Phone Number option, and make sure that the phone number shown for the host PC is correct.**

7. **Click the Dialing Properties button.**

   The Dialing Properties dialog box appears, as shown in Figure 9-3.

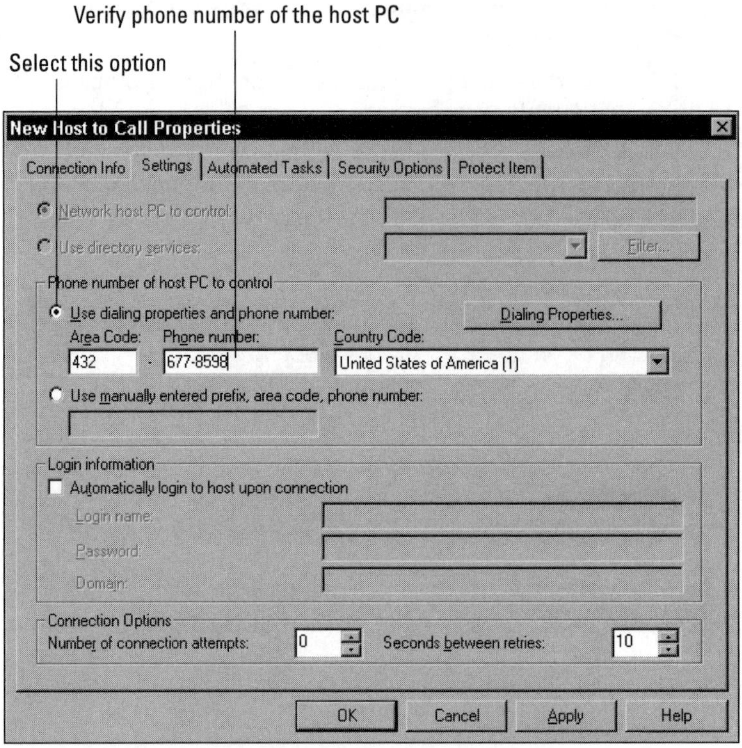

Verify phone number of the host PC

Select this option

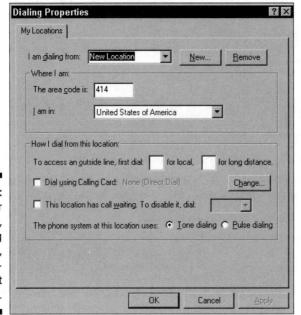

Figure 9-2:
Verify that
the phone
number for
the host PC
is entered
correctly.

Figure 9-3:
Enter your
location,
dialing
instructions,
and pay-
ment
method.

8. **Choose the country of the host PC from the I Am In drop-down box.**

   pcAnywhere maintains a list of telephone area codes for each country so that you don't have to look them up. When you select a country from the drop-down list, pcAnywhere enters the area code for the country automatically.

9. **If a special number must first be dialed from your location to access an outside line or to make long-distance calls (for example, 9 or 1), type that number in the To Access an Outside Line, First Dial text box.**

10. **(Optional) If you're paying for the call to the host PC with a calling card, select the Dial Using Calling Card option and click the Change button.**

    The Change Calling Card dialog box appears, as shown in Figure 9-4.

11. **(Optional) Select your calling card type (the issuing company) from the Calling Card to Use drop-down list, and type your account number in the Calling Card Number text box and click OK to exit the Change Calling Card dialog box.**

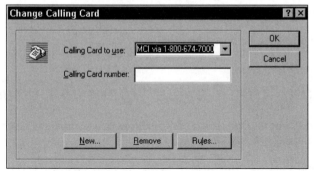

Figure 9-4:
Enter your
calling card
information
to pay for
the call to
the host PC.

12. **Back in the Dialing Properties dialog box, select the This Location Has Call Waiting check box if the location from which you are dialing has call waiting. To disable it, select one of the codes for the various call waiting systems from the To Disable It, Dial drop-down list. (If you're not sure which code to use, call your local phone company and ask them.)**

    The call-waiting feature can interfere with your connection to the host computer. It's best to eliminate it as a possible cause of any problem that you may have with your connection.

13. **Select either the Tone Dialing or Pulse dialing option to indicate whether the phone system from which you're dialing uses pulse or tone dialing.**

14. **Click OK to save your changes and exit the Dialing Properties dialog box.**

Your remote PC is now configured to dial a host PC from a new and distant location. Bon Voyage!

Fine-Tuning Remote Control Operations

During your travels, you may find it necessary to adjust the image that appears on the screen of the remote computer. For example, you may find that the connection is too slow, or that the host screen that appears on your desktop is too small to work from.

Settings that affect what you see during a remote session are adjusted by using the Remote Operation page, which is accessed from the Tools menu. These settings can be modified even during an active session.

Don't like what you see? Even if you're in the middle of an active communication session, you can adjust the settings on the Remote Operation page without disconnecting. However, the settings that you modify during an active session affect only the current session.

Accessing the Remote Operation page

To access the Remote Operation page, from which you can adjust all remote control settings, follow these steps:

1. **Click the Remote Control button on the pcAnywhere Action bar.**

2. **Select the connection item icon of the current session you want to modify by clicking it once, or begin an active session by double-clicking the icon.**

   If you adjust Remote Operation settings during an active session, the adjustments take effect only for the duration of the session.

3. **Choose Tools➪Application Options.**

   The Applications Options dialog box appears on your screen.

4. **Click the Remote Operation tab.**

   The Remote Operation page appears, as shown in Figure 9-5.

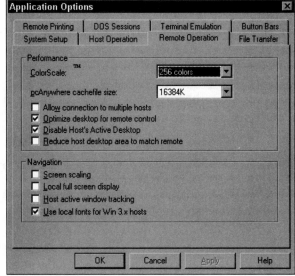

Figure 9-5:
The Remote
Operation
page con-
tains set-
tings that
affect all
remote
control
sessions.

Adjusting Remote Operation settings

You can enable the following settings from the Remote Operation page of the Application Options dialog box by placing a check mark in the box beside the setting:

- ✔ **ColorScale:** This option determines the number of colors that appear on the host PC screen as displayed on the remote PC's desktop. Selecting two or four, as opposed to 256 colors, reduces the amount of image data pcAnywhere must transmit and improves the speed of your connection.

- ✔ **pcAnywhere Cachefile Size:** The cachefile stores images from the host computer so that the image doesn't have to be retransmitted when the remote PC accesses it. This saves time. The larger the cachefile, the more host images are stored for expedited access. When available memory is a concern, you can reduce the cachefile size.

- ✔ **Allow Connection to Multiple Hosts:** This option enables the remote PC to connect to multiple hosts. Each host screen is displayed in a separate window that can be minimized.

- ✔ **Optimize Desktop for Remote Control:** This option improves transmission during a session by cleaning up the host's desktop and decreasing the amount of image data pcAnywhere has to transmit over phone lines. Any wallpaper, patterns, screen savers, power savers, and similar options are disabled on the host desktop, which means that all the colors and dots of image data that comprise them don't have to be transmitted.

✔ **Disable Host's Active Desktop:** The Active Desktop function is a feature of Internet Explorer 4.0 and Windows 98. This feature enables Web pages to be turned into items that reside on the desktop and are updated automatically. Disabling this feature enhances the functionality of pcAnywhere.

✔ **Reduce Host Desktop Area to Match Remote:** Enabling this feature automatically reduces the host PC screen resolution to match the resolution used on the remote PC. This eliminates the potential problem of an image being distorted because the host is using a higher resolution than what is supported on the remote PC.

Resolution is the degree of sharpness of a printed character or displayed image; it's usually expressed as a matrix of pixels (dots) on lines. For example, 640 x 480 is a standard resolution setting that means 640 dots on 480 lines. Another common resolution setting is 800 x 600.

✔ **Screen Scaling:** This option scales down the size of the host PC screen so that it fits comfortably on the remote PC desktop, as opposed to requiring the user to scroll to view different parts.

✔ **Local Full Screen Display:** This option lets the host PC use all of the remote PC desktop, instead of appearing in a window on the remote screen. This makes the host screen easier to view and work from because it appears as a larger image on the remote desktop.

✔ **Host Active Window Tracking:** This option ensures that the remote PC user sees any screen that's currently active on the host PC, such as an error message.

✔ **Use Local Fonts for Win 3.x Hosts:** If you're using an early version of Windows (3.*x* series), this option improves performance by closely matching the fonts on the remote and host PCs. If you're using Windows 95 or a later version on both machines, you can ignore this option.

Customizing the pcAnywhere Button Bar

You can customize the pcAnywhere Action bar and toolbars by using the Button Bars page in the Application Options dialog box. By using the settings on the Button Bars page, you can determine which buttons appear on the Action bar and the size of the Action buttons. You can also specify additional information to display on the toolbar located directly beneath the Action Bar on the pcAnywhere desktop.

Accessing the Button Bars page

To access the Button Bars page of the Application Options dialog box, follow these steps:

1. **Choose Tools➪Application Options.**

   The Application Options dialog box appears.

2. **Click the Button Bars tab.**

   The Button Bars page appears, as shown in Figure 9-6.

Figure 9-6:
The Button
Bars page
enables you
to add
Action
buttons to
your screen
and to
display
additional
information
on the
toolbar.

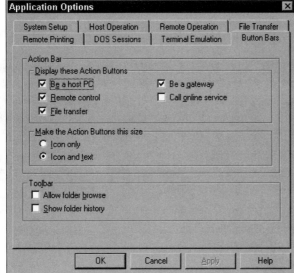

Selecting options on the Button Bars page

The Button Bars page offers the following three types of configuration options:

> ✔ **Display These Action Buttons:** Select the check box beside each Action button that you want displayed on the Action bar. Available buttons include Be a Host PC, Remote Control, File Transfer, Be a Gateway, and Call Online Service.

✔ **Make the Action Buttons This Size:** Indicate whether you want to display only an icon for each Action button or you want the icon to be accompanied by some descriptive text.

✔ **Toolbar:** You can display two types of additional information on the toolbar, as shown in Figure 9-7:

- **Allow Folder Browse:** This option displays the folder browse box on the toolbar, allowing you to change folders directly from the toolbar.

- **Show Folder History:** This option displays a list of the most recently selected folders.

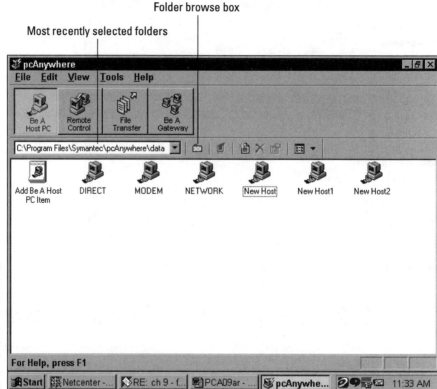

Folder browse box

Most recently selected folders

Figure 9-7:
You can display optional file information on the toolbar.

Look, No Hands! Remote Printing

Remote printing is a feature that enables you to execute a print command on the host PC. The document is produced on the printer that the host PC is connected to at the host location.

To configure the remote PC so that you can print a file from a printer where the host PC is located, follow these steps:

1. **Choose Tools⇨Application Options.**

   The Application Options dialog box appears.

2. **Click the Remote Printing tab.**

   The screen shown in Figure 9-8 appears. (This figure shows that a printer named Office Printer is already configured for remote printing.)

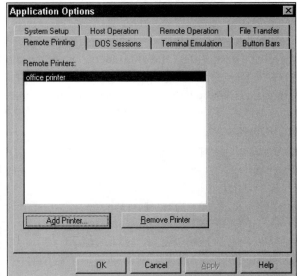

Figure 9-8:
List of available printers at the host location.

3. **Click the Add Printer button.**

   The Add Printer Wizard dialog box appears, as shown in Figure 9-9.

Manufacturer   Model

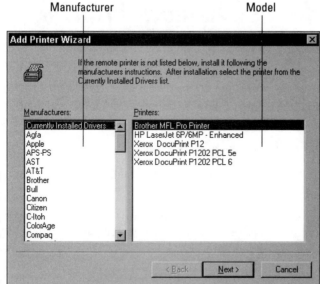

Figure 9-9:
Select a
printer
manufacturer
and model
from the list.

4. **From the two list boxes, select the manufacturer and model for the printer to which you want to send the print job; then click Next.**

Another Add Printer dialog box appears, as shown in Figure 9-10, asking you to name the printer that you're configuring for the print job.

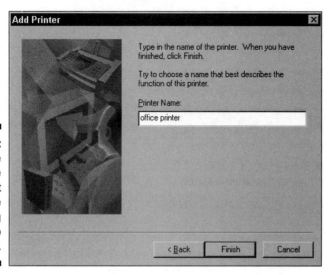

Figure 9-10:
Type a name
here for the
printer that
you're
configuring
to print to
remotely.

5. **Type a name for the printer.**

   This name appears on the list of available printers on the remote PC. It can be selected the next time the remote user prints a document. Select this printer when you want to print a document at the location of the host computer.

6. **Click Finish.**

If your printer isn't listed in the Add Printer Wizard, you may need to get a driver from the manufacturer. Chapter 15 tells you how to obtain an updated printer driver.

Part III

For Network Administrators Only

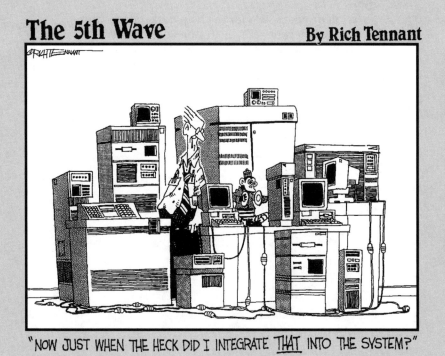

"NOW JUST WHEN THE HECK DID I INTEGRATE THAT INTO THE SYSTEM?"

In this part . . .

*P*art III provides help for the help desk. pcAnywhere can be a network administrator's best friend. You learn to remotely access troubled workstations and audit daily activity. You also learn how to configure a gateway to link your entire local area network (LAN) to the outside world using a single modem.

Chapter 10

Dial Up and Say A-h-h-h!

· ·

· ·

*I*f you're like most network administrators, you're constantly scrambling to placate frustrated users and put out fires. You don't have a lot of extra time on your hands to wander the halls of your workplace listening to the clicking keyboards of contented users and perfectly cooperating computers.

This chapter is intended to help you do a little less scrambling. You gain a new appreciation of pcAnywhere as a diagnostic tool, and you find out how to avoid a few headaches by mastering some basic troubleshooting techniques for telephone line problems and hardware conflicts.

Knowing Your Network

A network, in its simplest and purest form, is a system of two or more computers that can communicate with each other and share resources. *Resources* consist of all the pieces of the network, including drives, disks, printers, modems, processors, software, and data files. Computers on a network can share their own resources and access the resources of other computers.

The two basic types of networks are peer-to-peer and server-based. In a *peer-to-peer* network, all the computers are equal (thus, the term *peer*). They share and access data from each other, with no computer being specially designated to store resources for the other computers. There is no hierarchy of computers.

In contrast, a *server-based* network has (surprise!) a *server,* which is a computer designated to provide shared, centrally located resources to other computers on the network. These other computers are called *workstations,* and they can access the resources stored on one or more servers.

A single server can provide centralized, shared access to printers, applications, and files. Alternatively, multiple *dedicated servers* can each provide distinct functions for workstations on the network. For example, a *print server* can make printers available to workstations; an *application server* can provide access to software programs for workstations to install or run; and a *file server* can store and manage data and documents in a centralized location and provide workstations with access to those files.

A server often fulfills another important role: It may maintain a database to validate the passwords or names of users seeking access to network resources. Servers that perform this function are often locked or secured to prevent tampering. These locked areas are referred to as *server closets.*

Server-based networks are the standard model for networks serving more than ten users. Peer-to-peer networks usually service smaller networks. Throughout this book, the term *network* applies to all networks, whether they're peer-to-peer or server based. (In Chapter 2, I explain that either the standard or the network version of pcAnywhere can be installed on a network. The network version, however, is more economical and generally used on server-based networks.)

If you purchase the standard (as opposed to the network) version of pcAnywhere, you must install it on each workstation individually by performing a *standard* installation. If you buy the network version, you can install it first on the server and then install it on all the workstations at once using a special *shared installation file.* (For more information on installing pcAnywhere on a network, see Chapter 2.) This process is called a *network installation*, and it affects many aspects of pcAnywhere configuration. Because the network installation files are in the shared directory, you need to take extra steps to access them when reconfiguring certain options on the workstation.

You may have noticed that some of the pcAnywhere installation terminology is pretty generic, which can make it a little confusing. A *standard installation* refers to an installation of pcAnywhere on an individual PC, as opposed to a *network installation,* in which you create a shared installation directory so that all network users have access to the installation files. A *Typical* installation, on the other hand (see Chapter 2) means that you are choosing to install all the pcAnywhere features without picking and choosing, whereas a *Custom* installation means that you are choosing to install only certain features.

Help for the Help Desk

The *help desk* isn't simply a desk. It's a phone that sits on a desk, answered by a person called the *help desk operator.* The help desk operator is a term affectionately used to describe a person charged with providing technical assistance to computer users in the workplace. For example, an executive in a corner office may call up the help desk and complain that his computer won't boot up. The help desk operator dutifully hurries off to the executive's office only to find that the computer isn't plugged in. Often, however, the dutiful help desk operator faces far more complicated problems.

Help desk operators are a diverse group. In smaller companies, the network administrator may field users' technical questions in addition to keeping the network up, running, and current. Some larger companies may hire one or more help desk operators whose sole responsibility is to provide this type of hands-on technical support. And in yet another scenario, a company may contract with one or many outside consultants to answer questions and provide technical support for employees.

Regardless of who is providing the help, pcAnywhere can serve as an important diagnostic tool. pcAnywhere allows a help desk operator on a network to view the screen of a problematic PC without being physically located in front of it. Instead, he or she can troubleshoot the problem from a remote workstation, or even from home. This is great news for any network administrator who receives an unwelcome weekend or late night beeper page. It also allows an outside consultant who has pcAnywhere to provide help without billing for a "trip" charge.

For a help desk operator to troubleshoot without being physically present, the troubled workstation must be in *host mode*. Host mode means that the workstation has launched the pcAnywhere program so that it can receive a call from a remote computer and begin a pcAnywhere remote communication session. The help desk operator, sitting at a remote computer, can then dial into the recalcitrant PC and see what's upsetting the user. Because the remote PC takes control of the host computer during the pcAnywhere session, the help desk guru can even make changes to settings on the host without being physically in front of it.

It's also necessary for the help desk operator to be able to bypass any security that's part of the Windows operating system. For example, a help desk operator may be able to remotely connect to a workstation launched in host mode, but may not be able to get into the file that is causing the trouble because of a Windows security option that's been enabled. These issues are usually associated with the Windows NT operating system. The next section, "Required Rights to Run With (Say That Three Times Fast!)," talks about Windows NT and its security features.

A help desk operator or network administrator can use pcAnywhere to gain easy access to a server that's off-site or in a server closet. If the server has been launched in host mode, the administrator can make the necessary changes on the server without ever having to fumble for a key to the closet.

Required Rights to Run With (Say That Three Times Fast!)

Windows NT is an operating system designed especially for networks. It has special features (not offered in other versions of Windows) that give the network administrator more control over resources and provide greater security on a network. For example, the administrator can limit the user's ability to tamper with a centralized database on a server or to install and delete software on the network. The administrator can also regulate access to sensitive files.

NT users' rights and permissions usually vary with their job descriptions. For example, a company's sales staff generally doesn't need the rights and permissions to access sensitive personnel data and medical records.

Rights differ from access permissions. NT *rights* span the entire network, such as the ability to access, back up, or shut down the network. A user, for example, may be given the right to back up a system.

Access permissions, on the other hand, are specific to individual resources and limit access to things such as a client billing program, a personnel file, or a color printer.

Understanding access permissions

The sharing of resources in Microsoft Windows NT is regulated by access permissions. Access permissions determine the extent to which users can access and modify folders and files.

Access permissions apply to directories, as well as to individual files. If a user is denied access to a directory, the user cannot access any files or folders within the directory.

NT access permissions affect the tasks users can perform and the files that they can access when they use pcAnywhere. You can make files and other resources more secure by using NT access permissions along with, or in place of, pcAnywhere password protections. (I talk about security issues in much more detail in Chapter 11.)

NT access permissions are as follows:

- ✔ **No Access:** Prevents access to a resource by excluding the user from the directories, subdirectories, and files (including application files or files used to access a hardware device, such as a printer).

- ✔ **Read:** Allows the user to view directories, subdirectories, files, and all data within those elements, but the user cannot change, add to, or delete from those directories or files.

- ✔ **Change:** Allows the user to view and change directories, subdirectories, files, and all data within those elements.

- ✔ **Full Control:** Allows the user to "take ownership" of a directory and its subdirectories and files. Taking ownership means that the user cannot only modify a directory or file for which she has full control permission, but that she can also specify the access that everyone else has to that directory or file.

What file permissions to check

You must have appropriate access permissions to install pcAnywhere on a network, regardless of whether you're performing an installation on one computer or on a network. Remember, to perform a network installation using a shared installation file, you must have the network version of pcAnywhere. (See Chapter 2 for more about installing pcAnywhere on a network.)

To be able to run all the pcAnywhere services and features after you install the program, the remote PC must have the correct access permissions to both remote files and host files. You can see what access permissions are granted for a particular file by following these steps:

1. **Right-click the Start button on the Windows NT desktop, and choose Explore from the pop-up menu.**

    The Explorer window opens, displaying drives, folders, and files stored on the computer.

2. **Right-click the icon of the folder or file for which you want to view the access permissions, and choose Properties from the pop-up menu.**

    The Properties dialog box for that folder or file appears.

3. **Click the Security tab.**

    The Security page for the file appears, displaying buttons to click to display further information about file settings related to security.

4. **Click the Permissions button.**

    A dialog box appears, displaying all permissions granted for that particular file or folder.

To run pcAnywhere properly and to be able to use all its features, you must set appropriate access permissions for its files. The access permissions needed for the pcAnywhere files on the remote PC are listed in Table 10-1. Table 10-2 summarizes the required file permissions for pcAnywhere files on the host computer.

Table 10-1 Access Permissions Required for Files on the Remote PC

Name of File	Required Access Permission
/pcANYWHERE	Read
/pcANYWHERE/DATA	Read
/pcANYWHERE/DATA/AW.RL7	Change (If the remote is logging sessions.)
/pcANYWHERE/LICENSE	Change

Table 10-2 Access Permissions Required for Files on the Host PC

Name of File	Required Access Permission
/pcANYWHERE	Read
/pcANYWHERE/DATA	Read
/pcANYWHERE/DATA/CALLERS.IDX	Change
/pcANYWHERE/DATA	Change
/pcANYWHERE/DATA/AW.HL7	Change (If the remote is logging sessions.)
/pcANYWHERE/LICENSE	Change

Changing access permissions

Ownership is the ability to establish access permissions. If you have ownership, you can assign access permissions to control what users can do with files. This is an NT option available only to the NT network administrator — and it's a trump card. Ownership enables the NT network administrator to assign access permissions to others, such as read, change, full control, and so on. A network administrator can generally take ownership of any file on the network.

To change access permissions for a file, follow these steps:

1. **Press Ctrl+Alt+Del to bring up the NT login box.**

   A dialog box appears prompting you to enter your name, password, and domain name, if applicable.

2. **Type your login name, password, and domain name, if applicable, in the NT login dialog box.**

3. **Right-click the Start button and choose Explore from the pop-up menu that appears.**

   The Windows Explorer appears on your desktop.

4. **In the Explorer window, right-click the file for which you want to modify or verify the access permissions, and choose Properties from the pop-up menu.**

   The Properties dialog box for the file appears, as shown in Figure 10-1. (You may see additional tabs on your screen, depending on the NT options enabled on your system.)

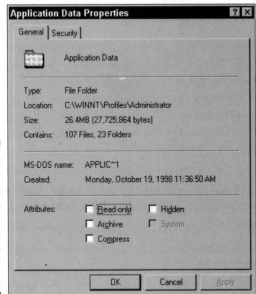

Figure 10-1:
The Properties dialog box displays the properties of the selected file.

5. **Click the Security tab.**

   The screen shown in Figure 10-2 appears.

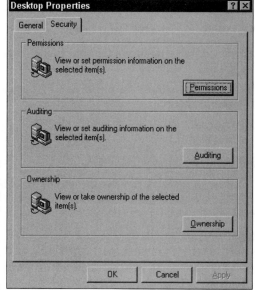

Figure 10-2:
You set
security
options from
the
Properties
dialog box.

6. **Click the Permissions button.**

   The Directory Permissions dialog box appears, as shown in Figure 10-3. A list of current users and groups having access to the file appears in the Name section of the dialog box.

7. **If the name of the remote user for whom you want to change access permissions appears in the Name section of the Directory Permissions dialog box, select it, and modify the permissions by using the Type of Access drop-down list. Then skip to Step 13.**

   If the remote user doesn't appear in the list, proceed to Step 8.

8. **If the name of the remote user doesn't appear in the Name section of the Directory Permissions dialog box, click the Add button.**

   The Add Users and Groups dialog box appears, as shown in Figure 10-4.

9. **In the List Names From drop-down box, select the name of the domain on which the remote PC is located.**

   A list of user groups appears. (For administrative purposes, users can be organized into groups having the same set of access permissions.)

10. **Click the Show Users button to display all the users on the system within the groups.**

11. **In the Names box, select the name of the user or group to whom you want to grant access permission.**

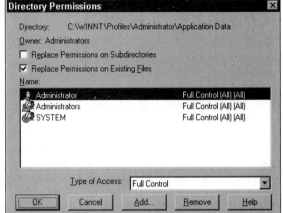

Figure 10-3:
Locate the
remote user
in the
Directory
Permissions
dialog box.

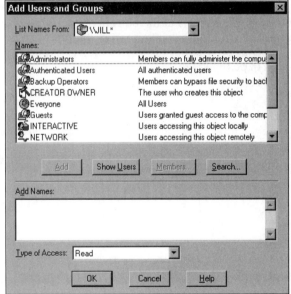

Figure 10-4:
Use this
dialog box
to add users
or groups
who don't
already
have access
to the file.

12. Click **Add**.

13. In the **Type** of Access drop-down list, specify the appropriate level of access permission for the remote user (see Figure 10-3).

14. Click OK three times to exit each open dialog box.

Using pcAnywhere as a Diagnostic Tool

pcAnywhere is a valuable diagnostic tool that enables you to view the activity on a workstation from another computer. The value of pcAnywhere as a troubleshooting tool depends on whether you, as an administrator, can access other workstations on the network. Troubled workstations must launch their computers in host mode, and you must be able to access and select them from a browse list.

Ensuring that users launch in host mode

As a network administrator, you may want to make an administrative decision that all workstations on the network will automatically initiate the host mode at startup. This means that every time a workstation user starts a version of Windows NT, Windows 95, or Windows 98 or later, pcAnywhere automatically launches in host mode. After this occurs, the small Host Waiting icon appears in the Windows taskbar (most likely at the bottom of your screen), as shown in Figure 10-5. The method you use to configure workstations to launch the host mode at startup depends on whether the workstation is running a standard or network installation of pcAnywhere.

Figure 10-5:
This familiar icon tells you that the host mode launched successfully.

Host Waiting icon

Configuring a standard installation to launch the host automatically

If you installed pcAnywhere using a standard installation, configuring the host to automatically launch at startup is a matter of selecting the appropriate check box.

Configuring a workstation to launch in host mode at startup

To set up a workstation to launch in host mode at startup, follow these steps:

1. **Launch the pcAnywhere program.**

2. **Click the Be A Host button on the Action bar.**

3. **Right-click the icon of the host PC that you want to launch at startup, and select Properties from the pop-up menu.**

    The Properties dialog box appears.

4. **Click the Settings tab.**

    The Settings page appears, as shown in Figure 10-6.

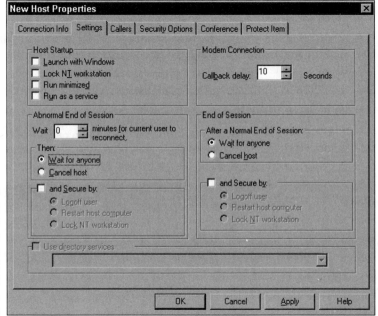

Figure 10-6:
Use the
Settings tab
to configure
the host PC
to launch at
startup.

5. **In the Host Startup section, click to place a check mark in the Launch with Windows box.**

    If this option is grayed out, it may be because it is password protected. To disable the password protection, follow the steps in the next section.

6. **(Optional) Click to place a check mark in the box next to Run Minimized.**

    If you select this check box, a tiny host icon appears on the taskbar at the bottom of your screen, letting you know that the host is waiting for a remote call.

7. (Optional) Click to place a check mark in the R<u>u</u>n as a Service check box if the workstation is to be used as a database, which stores files that can be retrieved by other computers on the network.

8. Click OK.

Disabling password protection on the host connection item

If the Launch with Windows option in the Host Startup box is grayed out and you're not on a network installation, the host connection item is probably password protected. You can disable the password protection by following these steps:

1. Click the Be A Host button on the pcAnywhere Action bar.

2. Right-click the icon of the host connection item for which you want to disable the password, and then choose <u>P</u>roperties from the pop-up menu.

   The Properties dialog box for the host connection item appears.

3. Click the Protect Item tab.

   The Protect Item page of the Properties dialog box appears, as shown in Figure 10-7.

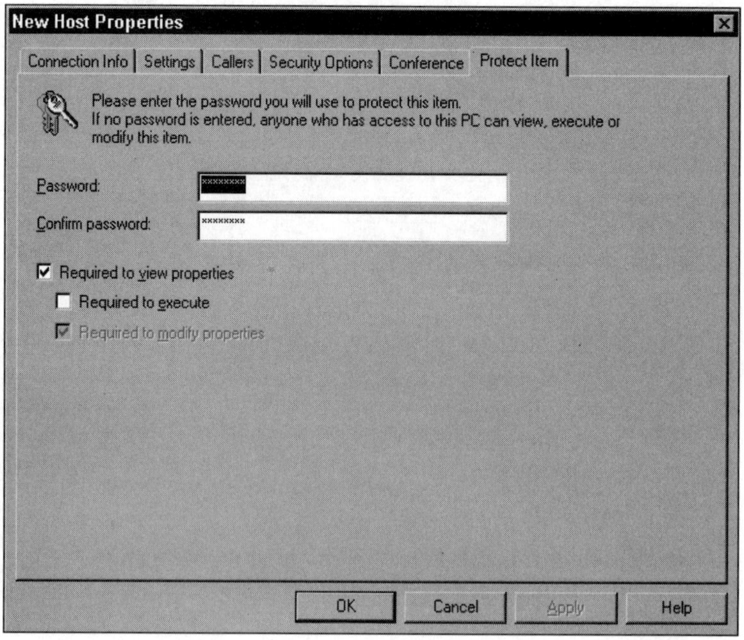

New Host Properties

Connection Info | Settings | Callers | Security Options | Conference | Protect Item

Please enter the password you will use to protect this item.
If no password is entered, anyone who has access to this PC can view, execute or modify this item.

Password: `xxxxxxxx`

Confirm password: `xxxxxxxx`

☑ Required to <u>v</u>iew properties

☐ Required to <u>e</u>xecute

☑ Required to <u>m</u>odify properties

OK | Cancel | Apply | Help

Figure 10-7:
Use the Protect Item tab of the Properties dialog box to disable a password.

4. **Click to remove the check mark from the Required to Execute box.**

5. **Click Apply to save any change that you've made to this page and then click OK. If you haven't made any changes, the Apply button is grayed out and you can simply click OK.**

Configuring a network installation to launch the host automatically

If you're running the network version of pcAnywhere, you have several options. You can configure the shared network directory to launch the host at startup for every computer, or you can allow users to change the location of their configuration files and configure their own computers to launch the host at startup.

You can find information about how to accomplish either of these configuration options in the pcAnywhere Administrator Guide included on the pcAnywhere installation CD. (Chapter 14 tells you how to access and view the manuals on the CD.) You can also read a wonderful article on the Symantec Web site (`www.symantec.com`) titled "Launching the Host Mode at Startup."

Configuring the workstations

After you set up the appropriate options on the network, you can configure individual pcAnywhere workstations to launch the host at startup by following these steps:

1. **Launch the pcAnywhere program on any workstation that you want to configure.**

2. **Click the Be A Host button on the Action bar.**

3. **Choose Tools⇨Application.**

   The Application Options dialog box appears.

4. **Click the Button Bars tab.**

   The Button Bars page appears, as shown in Figure 10-8.

5. **Under Toolbar, click to place a check mark in both the Allow Folder Browse and Show Folder History check boxes.**

6. **Click OK to close the Application Options dialog box.**

   A yellow folder icon now appears under the Action bar on the main pcAnywhere screen.

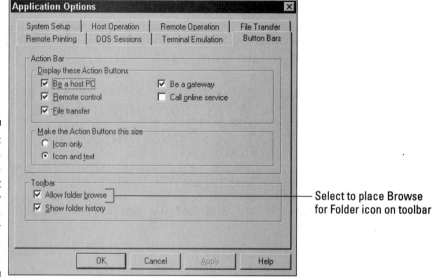

Figure 10-8:
Select the option here if you want to display the Browse for Folder button on the toolbar.

Select to place Browse for Folder icon on toolbar

7. **Click the yellow folder icon as shown in Figure 10-9.**

   The Browse for Folder dialog box appears, as shown in Figure 10-10, showing a list of folders on the local drive.

8. **Locate the folder in which you want to store the files you copy from the server.**

   These are the files that enable the workstation user to launch at startup.

9. **Without closing the Browse for Folder dialog box, right-click the Start button on the taskbar and choose Explore from the pop-up window to open the Explorer window.**

Click to display Browse for Folder dialog box

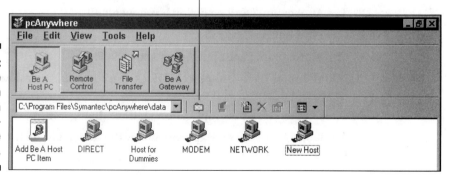

Figure 10-9:
Click the folder icon to display a list of folders on the local drive.

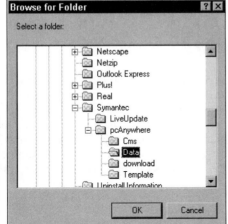

Figure 10-10:
This dialog
box displays
the folders
on the local
drive.

10. **In the Explorer window, locate the *.BHF folder on the shared network drive. (The shared network drive is explained in Chapter 4.)**

11. **Right-click the *.BHF folder and select Copy from the pop-up menu.**

12. **Locate the folder that you identified in Step 8, and right-click it.**

    A pop-up menu appears.

13. **Select Paste from the pop-up menu.**

    A dialog box tells you that the *.BHF folder on the shared network drive is being copied to the file on the workstation computer.

After the configuration is complete, you can set the workstation to launch the host at startup by following these steps:

1. **Click the Be a Host button on the Action bar.**

2. **Right-click the icon for the host PC that you want to launch at startup and choose Properties from the pop-up menu.**

    The Properties dialog box appears.

3. **Click the Settings tab.**

    The Settings page appears.

4. **In the Host Startup section, click to place a check mark in the Launch with Windows box.**

5. **Click OK to close the Properties dialog box.**

Troubleshooting Telephone Line and Modem Problems

Telephone line problems are particularly frustrating because they can involve equipment that you don't own or have full control over. The problems associated with modems and phone lines can taunt you by appearing sporadically or in a pattern that doesn't seem to make sense. Sometimes, you may be able to connect two computers that are using pcAnywhere; other times, not at all. Or you may be able to initiate a connection in one direction, but not the other. This section offers a few pointers for diagnosing and correcting telephone line problems.

Updating your modem

International standards for modem performance are established by the International Telecommunications Union (ITU). The ITU is headquartered in Geneva and has been setting standards for communications hardware since 1865.

The current ITU standard for modems in the United States is something called the V.90 standard. This standard incorporates 112 different programming *algorithms*, intended to take into account 168 different telephone line conditions.

An *algorithm* is a complex set of program instructions used in a particular set of circumstances. For example, algorithms are used for determining the fastest path for a signal to travel from one computer to another on a large network, or to re-route a signal when telephone circuits are busy.

Many older modems do not incorporate all 112 of the algorithms specified in the V.90 standards. Fewer algorithms mean that your modem's ability to take into account different line conditions is limited. This can result in problems making a connection, lost connections, and slow connections. If you're using an older modem, such as a V.34, consider upgrading to a V.90 modem.

Set the modem speed lower

If the rate of transmission for your modem is set higher than your old phone lines can accommodate, it can slow up the connection. If transmission is too rapid for the phone lines to accommodate, the result can be compromised data and lost connections. The need for increased error checking can also result in data having to be retransmitted, which certainly slows things down.

Checking your modem settings

Here are two things that you can do to avoid invoking the cumbersome error-checking feature (as a result of a large amount of compromised data coming across your modem) and keep data flowing smoothly:

✔ Experiment with maximum transmission speeds to see what your telephone lines can comfortably accommodate.

✔ Make sure that both the host and the remote modems are set to transfer data at the same rate.

If data is transferred only as fast as both the telephone line and receiving modem can accommodate it, you can substantially reduce the occurrence of data corruption and eliminate the slow process of reconstructing data via error checking.

Adjusting the modem speed

You may want to adjust your modem speed if you're experiencing problems with garbled data or lost connections. It may be that your modem is set to transmit data at a higher speed than the phone lines allow.

To set the modem speed for a connection item, follow these steps:

1. **From either the host or the remote computer, right-click the connection item for which you want to adjust the modem transmission speed, and choose** <u>P</u>**roperties from the pop-up menu.**

   The Properties dialog box for the connection item appears, with the Connection Info page on top.

2. **Click the** <u>D</u>**etails button.**

   The details dialog box, as shown in Figure 10-11, displays information about the modem, including the speed at which it's set to transmit data.

3. **In the** <u>M</u>**aximum Speed section, use the drop-down box to adjust your modem transmission speed.**

4. **Click OK to exit the details dialog box.**

5. **Click OK to exit the Properties dialog box.**

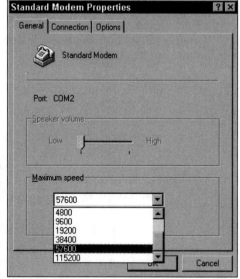

Strip!

Another step you may want to take in your modem troubleshooting effort is to remove all the following devices from the telephone line that you're using for the modem to your pcAnywhere connection:

- ✔ Telephones
- ✔ Fax Machines
- ✔ Answering Machines
- ✔ Caller ID Machines

If the phone line is loaded up with too many devices, the signal you're transmitting to establish the pcAnywhere connection may become degraded and corrupt.

Call the phone company

Some problems are beyond your control and require a call to the friendly customer service representative of your local telephone company. Here are a few of the options you may want to explore with the representative:

- ✔ **Line Testing:** Ask the telephone company to test the quality of the telephone line and let you know what they find out. Is the line capable of sustaining the 53-kilobits connection required by most modems?

✔ **Inside Wiring:** Ask the phone company to test the wiring inside your building. (There is usually a charge for this service.)

✔ **Line Conditioning:** The phone company may offer special *line conditioning* services that may enhance transmission. Although they cost extra, these are worth inquiring about. Line conditioning refers to special, extra-cost options on a telephone line that improve performance by reducing distortion and amplifying weak signals.

✔ **Digital Connections:** Switching to a digital connection, such as ISDN (which is discussed in the "Faster! Faster! ISDN that data now!" sidebar in Chapter 3), can enhance considerably the speed, reliability, and quality of your connection.

Dealing with IRQ/COM Port Conflicts

IRQ is one of those forced acronyms. It stands for Interrupt ReQuest. An *Interrupt Request* is a signal sent by a hardware device, such as a modem, to the computer's processor to let it know that it needs the processor's resources. A computer usually has 16 IRQ "lines" or settings, with each port or device configured to use a specific IRQ line. Each line has a different priority so that in the event of a conflict (a simultaneous request for use of a hardware device) the processor knows which IRQ request to process first.

An external modem connects to a serial port, which has one of four possible addresses: COM1, COM2, COM3, or COM4. These ports generally have one of two interrupt settings: IRQ3 or IRQ4.

If you have installed other programs or devices using the IRQ3 and IRQ4 settings, you may have a conflict, which causes one or more of the following problems:

✔ A really slow connection

✔ Problems getting the system to recognize or initialize your modem

✔ Other devices, such as a mouse, no longer work

✔ Lost connections

Not all IRQ conflicts cause problems, but you need to be able to diagnose problems attributable to them. One way to recognize an IRQ conflict is to make use of special programs, such as Microsoft Diagnostics, which enables you to see which IRQ requests are in use and which ones are available. You can then review the manufacturer's instructions for any conflicting device and change the IRQ settings.

If you suspect an IRQ conflict, check the System Properties dialog box on your computer running Windows or Windows NT. Right-click the My Computer icon on the Windows desktop and select Properties. Then click the Device manager tab. If there are IRQ conflicts, the offending device will appear with a yellow question mark.

Chapter 11

Shhhh! Security!

● ●

In This Chapter

▶ Configuring host PC security options

▶ Securing the remote connection items

▶ Allowing only authorized callers

▶ Invoking the Windows NT security features

● ●

*p*cAnywhere is a sociable program that lets a user access and control a host computer from a remote computer. It isn't difficult to imagine scenarios for abuse of this technological hospitality (in the form of unauthorized people connecting to your system and rooting around in your files).

In this chapter, I provide you with an inventory of the security options available to protect the host and remote computers. pcAnywhere is flexible when it comes to security issues. You can pick and choose the options you want to use to protect you and forgo those that you find unnecessarily cumbersome.

Protecting the Host PC

Certain types of protections are available exclusively on the host computer. For example, the host PC screen can be made blank during a session for privacy, or its keyboard can be locked to prevent file tampering. You can also configure the host PC to receive an alert message to validate each remote user that attempts to connect. (Chapter 4 covers these protections in further detail.)

Viewing the host security options page

Each connection item has unique settings that you can view by opening the Properties dialog box for that particular item. You can enable or disable all security options for a host connection item from the Security Options tab of the Properties dialog box on the host computer.

To view the security options for a host connection item, follow these steps:

1. **On the host PC, click the Be A Host PC button on the pcAnywhere Action bar.**

   All the existing host connection items appear on the screen.

2. **Right-click the host connection item for which you want to configure security options, and choose Properties from the pop-up menu.**

   The Properties dialog box for the host connection item appears.

3. **Click the Security Options tab.**

   The Security Options page appears.

Making the host screen, keyboard, and mouse inaccessible

pcAnywhere enables you to render the host computer's monitor, keyboard, and mouse unusable during an active session. Selecting these security options prevents unauthorized persons from viewing information that may otherwise be openly displayed during an active, unattended session. It also prevents interference with the tasks being performed on the host PC during the remote control session.

All these options must be configured from the host PC.

Blanking the host screen

To blank the host PC screen during a remote control session, open the Security Options page of the Properties dialog box on the host computer (as described in the preceding section) and then follow these steps:

1. **Select the Blank PC Screen After Connection check box (see Figure 11-1).**

2. **Click OK.**

   This causes the screen on the host computer to remain blank during the pcAnywhere remote control session.

To blank host screen   To control mouse and keyboard

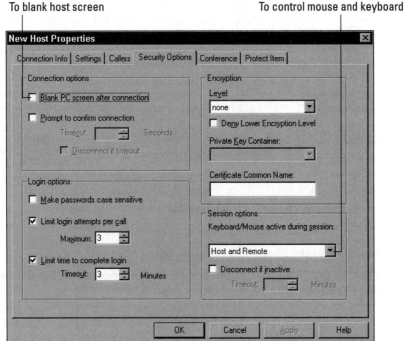

Figure 11-1:
You can set
host PC
security
options from
the Security
Options tab.

Controlling the host keyboard and mouse

On the host computer, from the Security Options page of the Properties
dialog box, you can determine who has control of the host's keyboard and
mouse during a communication session. In the Session Options section, the
Keyboard/Mouse Active During Session drop-down list provides the following
options:

- **Host and Remote:** Both the host and remote computers have access to
  the host keyboard and mouse during an active session.

- **Host:** The host keyboard and mouse can be accessed only from the host
  computer.

- **Remote:** Only the remote user can access the host keyboard and mouse,
  preventing someone at an unattended host from inadvertently interfer-
  ing with an active session.

Alerting the host to a connection

You can set options on the Security Options page of the host computer so
that the host PC is notified when a remote connection is being attempted. A

connection alert message flashes on the host PC screen showing that a connection attempt is pending. The message includes a dialog box with a Yes/No prompt asking the host whether the connection attempt is permitted to continue. The host PC then has a specific number of seconds to authorize the connection before the remote PC is disconnected.

To enable the connection alert message and to configure the number of seconds the host has to authorize an attempted connection, follow these steps:

1. **Right-click the host connection item for which you want to configure a connection alert message; then select _P_roperties from the pop-up menu.**

   The host Properties dialog box appears.

2. **Click the Security Options tab.**

   The Security Options page appears.

3. **Select the _P_rompt to Confirm Connection check box.**

4. **In the Time_o_ut box, enter the number of seconds that the host has to authorize the connection.**

   The default is ten seconds. This box is grayed out if you haven't selected the _P_rompt to Confirm Connection check box, as instructed in Step 3.

5. **(Optional) Click to place a check mark in the _D_isconnect If Timeout check box.**

   If you select this option, the host disconnects the remote PC if it doesn't confirm the connection in the designated number of seconds.

6. **Click OK to save the changes that you've made to the Security Options page and exit the host Properties dialog box.**

Securing the Remote PC

Security on the remote PC is less of a concern and involves fewer configurations than security on the host PC. Unlike the host PC, the remote PC doesn't make its directories and files available to users who are not physically present at the workstation.

You can limit access to the remote PC in two different ways. First, you can protect the remote connection items with passwords. Second, you can enable encryption to correspond to the encryption method used by the host computer. These two types of protections are covered in the sections that follow, and you can configure them on both the host and the remote PC.

Password Protection for Host and Remote Connection Items

You can enable password protection for both host and remote connection items. You can require a password before a user can *view* a connection item's properties or before the user can *change* the connection item's properties. You designate the initial password by using the Protect Item page of the host or remote Properties dialog box. Then you can configure additional password options by using the Security Options tab.

To password protect a host or remote connection item

To password protect a host or remote connection item, follow these steps:

1. **Right-click the icon of the host or remote connection item that you want to password protect; then select Properties from the menu.**

   The host Properties dialog box appears.

2. **Click the Protect Item tab.**

   The Protect Item page appears, as shown in Figure 11-2.

3. **Type a password in the Password text box.**

   For the purpose of security, your password appears as asterisks.

4. **Type the password again in the Confirm Password text box.**

5. **Select one of the following check box options beneath the Confirm Password text box:**

   - **Required to View Properties:** If you check this option, a dialog box requesting a password appears when you attempt to view properties of the connection item. (If you select this option, the Required to Modify Properties box is automatically selected and grayed out.)

   - **Required to Modify Properties:** If you check this option, you can view connection item properties without typing a password, but you must type a password before you can modify any properties.

   - **Required to Execute:** If you check this option, you can't make a connection using this item without entering a password.

6. **Click Apply to save your changes to the Protect Item page; then click OK to close the Properties dialog box.**

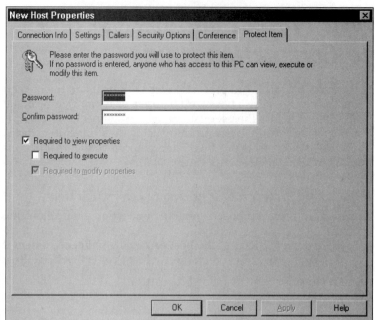

Figure 11-2:
Type a pass-
word here.

To set additional password options

You can make passwords case sensitive or regulate login attempts by using options that appear on the Security Options page.

To set additional password options, follow these steps:

1. **Open the Security Options page for the host connection item or the remote connection item for which you want to add additional passwords. Then configure the following options, as applicable:**

    -   **Make Passwords Case Sensitive:** Selecting this check box forces the user to type the password using the proper upper- and lower-case letters.

    -   **Limit Login Attempts Per Call:** Selecting this check box allows you to determine the number of incorrect login attempts that the user can make before being disconnected. The default number is three.

    -   **Limit Time to Complete Login:** Selecting this check box enables you to determine the amount of time you want the user to be allowed to fumble around for the correct password. The default is three minutes.

2. **Click OK to save your changes and close the Properties dialog box.**

Enabling Encryption

In the not-so-distant past, encryption was a sophisticated security option limited to government espionage. Now encryption is a household word and has made its way onto the pcAnywhere screen. (See the sidebar "Breaking the code — everyday encryption.") If you want to use encryption, you must select the option for both the PC sending data and the PC receiving it.

To view the pcAnywhere encryption options set on either the host or remote computer, follow these steps:

1. **Right-click the connection item for which you want to enable encryption and choose Properties from the pop-up menu.**

   The Properties dialog box for the connection item appears.

2. **Click the Security Options tab.**

   The encryption options shown in Figure 11-3 appear on the Security Options page whether you are viewing this page for a host connection item or a remote connection item.

Figure 11-3: These encryption options appear on both the host and remote PCs.

pcAnywhere encryption options

pcAnywhere provides four encryption options. You select one of the following encryption options from the Level drop-down box on the Security Options page of either the host or remote connection item (refer to Figure 11-3):

- ✔ **None:** No encryption whatsoever. Zilch.

- ✔ **pcAnywhere:** This encryption method is a part of the pcAnywhere program. It provides a minimum level of data security to prevent interception by parties who aren't supposed to be privy to the pcAnywhere session. This method does not require separate installation of an encryption program, as is the requirement for a public key or symmetric system. (See the "Breaking the code — everyday encryption" sidebar later in this chapter.)

pcAnywhere 9.0 encryption is compatible with earlier versions of the software. In other words, you can send and receive data from a computer by using an older version of pcAnywhere without a problem.

✔ **Public Key:** A public key encryption system is separately installed by using the CryptoAPI 2.0 program that is manufactured by a third-party software vendor and is available with Windows NT 4.0 Service Pack 3, or Microsoft Internet Explorer 4.0. This system requires the sender to encrypt data by using one key and the recipient to decode it by using another key.

✔ **Symmetric:** This level of security doesn't provide the same protection as public key encryption because pcAnywhere creates a single key used to encrypt and decode data, as opposed to a third-party vendor generating one of the keys. Symmetric encryption systems are separately installed and are available with Windows 4.0 and Window 95 and later versions.

Breaking the code — everyday encryption

Encryption is the process of turning ordinary data into secret code. The data is scrambled and unscrambled by a special mathematical formula called an *algorithm*.

Encryption is no longer just for espionage. For example, your Web browsing software (which allows you to download and view Web pages from the Internet) probably provides some level of encryption. If you're a Netscape user, you may have wondered about the little broken key or padlock icon in the bottom corner of the screen. This icon denotes a secure, encrypted link between your browser and the Web server.

A number of companies provide encryption software and services. The encryption systems you purchase from these companies rely on keys and digital certificates.

A *key* is a numeric code used to scramble data for encryption. It's also used to unscramble encrypted data so that the recipient can read it.

Encryption systems can be either *public key* systems or *symmetric* systems. (A key is a form of numeric code.) Public key systems use a code known as a *public key* to send data, and a *private key* issued to individual recipients of the data to unscramble it. A symmetric cryptography system uses a single key, or algorithm, to encode and decode data.

A *digital certificate* is another term for a private key. A certificate is like an ID card that you can use with a public key encryption system. You must enter your certificate number in the system before encrypted data can be unscrambled. Third-party commercial companies issue certificates along with their public key encryption systems.

Other encryption information

After you select one of the available encryption options listed in the preceding section, you may need to select one of the following options and provide additional information:

- ✔ **Deny Lower Encryption Level:** Choose this option if you want the host PC to end connections with any remote PC not using the same level of encryption.

- ✔ **Private Key Container:** If a key was issued from a commercial software vendor, type the name of the user to whom the private key was issued by the vendor of the program. (You only need to enter this information if you're using a public key encryption method as explained in the earlier sidebar "Breaking the code — everyday encryption.")

- ✔ **Certificate Common Name:** If you are using a key from a commercial certificate provider, type the name of the user to whom the certificate was issued. (You only need to enter this information if you're using a public key encryption method as explained in the sidebar "Breaking the code — everyday encryption.")

Protecting Caller Items

Chapter 4 explains setting up a new caller connection item for each remote caller dialing into the host computer. Chapter 4 also covers the steps of limiting access from a remote computer to certain hardware devices and files on the host computer.

But what can prevent a caller from accessing the host computer and modifying his or her own privileges? The answer is password protection. It's a good idea to password protect the caller connection items from modification when a remote caller has less than full access to all the hardware devices and files on the host computer.

To limit access to a caller connection item by using the pcAnywhere password authentication system, follow these steps:

1. **Click the Be A Host button on the pcAnywhere Action bar.**

   All host connection items appear on the pcAnywhere desktop.

2. **Right-click the icon of the host connection item for which you want to require a password, and choose Properties from the pop-up menu.**

   The Properties dialog box for the connection item appears.

3. **Click the Callers tab.**

   An icon appears for each caller authorized to access that host connection item, as shown in Figure 11-4.

4. **Select the option Use pcAnywhere Authentication with pcAnywhere Privileges.**

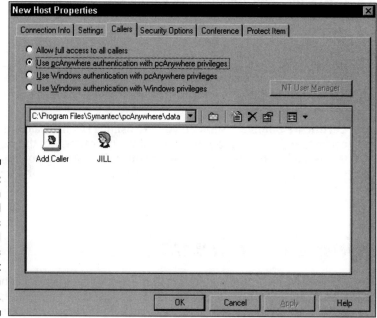

Figure 11-4:
This screen
displays all
callers
authorized
to access
the host
connection
item.

5. **Right-click the icon for the caller connection item to which you want to assign a password, and choose Properties from the pop-up menu.**

   The Properties dialog box for the caller connection item appears.

   You must select a security option other than Allow Full Access to All Callers before you can access and configure the properties for a specific caller (refer to Figure 11-4).

6. **Click the Protect Item tab.**

   The Protect Item page appears, as shown in Figure 11-5.

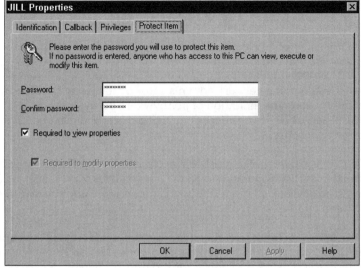

Figure 11-5:
Use this
screen to
assign a
password to
a caller
item.

7. **Type a password in the P̲assword text box.**

   The password appears as a series of asterisks.

8. **Type the password again in the C̲onfirm Password text box.**

9. **Select one of the following options:**

   - **Required to V̲iew Properties:** If you select this option, a dialog box requesting a password appears when the caller attempts to view properties of the connection item, as shown in Figure 11-6. When this option is selected, the Required to Modify Properties option is selected and grayed out automatically.

   - **Required to M̲odify Properties:** If you select this option, the caller must enter a password before she can modify any connection item properties. (But she can view the properties.)

10. **Click A̲pply to save your changes to the Security Options Page; then click OK to close the Protect Item page and click OK again to close the Properties dialog box.**

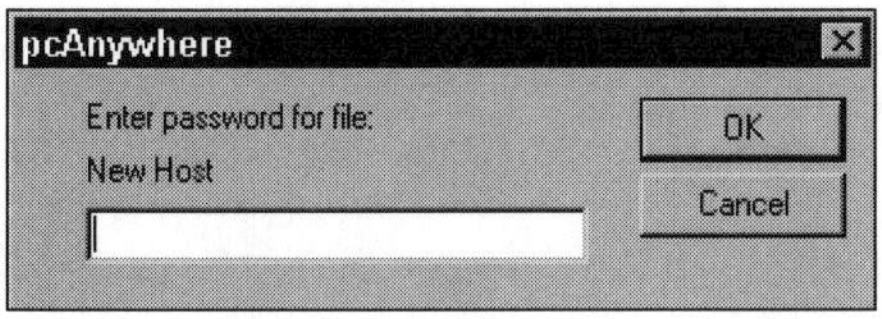

Figure 11-6:
Enter a
password to
view or
modify
properties.

pcAnywhere

Enter password for file:

New Host

OK

Cancel

Using NT Security Features

If you're using pcAnywhere on a network that uses the Windows NT operating system, you can assign passwords to callers by using either pcAnywhere or NT. The advantage in using pcAnywhere is that you can assign passwords even if you're not a network administrator by following the steps in the preceding section. The limitation of pcAnywhere passwords is that they only control access to pcAnywhere connection items and can't control access to any other resources.

A network administrator must assign NT passwords. NT passwords determine the level of access that callers have to all resources, such as files and hardware devices, on the NT network. (I talk more about network resources in Chapter 10.)

The Windows NT network administrator maintains a list of authorized users and their access permissions on the network. Only an NT network administrator can add users, and only appropriately designated NT users can modify privileges.

To require pcAnywhere callers to use the NT login names and passwords assigned by the NT network administrator, follow these steps:

1. **Click the Be A Host button on the pcAnywhere Action bar.**

   All host connection items appear on the pcAnywhere desktop.

2. **Right-click the icon of the host connection item used by the caller for whom you want to require a password, and choose Properties from the pop-up menu.**

   The Properties dialog box for the connection item appears.

3. **Click the Callers tab.**

   Icons for the callers authorized to access the host connection item appear.

4. **Select the option Use Windows Authentication with Windows Privileges.**

   This option allows you to apply any privileges and passwords configured for a caller using the Windows operating system to the same caller dialing into the host using pcAnywhere.

5. **Click Apply to save your changes to the Security Options Page; then click OK to close the Callers page.**

Chapter 12

Going with a Gateway

A pcAnywhere *gateway* is a networked computer that lets other computers on the network share its modem. If a network using pcAnywhere has a computer that's configured as a gateway, a modem-less PC on that network can communicate with a computer on a different network.

In this chapter, I explain how pcAnywhere gateways work. I also show you how to modify gateway connection items and start a gateway session.

Grasping the Gateway Concept

The sole function of your pcAnywhere gateway is to enable computers on your network to share modems. Besides having a modem, a pcAnywhere gateway also has special gateway connection items that enable it to share its modem with other computers on the network.

Using a pcAnywhere gateway also can help stretch hardware resources. A computer serving as a gateway can also be used as an ordinary workstation; and modem-sharing limits the number of telephone lines that you need. In addition, using a pcAnywhere gateway can enhance network security because it limits the number of points at which outsiders can dial into your network.

If you're a computer guru, forget everything you ever knew about gateways: gateway means something different in the world of pcAnywhere. The term *gateway* usually refers to a computer that translates protocols so that computers on the network can talk to each other. But this is not what a gateway is in the context of pcAnywhere. Protocol translation is not the function of a pcAnywhere gateway.

The concept of how a pcAnywhere gateway works is easier to understand with an example. Assume the following:

- XYZ Company has two branch offices — one in Chicago and one in New York.
- Each branch office has its own local area network (LAN).

How a gateway works

Ursula User from New York wants to dial Wendy Workstation in Chicago, but neither Wendy nor Ursula has a modem on her PC.

Ursula and Wendy *can* connect, even though neither of them has a modem, as long as each LAN (one in Chicago, one in New York) has a separate computer configured to be a gateway. Here's how it works:

1. Ursula's modem-less workstation in New York sends a signal to the gateway computer on the New York LAN.
2. The New York gateway dials the gateway on the Chicago LAN.
3. The Chicago LAN gateway passes the signal to Wendy's modem-less workstation.

All of this takes place, as shown in Figure 12-1, without interrupting users who may be working on the PCs configured to operate as gateways.

Is your gateway unidirectional or bidirectional?

Gateways are configured to be either unidirectional or bidirectional. A *unidirectional* gateway can receive one of the following types of calls, but not both:

- **Incoming calls:** Calls from outside the network accessing workstations on the network through the modem
- **Outgoing calls:** Calls initiated from users on the network to contact PCs outside the network

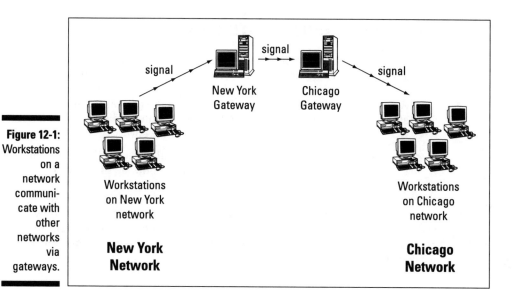

Figure 12-1:
Workstations
on a
network
communi-
cate with
other
networks
via
gateways.

A *bidirectional* gateway can handle both incoming and outgoing calls. Workstations on the network can initiate and send calls through the gateway and can also receive incoming calls.

A unidirectional gateway can provide better security for the network, as opposed to its bidirectional counterpart: If the gateway accepts only outgoing calls, unauthorized users can't dial into the network.

Gateway Connection Devices

Gateways must be configured to use particular connection devices and items. A connection device is a modem, network interface card, or other hardware component used for data transfer between PCs. A connection item is a type of file that identifies one or more connection devices and contains the settings that you need to begin a remote communication session. Connection items are represented as icons on the pcAnywhere desktop. (If you need a refresher on connection devices or connection items, see Chapters 3, 4, and 5.)

A *network interface card* is a hardware device that allows computers on a network to communicate with each other. Network interface cards use one or more protocols to talk to each other. A *protocol* is a set of rules or communication standards — sort of like a common dialect for computers. Examples of protocols include TCP/IP and SPX.

The dual device requirement

Every gateway, whether unidirectional or bidirectional, requires two connection devices: a *network connection device* and a *modem connection device:*

- ✓ **A network connection device:** Transmits signals to and from workstations on the network to the gateway computer. An example of a network connection device is a network interface card.
- ✓ **A modem connection device:** A modem configured to either dial outside the network or receive calls from computers outside the network.

Every gateway connection item must specify two connection devices. This confuses a lot of network administrators because they assume that only bidirectional gateways require two connection devices. It's important to remember that you must have both incoming and outgoing connection devices for unidirectional gateways, as well.

Coming or going?

All gateway connection devices are either *incoming* or *outgoing*, depending on whether they're being used to transmit incoming signals *to the gateway* computer or outgoing signals *away from the gateway* computer. The gateway PC receives calls from within the network or outside the network by using an incoming device. The gateway PC uses the outgoing device to call a waiting host PC located either on the network or outside the network.

Don't confuse the concept of calls coming into the network and calls being made from the network with the terms "incoming" and "outgoing" as used to describe the function of connection devices. They don't always correspond. A reference to a connection device as *incoming* or *outgoing* describes whether a signal is coming into or going out of the gateway. For example, an incoming connection device on the gateway may receive a signal from a network computer to be transmitted to the outgoing device (the modem) as an outgoing call. It can be pretty confusing!

To make things a bit less daunting, pcAnywhere refers to calls coming into the network as DIALIN connections, and outgoing calls made from the network as DIALOUT connections. The diagrams in Figures 12-2 and 12-3 show how incoming and outgoing connection devices make DIALIN and DIALOUT connections. Don't feel bad if you have to refer to these diagrams periodically to keep it straight.

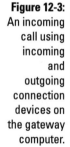

Figure 12-2:
An outgoing call using incoming and outgoing connection devices on the gateway computer.

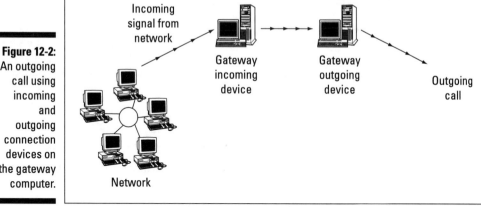

Figure 12-3:
An incoming call using incoming and outgoing connection devices on the gateway computer.

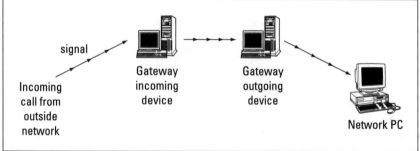

Creating Gateway Connection Items

pcAnywhere lets you create a gateway connection item, specifying both an incoming and outgoing device, by using the following three methods:

- ✔ Launching the convenient Be A Gateway Wizard
- ✔ Modifying the preconfigured DIALIN and DIALOUT items that appear on the screen when you click the Be A Gateway button on the Action bar
- ✔ Choosing File⇨New from the Be A Gateway screen

Using the Be A Gateway Wizard

The Be A Gateway Wizard is the easiest way to configure a new gateway connection item. The only information you have to provide is a name for the connection item, whether you want the connection to be bidirectional, and what incoming and outgoing connection devices you are using. The rest is plugged in for you by default settings.

To create a new gateway connection item, follow these steps:

1. **Click the Be A Gateway button on the pcAnywhere Action bar.**

   A screen appears showing icons for the wizard and for any existing gateway connection items.

2. **Double-click the Add Be A Gateway Item icon.**

   The Be A Gateway Wizard screen appears, as shown in Figure 12-4.

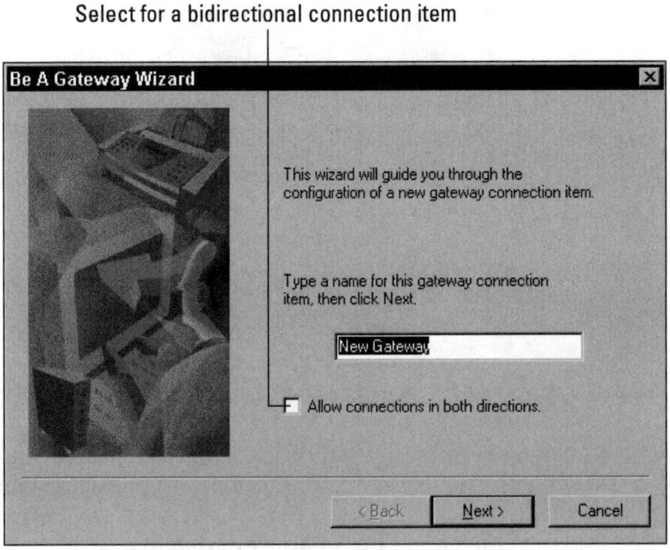

Select for a bidirectional connection item

Figure 12-4:
Type a name for the connection item and select the check box if it's bidirectional.

Be A Gateway Wizard

This wizard will guide you through the configuration of a new gateway connection item.

Type a name for this gateway connection item, then click Next.

New Gateway

☐ Allow connections in both directions.

< Back   Next >   Cancel

3. **Type a name for the new connection item or leave the default name in the text box.**

   The default name is New Gateway. Each subsequent connection item you create using the default name will be numbered sequentially (New Connection Item1, New Connection Item2, and so on).

4. If you're creating a bidirectional connection item, click to place a check in the Allow Connections in Both Directions box.

A bidirectional connection item can receive calls coming into the network and make outgoing calls to PCs outside the network. If the check box isn't selected, the gateway can receive only incoming *or* only send outgoing calls.

Do not select this check box if you are configuring a unidirectional gateway. The bidirectional check box, in conjunction with the connection devices you choose in Steps 6 and 7, determines how and whether your gateway can receive incoming calls, send outgoing calls, or do both.

5. Click Next.

The Be A Gateway Wizard screen appears, as shown in Figure 12-5.

Choose incoming connection device

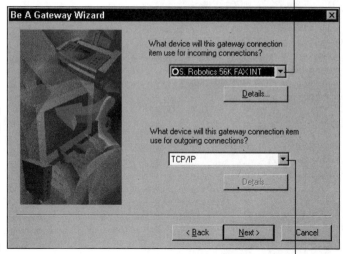

Figure 12-5:
Specify the incoming and outgoing connection devices in this screen.

Choose outgoing connection device

6. Choose the incoming connection device from the topmost drop-down menu.

The incoming connection device receives the signals transmitted to the gateway from other computers. The default device entered in this field is the modem used by your Windows operating system, which was specified when you installed either Windows or the modem.

7. **Choose the outgoing connection device from the bottom drop-down list.**

   pcAnywhere assumes that you're using your network interface card and specifies a default protocol. You can change the default by choosing a different option from the drop-down list.

8. **(Optional) To adjust the modem speed (for example, to accommodate a phone line that cannot transmit data as rapidly as your modem allows) and speaker volume (to increase or decrease the sound of your modem dialing), click the Details button beneath the box for either the incoming or outgoing device fields in which you entered a modem.**

   The Properties dialog box for the modem appears, as shown in Figure 12-6. After you make any changes, click OK to save your settings and exit the Properties dialog box.

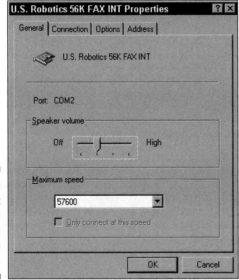

Figure 12-6:
Adjust
modem
settings
using this
dialog box.

9. **Click Next.**

   The final screen of the Be A Gateway Wizard appears.

10. **Click to place a check mark in the Automatically Launch This Gateway upon Wizard Completion check box.**

    Select this option to make outgoing calls or to receive incoming calls immediately upon completion of the wizard (see Figure 12-7).

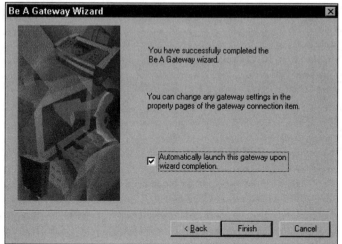

Figure 12-7:
You've successfully configured a new gateway connection item.

11. **Click Finish.**

An icon for the newly configured gateway connection item appears on your pcAnywhere desktop.

Using preconfigured gateway connection items

For your convenience, pcAnywhere comes with two preconfigured gateway connection items: DIALIN and DIALOUT. Their labels are helpful because it can be easy to confuse incoming and outgoing *devices* with incoming and outgoing *calls*. As explained earlier in this chapter, they're not the same.

The preconfigured DIALIN and DIALOUT connection item icons appear on your pcAnywhere screen, as shown in Figure 12-8. You can modify the preconfigured DIALIN and DIALOUT default settings, as discussed later in this chapter under "Setting and Modifying Gateway Connection Item Properties."

DIALIN connection item

The DIALIN connection item is preconfigured to accept incoming calls to computers on the network from outside the network. To view the Properties dialog box for the DIALIN connection item, right-click the item and select Properties from the pop-up menu. The Connection Info page of the DIALIN Properties dialog box appears on top, as shown in Figure 12-9. The default for the incoming connection device is your modem. The default for the outgoing device is the protocol for the network adapter card that connects the computer to the cable it uses to communicate with the network (the most common protocol is TCP/IP).

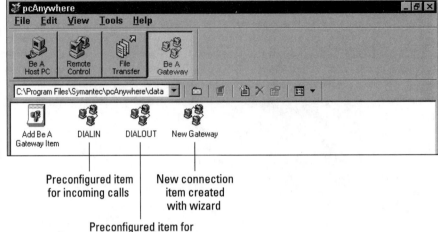

Figure 12-8:
pcAnywhere
provides
preconfig-
ured
connection
items.

Preconfigured item
for incoming calls

New connection
item created
with wizard

Preconfigured item for
outgoing calls

A network adapter card is a circuit board in a PC that looks like a card with
wires on it. It enables the PC to communicate with other computers on the
network through a cable, which actually attaches to the network adapter
card.

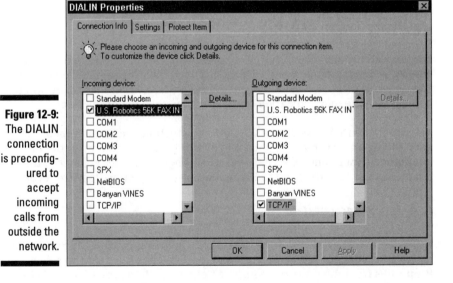

Figure 12-9:
The DIALIN
connection
is preconfig-
ured to
accept
incoming
calls from
outside the
network.

DIALOUT connection item

The DIALOUT connection item is preconfigured to make outgoing calls from the network to computers located outside the network. To view the Properties dialog box for the DIALOUT connection item, right-click the item and select Properties from the pop-up menu. The Connection Info page of the DIALOUT Properties dialog box appears on top, as shown in Figure 12-10. The default for the incoming connection device is the protocol for the network interface card, which connects the computer to the cable it uses to communicate with the network (the most common protocol is TCP/IP). The default for the outgoing device is your modem.

Figure 12-10: The DIALOUT connection is preconfigured to make outgoing calls from the network.

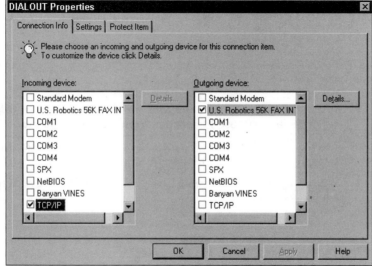

Creating a connection item from the File menu

You can create a pcAnywhere gateway connection item without using the wizard. To do so, follow these steps:

1. **Click the Be A Gateway button on the Action bar.**

   A screen appears showing all existing gateway connection items.

2. **Choose File⇨New.**

   The Properties dialog box appears but doesn't display any default settings.

You can use the Properties dialog box to configure connection devices, select unidirectional and bidirectional options, and enable password protection for the new item (explained in the following section). If you're creating a new connection item from the File menu, you need to do it all from scratch. No default settings are plugged in for you.

Setting and Modifying Gateway Connection Item Properties

The Properties dialog box for each connection item contains three tabs that give you access to various settings. The next three subsections explain the details of these tabs.

To open the Properties dialog box for an existing gateway connection item, follow these steps:

1. **Right-click the connection item for which you want to modify the properties and choose Properties from the pop-up menu.**

    The Properties dialog box for the connection item appears, with the Connection Info page open on top.

2. **Click among the three Properties tabs and modify the settings on each page as needed.**

The Connection Info page

The information on the Connection Info page determines the incoming and outgoing hardware devices that the connection item uses for each session.

Click the Connection Info tab. With the Connection Info page open, you can configure, change, or specify connection devices by following these steps:

1. **In the Incoming Device box, select the hardware device to be used to receive signals from the network or from a computer outside the network.**

    The incoming device simply receives the signals coming into the gateway. It doesn't route them to their destination.

2. **In the Outgoing Device box, select the hardware device (or protocol for a network connection device) to be used for routing calls to their final destination.**

    The outgoing device routes the signal to a waiting host PC on the network or outside the network.

3. **Click the Details button to the right of the Incoming Device or Outgoing Device box, and adjust the modem speed and modem speaker volume, if applicable.**

   Chapter 10 explains some ways to figure out the maximum speed at which your modem can be set. If the modem speed is set too high, it can result in data corruption and error-checking procedures that can actually slow down transmission. You also need to remember that not all modems have an adjustable volume option. If yours has one, it can come in handy if you like to hear the sound of your modem dialing so that you know it's working properly, or if you like to turn the volume down so that you don't have to listen to the background noise.

4. **Click Apply to save the changes you made on the Connection Info page and then move on to another tab. If you are finished adjusting properties settings, click OK to both save your changes and exit the Properties dialog box.**

The Settings page

When you click the Settings tab for a gateway connection item, the page displays the following options (see Figure 12-11):

- ✔ **Bidirectional:** Select this check box if you want the gateway connection item to be bidirectional. A bidirectional gateway can receive both incoming and outgoing calls.

- ✔ **Inactivity Timeout:** Select this check box and enter a number in the accompanying Minutes box to specify the amount of time a session can be idle before the gateway computer disconnects. The default is 60 minutes, which means that an inactive session is disconnected after an hour.

- ✔ **Class:** If you have multiple gateways on your network and you want this gateway to be part of a particular group or class, type a class name in this field.

The Protect Item page

You can protect a gateway connection item from being used, viewed, or modified by an unauthorized person by using the Protect Item page to assign a password to the connection item.

Click the Protect Item tab (see Figure 12-12). With the Protect Item page open, you can protect a gateway connection item with a password by following these steps:

1. **Type a password in the <u>P</u>assword text box.**

   The password is displayed as a series of asterisks.

2. **Type your password again in the <u>C</u>onfirm Password text box.**

   The options beneath the <u>C</u>onfirm Password box are no longer grayed out.

3. **Select any or all of the following options appropriate for your situation:**

   • **Required to <u>V</u>iew Properties:** A user must type a password before he can view the properties of the connection item. If you select this option, the Required to Modify Properties box is automatically selected and grayed out.

   • **Required to <u>M</u>odify Properties:** A user must type a password before she can change or modify any connection item properties.

   • **Required to Execute:** A user cannot make a connection without typing a password.

4. **Click <u>A</u>pply to save the changes you made on the Protect Item page and then move on to another tab. If you are finished adjusting properties settings, click OK to save your changes and exit the Properties dialog box.**

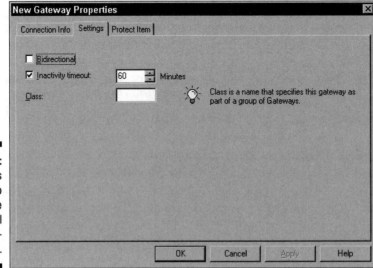

Figure 12-11:
Use this page to indicate bidirectional or unidirectional.

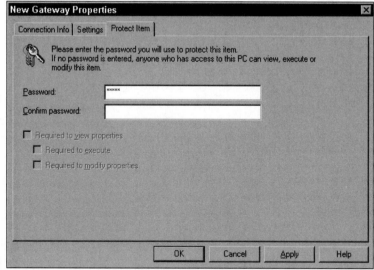

Figure 12-12:
This page
provides
options to
enable you
to password
protect the
gateway
connection
item.

Launching a Gateway Session

This is the easy part!

To begin a communication session by using a gateway computer, simply do
one of the following:

- **For an outgoing call:** Double-click the DIALOUT icon (or the icon of
  another connection item that you've configured for this purpose).
  pcAnywhere begins dialing by using the connection devices and settings
  specified for the item.

- **For an incoming call:** Right-click the DIALIN icon (or the icon of another
  connection item that you've configured for this purpose) and select
  Launch Gateway from the pop-up menu. A small pcAnywhere icon
  appears on your Windows taskbar. This indicates that the host is waiting
  to receive an incoming call from a remote computer.

Part IV

To Infinity and Beyond — Advanced Program Features

The 5th Wave

©RICHTENNANT

By Rich Tennant

Ever the innovator, Larry beta-tests the Personal Belt Buckle Assistant/Wireless Fax

Hold on a second, Stu, I'm getting a fax.

In this part . . .

Some people like to see how fast they can drive a new car. Others like to see what extra things they can do with a program.

After you've mastered the basics of pcAnywhere, you may want to try automating tasks by writing your own programming code, or *script*. You may want to explore online services, which are like Web sites with their own unlisted phone numbers. Online services are packed with useful, specialized information you can't find by surfing the net.

Chapter 13

Look, No Net! Opting for Online Services

● ●

In This Chapter

▶ Contacting online services

▶ Mimicking an online service terminal

▶ Starting an online session

▶ Refining your online communications

● ●

*A*lthough the Internet is largely replacing online services, these services still fill a special niche in the info-tech community. Online services often offer databases, forums, and registration capabilities that you can't get elsewhere. Some special interest groups find online services particularly useful because they can't be "surfed" on the Net — you need a separate phone number to access them. The Internet is stuffed with information, but there will always be room for online services.

Introduction to Online Services

Online services may be an integral part of your business. For example, you may use these services to place orders with particular suppliers or to check the status of equipment updates. Symantec realizes that if you use a specialized online service, you're likely to access it frequently. So pcAnywhere enables you to set up special connection items to dial those services quickly and painlessly.

What do online services offer?

The most common type of online service is the Bulletin Board Service (BBS). A BBS has been likened to a stand-alone Web site with its own phone number and no graphics. It usually serves as a forum or database for a particular group. A BBS can also be used as a customer support resource or to distribute free software, updates, and special programs called *drivers* that help you run hardware that you've purchased, such as a printer.

Until recently, Symantec maintained a BBS to distribute much of the information that you can now obtain from its LiveUpdate Server (which I discuss in Chapter 16). Many universities also use an online service to register their students for classes each semester.

How do online services work?

Online services are commercial operations that sometimes charge you for accessing their databases. They have their own phone numbers, which means that you can't access them while you're out cruising the Internet. You get billed for the time that you're connected — unless it's some sort of freebie service.

Each online service has its own procedures for how you log in, and each service may also use your screen and keyboard in a particular manner during your online session. pcAnywhere provides several *terminal emulation* options that allow your video display and keyboard to operate in the way required by the online service.

Bright, flashy Internet Web pages are replacing dowdy BBS services that lack graphics and excitement. The Internet now provides the secure connections and interactive links once offered only on a BBS. Interestingly, Symantec, which makes pcAnywhere, has dismantled its own BBS in favor of providing comprehensive information to customers on the Web.

Creating an Online Service Connection Item

Symantec considers Online Service Items an optional feature. The Call Online Service button doesn't automatically appear on the pcAnywhere Action bar — you have to put it there. After you place it on the Action bar, you can configure connection items to dial your online service directly.

Displaying the Call Online Service button

The Call Online Service button is the only action button that doesn't show up automatically on the Action bar after you first install pcAnywhere.

To display the Call Online Service action button, follow these steps:

1. **From the pcAnywhere desktop, choose Tools⇨Application Options.**

   The Application Options dialog box appears.

2. **Click the Button Bars tab.**

   The Button Bars page appears, as shown in Figure 13-1.

Select this check box

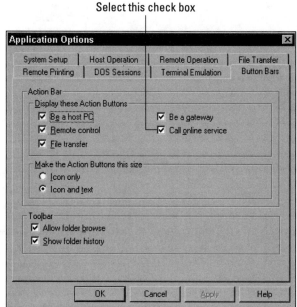

Figure 13-1:
Add the Call
Online
Service
button to
your Action
bar.

3. **Click to place a check mark in the Call Online Service check box.**

4. **Click OK to save your changes and exit the Application Options dialog box.**

Running the Call Online Service Wizard

It's really easy to set up an online service item by using the convenient Call Online Service Wizard. But it's nearly impossible to set up an online service item by configuring the properties from scratch.

To set up an online service item by using the Call Online Service Wizard, follow these steps:

1. **Click the Call Online Service button on the Action bar.**

   If the Call Online Service button isn't on your Action bar, follow the steps in the preceding section to put it there.

   The Add Online Service Item and any existing online service items are displayed on your desktop, as shown in Figure 13-2.

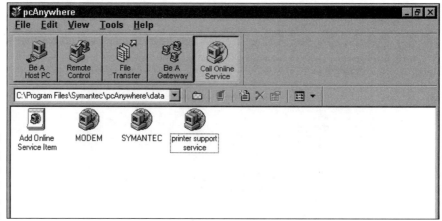

Figure 13-2:
The online service item icons.

2. **Double-click the Add Online Service Item icon on your desktop.**

   The first screen of the Call Online Service Wizard appears, as shown in Figure 13-3.

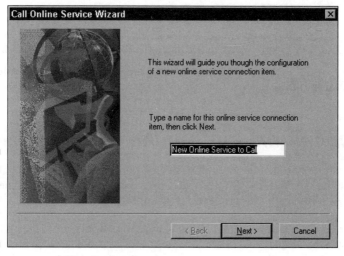

Figure 13-3:
Type a name for the online service item.

3. **Type a name for the online service item.**

   A good, logical choice for an online service item name is the name of the online service provider (for example, "Acme Customer Service BBS").

4. **Click Next.**

   A second Call Online Service Wizard screen appears.

5. **From the drop-down box, choose the COM port to which your modem is attached (see Figure 13-4).**

   Most modems use either COM1 or COM2. (See Chapter 3 for more details.)

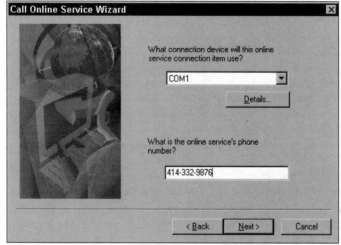

Figure 13-4:
Select the modem port and type the phone number for the online service.

6. **(Optional) Click the Details button if you want to adjust the speed and volume settings for your modem.**

   The details dialog box for the modem appears, as shown in Figure 13-5. Make any necessary adjustments to the settings, and then click OK to exit the dialog box. (See Chapter 3 for more about configuring modems.)

7. **Enter the phone number for the online service provider.**

8. **Click Next.**

   Another Call Online Service Wizard screen appears, displaying a drop-down list of terminal emulation options.

9. **From the drop-down list, select a terminal emulation mode that works with your online service (see Figure 13-6).**

   The terminal emulation mode dictates what appears on the screen and the different keyboard commands for a particular online service. pcAnywhere offers five menu options for terminal emulation. Consult with your online service provider to figure out which one works best with their service.

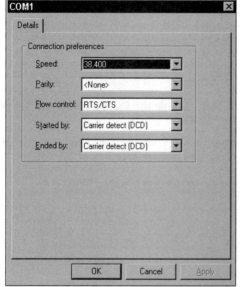

Figure 13-5:
Adjust
modem
settings by
using this
dialog box.

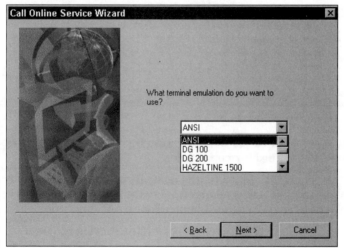

Figure 13-6:
Choose a
terminal
emulation
mode that
works with
your online
service.

10. **Click Next.**

The final Call Online Service Wizard screen appears, as shown in
Figure 13-7.

Select to dial online service upon completion

Figure 13-7:
The wizard
can be
launched
upon
completion.

11. **Select or deselect the Automatically Call the Online Service Upon Wizard Completion check box; then click Finish.**

    If you want pcAnywhere to begin dialing the online service as soon as you complete the Call Online Service Wizard, select the check box. Deselect it if you want to dial the connection later.

Modifying Online Connection Item Properties

You can modify the properties for an online connection item. The settings you can change include the hardware device, terminal emulation mode, options for viewing text on-screen, password protection, and session recording features.

Changing the connection

You almost always connect to an online service by using a modem. If you need to change the modem that is specified, follow these steps:

1. **From your pcAnywhere desktop, right-click the online service item for which you want to change the modem connection and choose Properties from the pop-up menu.**

   The Properties dialog box for the connection item appears with the Connection Info page open on top, as shown in Figure 13-8.

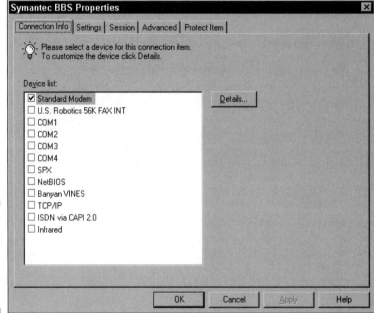

Figure 13-8:
The
Connection
Info page
appears
on top.

2. **Click to place a check mark in the check box of the connection device that you want to use for the online service item.**

3. **(Optional) Click the Details button if you want to adjust the speed and volume settings for your connection device.**

   The details dialog box for the modem appears. Make any necessary adjustments to the settings, and then click OK to exit the dialog box and return to the Connection Info page.

4. **Click Apply to save the changes you've made to the new connection device and its settings.**

   You may notice that the Apply button is grayed out until you make a change. Then it's available so that you can save your new settings.

5. **Click OK to exit the Properties dialog box, or click another tab to continue modifying settings.**

The following sections show you how to use the other tabs in the Properties dialog box to adjust the various settings for an online service item.

Configuring online service settings

You use the Settings page of the Properties dialog box to view and modify online service item settings, such as the terminal emulation mode, the file transfer protocol, and the phone number of the online service.

To view or modify the settings for an online service item, follow these steps:

1. **Open the Properties dialog box (refer to the preceding section if you need help with this task) and click the Settings tab.**

   The Settings page for the online service item appears, as shown in Figure 13-9.

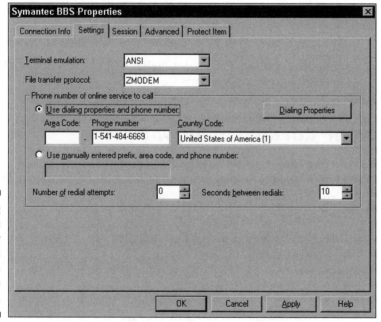

Figure 13-9:
The Settings page box for the selected online service item.

2. **Make any necessary changes to the following settings:**

   • **Terminal Emulation:** From the drop-down list, select a terminal emulation mode that works best with the online service you're using. (You may need to consult the online service.)

- **File Transfer Protocol:** From the drop-down list, choose the protocol recommended by the online service for transferring files.

- **Phone Number of Online Service to Call:** You can configure pcAnywhere to dial the number of the online service automatically by selecting the Use Dialing Properties and Phone Number option. If you don't, you'll be prompted to enter a phone number each time you launch the connection item.

- **Number of Redial Attempts:** Indicate how many times you want pcAnywhere to attempt to dial the online service before closing the connection item.

- **Seconds Between Redials:** Enter the number of seconds you want pcAnywhere to wait between redial attempts. This feature is useful in avoiding a busy signal because pcAnywhere redialed too quickly.

- **Dialing Properties button:** Pressing this button gives you access to the Dialing Properties dialog box, where you can set various phone number and dialing options, as well as choose to have your call charged to your calling card. (I talk about the Dialing Properties dialog box in detail in Chapter 9.)

3. **Click Apply to save any changes that you've made to the settings.**

4. **Click OK to exit the Properties dialog box, or click another tab to continue modifying settings.**

Some advanced options

You use the options on the Advanced tab of the Properties dialog box to designate how text appears on your screen during a session with an online service.

To view and modify the advanced settings, follow these steps:

1. **Open the Properties dialog box and click the Advanced tab.**

   The Advanced page for the online service item appears, as shown in Figure 13-10.

2. **Make any necessary adjustments to the following settings:**

   - **Line Wrap:** If you select this option, lines that exceed the width of your display window continue on the next line.

   - **Screen Wrap:** If you select this option, when text reaches the bottom of your screen, it begins overwriting the text at the top of your screen line-by-line. (This saves you the effort of scrolling downward after the last line on the current screen.)

   - **Destructive <BS> Key:** If you select this option, you can use the Backspace key to delete characters.

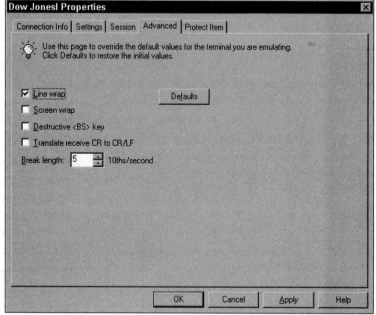

Figure 13-10:
These
options
affect how
text from
an online
service
appears on
your screen.

- **Translate Receive CR to CR/LF:** If you select this option, the cursor moves to the left side of the screen and advances one line at a time for each line transferred from the online service.

- **Break Length:** This applies to the length of the break signal used to interrupt programs running on a mainframe computer. To determine whether your online service is running from a mainframe computer, and to find out how to optimize this setting, consult the online service.

3. Click **Apply** to save any changes that you've made to the settings.

4. Click **OK** to exit the Properties dialog box, or click another tab to continue modifying settings.

Password protection

You use the Protect Item page to assign password protection to an online service Item, just as you would for any other type of remote connection item.

To password protect an online service item, follow these steps:

1. **Open the Properties dialog box and click the Protect Item Tab.**

   The Protect Item page appears, as shown in Figure 13-11.

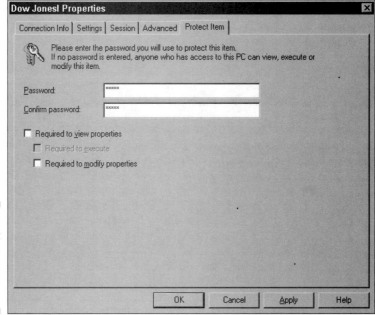

Figure 13-11:
Set
password
protection
on this
page.

2. **Type your password in the Password text box.**

   Your password appears as a series of asterisks.

3. **Type your password again in the Confirm Password box.**

   Notice that two of the options beneath the Confirm Password dialog box are no longer grayed out. The Required to Execute check box, however, is grayed unless the Required to View Properties option is selected. The designers of pcAnywhere presume that if you don't have the right to make a connection using the item, security considerations dictate that you certainly shouldn't be entitled to snoop around and view the item's properties.

4. **Select one or more of the following options:**

   • **Required to View Properties:** If you select this option, you must enter a password before you can view the properties of the online service item.

   • **Required to Modify Properties:** If you select this option, you must enter a password before you can change or modify any online service item properties. (This option is grayed if you've selected the Required to View Properties option.)

   • **Required to Execute:** If you select this option, you must enter a password before you can use this item to connect to an online service. (This option is grayed unless the Required to View Properties option is selected.)

5. Click <u>A</u>pply to save any changes that you've made to the settings.

6. Click OK to exit the Properties dialog box, or click another tab to continue modifying settings.

Setting session options

You can use the Session tab to enable some pretty sophisticated options for your online service session, such as recording a session, running a script, and creating a macro. I tell you more about how to do these advanced tasks in Chapters 14 and 16. Then, if these features appeal to you, you can come back to this tab to enable them.

Starting an Online Session

After you set up the online service item, connecting to the online service is quick and easy. Just double-click the item and let the dialing begin! If you didn't previously enter the number of the online service, the dialog box shown in Figure 13-12 appears, and you need to enter the online service number here. If you did enter the number during the setup process, the dialing occurs automatically, and a dialog box informs you that the connection has been made.

Figure 13-12:
Type the number for the online service if you didn't enter it on the Settings page when you set up the item.

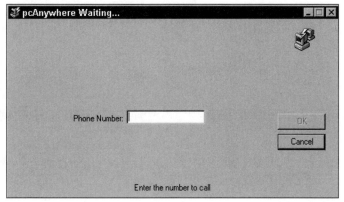

Chapter 14

Scoping Out Scripts

● ●

In This Chapter

▶ Understanding how scripts work

▶ Using the pcAnywhere Script Guide

▶ Figuring out what to include in a script

▶ Translating a script

▶ Activating a script

● ●

Scripting is like bungee jumping — it's a skill that not everyone feels compelled to acquire. You can use pcAnywhere without learning how to script, but it's an exciting skill to master. And unlike bungee jumping, it can make you more productive at work.

A *script* is a mini-program that you create to make using pcAnywhere more automatic. For example, you can write a script to automatically transfer and update files between computers in the middle of the night. Or you can write a script to log on to a special online service that you use.

Scripts save you time by automatically running a series of operations that you would otherwise have to initiate one at a time. They also enable you to perform certain tasks without being present, such as an unattended file transfer. And, theoretically, the more tasks that can be performed unattended, the more breaks you can take at work. Well-earned breaks, I'd say.

So, What's a Script?

A script is a series of instructions, called *commands,* written in a special language. The commands are then saved to an *ASCII text file*. ASCII is an acronym for American Standard Code for Information Exchange. It's a binary code that most computers can read. Saving data as an ASCII file is an important way for you to communicate with your computer on its own level. Later in this chapter, I tell you precisely how to create an ASCII file.

Your pcAnywhere installation disc includes the pcAnywhere Script Guide, which contains all the pcAnywhere script commands. You must use these commands exactly as they appear in the Script Guide. If you don't, the unfortunate result is something called a *syntax error*. A syntax error is a mistake, such as a spelling error, that makes the command unreadable to your computer.

Viewing the pcAnywhere Script Guide

The Script Guide is included with your pcAnywhere CD-ROM. The CD also includes a copy of the Adobe Acrobat Reader 4.0 software, which is the software program you need to load on your system to view the Script Guide.

What you can find in the Script Guide

The Script Guide contains the following elements:

- Explanations of key scripting concepts
- Detailed instructions for creating and running scripts
- An appendix of all script commands
- An appendix of *reserved words,* which have a special meaning to pcAnywhere and can't be chosen by you to name files or use in any way other than as a command

Viewing the Script Guide

To view the pcAnywhere Script Guide, follow these steps:

1. **Insert the pcAnywhere CD-ROM disc into the CD-ROM drive.**

   If the Windows AutoPlay feature is enabled, you hear a whirring sound and the pcAnywhere setup screen appears. You can then skip to Step 4.

   If the Windows AutoPlay feature isn't enabled, proceed to Step 2 to start the CD manually.

2. **Choose Start⇨Run.**

   The Run dialog box appears, as shown in Figure 14-1.

3. **In the Run dialog box, type** D:\setup.exe, **where** *D* **is the letter of the CD-ROM drive. (If your CD-ROM drive letter is not** *D*, **type the correct letter for your drive.) Click OK.**

The pcAnywhere installation screen appears, offering you the option of installing several versions of the pcAnywhere software or the option of viewing manuals.

Figure 14-1:
If AutoPlay
isn't
enabled,
enter this
command.

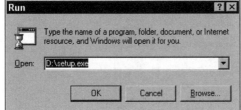

4. **Click the View Manuals button.**

   A screen appears listing the manuals available on the CD-ROM, as shown in Figure 14-2.

5. **Click the pcAnywhere Script Guide button.**

   If you already have Adobe Acrobat Reader installed on your computer, the pcAnywhere Script Guide appears. You can view it onscreen or print it out.

Click here for Script Guide

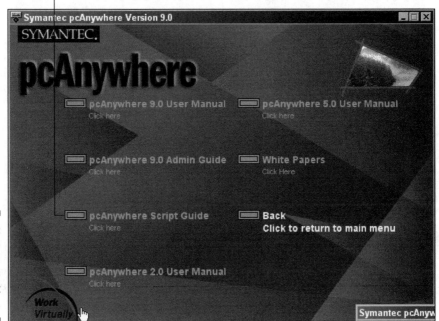

Figure 14-2:
The
CD-ROM
contains a
Script
Guide.

If you don't have the Adobe Acrobat Reader 4.0 software installed on your computer, the Symantec pcAnywhere dialog box shown in Figure 14-3 appears, explaining that you must have Adobe Acrobat Reader to view the pcAnywhere Script Guide.

Figure 14-3:
Acrobat
Reader
is required
to view the
Script
Guide.

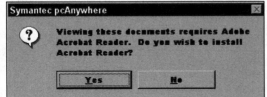

6. **If you don't have Adobe Acrobat installed on your computer, click Yes to install it.**

   The Adobe Acrobat Wizard installs the Reader program and prompts you to exit all programs and restart your computer. After you've restarted your PC, repeat Step 1 through Step 4 to access the pcAnywhere Script Guide.

Should I Try This if I'm Not a Programmer?

Scripting isn't for everyone. It takes time, patience, and lots of trial and error — mostly error — until you master the nuances of the *syntax,* or how the language is used. But once you've written a script that works, the timesaving dividends are yours to enjoy.

The following sections acquaint you with the three basic stages of the scripting process. Then you can decide if you're up for the challenge.

Step #1: Choosing What to Put in Your Script

Before you begin the process of writing a script, you need to make an inventory of each and every action pcAnywhere must perform to complete the task you're scripting.

The pcAnywhere Script Guide refers to this phase of the scripting process as writing your instructions out in *pseudocode*. Pseudocode is a series of plain-English instructions that you can methodically translate into scripting language

Now, assume that you want to create a script to have pcAnywhere automatically dial your Internet service provider, CheapServ. The following is an example of how you can document the process in pseudocode:

1. **I dial 555-943-4333.**

2. **A message appears on my screen that says, "Connecting to CheapServ . . . "**

3. **A box appears asking me to enter my CheapServ user identification number.**

4. **I type 007.**

5. **A screen appears asking for my password.**

6. **I type 5423.**

7. **A dialog box appears telling me that I am connected to CheapServ.**

These steps document in pseudocode all the things that you need to do to connect to CheapServ.

Step #2: Writing a Script

After you've listed the steps for your eventual script in pseudocode, you need to translate them into script commands. Each pseudocode line translates into one or more lines of script commands.

Scripts vary in complexity. To write a basic script, you need to master four concepts: commands, comments, parameters, and syntax.

Finding the right commands

Commands are basic instructions to pcAnywhere, telling it to perform a specific action. There are a finite number of commands, but an infinite number of ways to use them.

The pcAnywhere Script Guide gives you a complete list of the *reserved words* used for script commands. The Script Guide lists all the pcAnywhere script commands in alphabetical order and explains their functions.

If a term is included on the pcAnywhere reserved word list, you can use that term in the script only as a command. If you try to use the term differently, you get an error message. These words have special meanings to pcAnywhere — that's why they're reserved.

It's helpful to look at some commonly used commands. Take a look at the pseudocode example in the previous section. The actual script to connect to CheapServ might contain the following commands:

- ✔ `Dial Number "555-943-4333"`: The Dial Number command directs pcAnywhere to dial the number for CheapServ and make a connection. The telephone number you're dialing appears in quotation marks.

- ✔ `Wait String "Connecting to CheapServ . . . "`: The Wait String command tells pcAnywhere to wait for a *string* — a specific sequence of characters that aren't used for calculations. This command directs your computer to wait for the string "Connecting to CheapServe . . . " to appear on the screen before responding and carrying out the next command in the script.

A *string* is any sequence of consecutive characters, such as a password or phone number. A string is enclosed in quotation marks and can be up to 255 characters. It's referred to by a name, such as "phone number." Numbers in a string can't be used for calculations. Strings are commonly used for error messages, status messages, and onscreen prompts.

- ✔ `Send String "^M"`: The Send String Command directs pcAnywhere to send the string in quotation marks. In this case, the string "^M" is the code for Enter. You're telling pcAnywhere to press Enter using this sample command (like at the end of the CheapServ login process).

- ✔ `Send Line "007"`: The Send Line command tells pcAnywhere to send the line of text or characters that appear between the quotation marks. In this example, it's the password for the hypothetical CheapServ account.

According to the pcAnywhere Script Guide, a common scripting error is forgetting to tell pcAnywhere what to look for before it sends a response to a prompt — in other words, forgetting to put in a Wait String command followed by the text of what appears on the screen.

Including comments

Comments aren't technically part of the script. They're not commands to be carried out. Comments are lines of text, preceded by a semicolon, that are included for your reference to explain the commands in the script. The semicolon tells pcAnywhere to ignore the text that follows it.

In a pcAnywhere script, here is how you might add comment lines to describe a couple of the command lines used in my pseudocode example:

```
; Wait for screen to say Connecting . . .
Wait String "Connecting to CheapServ . . ."
; Press Enter
Send String "^M"
```

The lines with the semicolons — the comments — are only provided for the convenience of the reader. They don't affect the execution of the script.

Applying the syntax

Syntax is a set of rules governing how a command is written. Syntax determines capitalization, spacing, and what information must be included in the command.

If you don't enter a command correctly, pcAnywhere gives you a *syntax error* message when you attempt to convert script commands into a script file that pcAnywhere can execute. Here are some examples of common syntax error messages:

- ✔ Syntax Error: A command didn't follow the prescribed format for entering commands and string information.

- ✔ Invalid String Size: A string exceeds the maximum allowable 255 characters.

- ✔ Bad Command Name: A command you entered is incorrectly spelled, improperly capitalized, or doesn't exist at all.

- ✔ Illegal Arithmetic Expression: An arithmetic expression or formula you specified can't be executed and needs to be rewritten.

These are just a few of the things that can go wrong. The pcAnywhere Script Guide contains a list of all possible syntax errors.

You can easily locate an erroneous command. When you run your script and receive an error message, each message is preceded by the number of the line on which it occurred.

Specifying parameters

A *parameter* provides additional information that pcAnywhere needs to execute a command, and the parameter is part of the command. Parameter information is usually included in quotation marks, following the command itself (such as the Send String or Dial Number command).

For example, you might tell pcAnywhere to enter a certain phone number. The phone number is the parameter. It's information, in addition to the reserved words of the command, required to carry out the command.

There are two types of parameters: *literal* and *variable*. Literal parameters are unchanging — they're the same every time the script is run. An example of a literal parameter is the login phone number for CheapServ.

Variable parameters contain values that can change. An example of a variable parameter is the CheapServ password, assuming that it's different for each user in the company.

There are several types of variable parameters. They're discussed in detail in Chapter 2 of the pcAnywhere Script Guide on your CD-ROM.

Putting it all together: Writing the script

Now that you've been introduced to the essentials of commands, comments, syntax, and parameters, it's time to put it all together with a short sample script.

Looking at a sample script

You could write a login script for the hypothetical Internet service provider, CheapServ, like this:

```
; Dial Number for CheapServ
Dial Number "555-943-4333"
; Wait for the screen to say Connecting . . .
Wait String "Connecting to CheapServ . . ."
Wait String "User ID . . ."
; Enter User ID
Send Line "007"
; Press Enter
Send String "^M"
Wait String "Password . . ."

; Enter your password
Send Line "5423"
; Press Enter
Send String "^M"
```

Writing and saving an actual script

Now that you've taken a look at a sample script, you're ready to write and save an actual script as an ASCII text file. To write your script and save it to pcAnywhere, follow these steps:

1. **Choose Tools⇨Scripts.**

The Scripts dialog box appears, displaying all previously created scripts. Figure 14-4 shows a script named Sample.

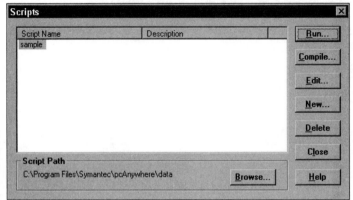

Figure 14-4:
The Scripts dialog box.

2. **Click the New Button.**

    The pcAnywhere Editor [Untitled] dialog box appears, as shown in Figure 14-5. (It's Untitled because you haven't yet named the new script.)

3. **Type your script in the dialog box.**

Figure 14-5:
Type the new script as shown here.

4. **After you finish typing your script, choose File⇨Save As.**

    The Save As dialog box appears.

5. **Type a name for the script in the File Name text box (see Figure 14-6), and click the Save button.**

The name of the new script that you've written appears in the Scripts dialog box.

Figure 14-6:
Save the
new script
using this
dialog box.

6. **Click the Close box (X) in the upper-right corner of the Scripts dialog box to close it.**

Step #3: Compiling a Script

After you write a script by using all the appropriate commands, syntax, and parameters, you still have more work to do. The script commands that you've written and saved to the ASCII file are called *source code*. You have to *compile* that source code so that it's translated into language that your computer can understand and execute.

Compiling also alerts you to errors in the script. You need to correct all the errors discovered during compilation before you can run the script.

The process of compiling a script is simple and involves little more than a click of your mouse.

To compile a script, follow these steps:

1. **Choose Tools⇨Scripts.**

   The Scripts dialog box appears, displaying all previously created scripts.

2. **Select the script you want to compile and click the Compile button.**

   pcAnywhere compiles the script. If there are no errors in the script, a pcAnywhere dialog box appears, as shown in Figure 14-7. If the script contains errors, you see a different pcAnywhere dialog box, as shown in Figure 14-8.

Figure 14-7:
This
message
appears if
no syntax
errors were
detected.

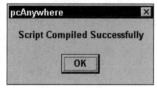

Figure 14-8:
This
unfortunate
message
appears
when
errors are
detected.

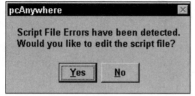

3. **If you get the "Script Compiled Successfully" message, click OK and skip to Step 5. You can now run your script. If you get the "Script File Errors Have Been Detected" message, click Yes to edit the script file.**

   If you click Yes to edit the script file, the pcAnywhere Editor dialog box appears, as shown in Figure 14-9.

Figure 14-9:
Correct
script errors
using this
dialog box.

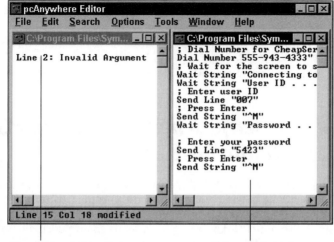

Shows line number of error   Edit script here

4. **Edit the script by using the right side of the dialog box (just as if you were editing a Microsoft Word document).**

   In my sample script, I received an error message because I left off the initial quotation mark around the phone number. So to correct my script, I would add those quotation marks at this time.

5. **When you've finished correcting the script, choose File⇨Save.**

6. **Exit the Script dialog box by clicking the Close box (X) in the upper-right corner.**

   When you try to compile the script again, it should be error-free.

Step #4: Running the Script

There are several ways to run a script. The two most common methods are by activating it through the Scripts dialog box or by programming it to run automatically when the remote PC connects to the host PC.

Running a script from the dialog box

To run a script from the Scripts dialog box, follow these steps:

1. **Choose Tools⇨Scripts.**

   The Scripts dialog box appears displaying all existing scripts. (If a script has not been successfully compiled, a dialog box appears telling you that errors have been detected and directing you to edit the script before you can run it.)

2. **Select a script and click the Run button.**

   The script begins running and executes the commands you have programmed (such as logging on to an Internet service provider, as in my earlier CheapServ example).

Running a script when the remote PC connects to the host PC

This is a useful feature that helps ensure that a task is regularly accomplished. An example of when you might want to run a script automatically upon connecting to the host is when you want to transfer files to or from the host PC to the remote PC. This is a great way to ensure periodic updates of files. (In Chapter 6, I tell you how to begin a session and establish a connection from the remote to the host.)

To configure the remote PC to automatically run a script whenever it connects to the host PC, follow these steps:

1. **From the remote pcAnywhere desktop, click the Remote Control button on the Action bar.**

   All existing remote control items appear on the pcAnywhere desktop.

2. **Right-click the icon for the connection item that you want to use when you run the script, and choose Properties from the pop-up menu.**

   The Properties dialog box for the remote control connection item appears.

3. **Click the Automated Tasks tab in the Properties dialog box.**

   The Automated Tasks page appears, as shown in Figure 14-10.

4. **Select the Run Upon Connection check box.**

5. **Click to select the Script option.**

   The text box next to this option is no longer grayed.

6. **Type the name of the script in the Script text box.**

   If you can't remember the name of the script, click the Browse button to search for the script.

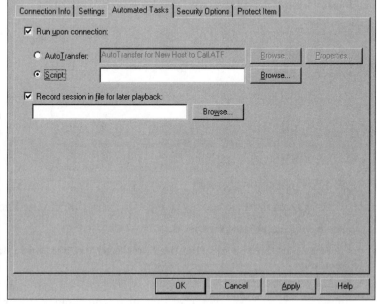

Figure 14-10:
From this dialog box, you can choose to run a script from the remote PC as soon as it connects to the host PC.

7. Click OK to save your changes and exit the Properties dialog box.

The next time the remote PC connects to the host PC, the script that you've designated runs automatically.

Modifying and Editing Scripts

At times, it may be more convenient to edit an existing script than to start a new one from scratch. To edit an existing script, follow these steps:

1. Choose Tools⇨Scripts.

The Scripts dialog box appears displaying all the previously created scripts.

2. Select a script and click the Edit button.

The pcAnywhere Editor dialog box appears, as shown in Figure 14-11.

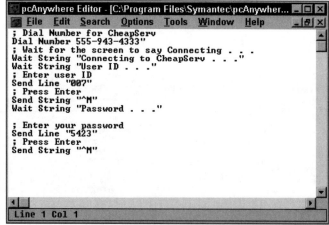

Figure 14-11:
Use this dialog box to edit an existing script.

3. Edit the script as necessary.

4. After you make the necessary changes to the script, choose File⇨Save As.

The Save As dialog box appears.

5. Type a name for the script in the File Name text box, and click the Save button.

If you want to preserve the original script, be sure to enter a new name in the File Name text box rather than using the name of the original script.

6. **Click the Close box (X) in the upper-right corner of the Scripts dialog box to close it.**

If you want to permanently modify the existing script that you were editing, you can choose File➪Save instead of Save As and save the changes to the script under its current name.

For Super Scripters: Where to Get More Information

If this chapter has left you hungry for more information about scripting, be sure to check out the pcAnywhere Script Guide. It is undoubtedly the most comprehensive source of information available for pcAnywhere scripts, and it's readily available on the pcAnywhere installation CD.

The Symantec Web site at www.symantec.com is another great resource for "super scripters." The site contains over 20 articles on scripting topics. You can locate these articles by clicking the Knowledge Base link under the technical support options. (In Chapter 17, I tell you more about how to locate articles on specific topics using the Symantec Web site.) Here are a few of the articles that you can find on the Web site:

- ✔ **"How to Transfer Files to or from a Host Computer Using a Script":** This article explains writing and running a script for an unattended file transfer.

- ✔ **"How to Troubleshoot a Script":** Sometimes those cryptic little syntax error messages don't tell the whole story. This article provides you with a checklist and explanations of common script problems.

- ✔ **"How to Transfer Files to or from an Online Service Using a Script":** This article details automating the process of updating your own bulletin board service (as discussed in Chapter 13) or streamlining the process of receiving updated information from a service someone else maintains.

- ✔ **"How to Obtain Support for the pcAnywhere Scripting Language":** This article provides you with phone numbers for both free and fee-based support personnel who can answer scripting questions.

Part V
The Part of Tens

The 5th Wave   By Rich Tennant

"You the guy having trouble staying connected to the network?"

In this part . . .

You may think that this section is just a bunch of stuff that didn't fit anywhere else. Not so. In fact, I had a lot more than ten things to include under each title. It was truly a struggle to come up with the cream of the cream. Part V includes chapters on tips for troubleshooting, some useful pcAnywhere tools, and information about the terrific Symantec Web site. This is my favorite part of the book.

Chapter 15

Ten Troubleshooting Tips

1 got the information in this chapter by posing as a frantic caller to the Symantec help desk. (Actually, it wasn't always an act.) During the course of my research into pcAnywhere, I discreetly interviewed six friendly help desk folk — people who really know their stuff. I polled them to find out the ten most common, but avoidable, calls received by the pcAnywhere support folks. In this chapter, I share the results with you.

The next time you have a problem with pcAnywhere (before you whip out your credit card — pcAnywhere technical support isn't always free), try these ten troubleshooting tips. You'll save on telephone and technical support charges — not to mention the bragging rights you'll earn because you figured out the problem on your own — okay, with just a little help!

Flee to the Web Site

The Symantec help desk staff with whom I spoke didn't always agree on which problems are most prevalent, or on the best ways to solve them. But they all agreed that if you run into a glitch, your first step should be to log on to the Web site at www.symantec.com.

Whatever problem you're having — no matter how traumatic or annoying — it's pretty darn likely that someone else has had it before. The Web site provides solutions and explanations for free. (In Chapter 17, I give you even more reasons to wander the Web site in your troubleshooting efforts.)

Combating the Evil Black Screen

One of the most disconcerting problems you can experience with pcAnywhere is to successfully connect to the host only to view a totally black screen. Fortunately, there are a couple of really simple steps you can take to shed some light.

Change the video display driver

If you can see the online toolbar (discussed in Chapter 7) and the main pcAnywhere menu at the top of your black screen, the likely culprit is an incompatible video *driver*. A driver is the software that lets your Windows operating system control your video display hardware.

To change the default video driver to an alternative one, follow these steps:

1. **From the host computer, choose Tools⇨Application Options.**

   The Application Options dialog box appears.

2. **Click the Host Operation tab.**

   The Host Operation page appears. The Default driver (it's actually called *Default*) appears in the Video Mode Selection box.

3. **In the Video Mode Selection box, click the arrow and select Compatibility from the drop-down list (see Figure 15-1).**

   The Compatibility driver is simply an alternative driver to the pcAnywhere default driver. You can choose this option to obtain a driver that is compatible with your system.

4. **Click OK to save your changes and exit the Application Options dialog box.**

If both the host PC and remote PC are on the same network, the problem is more likely to be incompatible video drivers than if the remote PC is dialing in from outside the network.

Select video driver

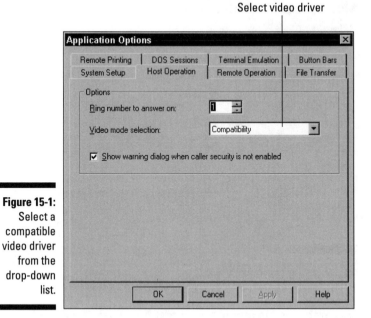

Figure 15-1:
Select a
compatible
video driver
from the
drop-down
list.

Decrease your modem speed

Still in the dark? The second-most-likely culprit is a modem speed that's set too high. Although your modem may be perfectly capable of handling data transmissions of 115,200 bits per second (bps), standard phone lines and most computer processors simply freak out trying to keep up. Try dropping your modem speed to 57,600 bps or 38,400 bps. To decrease your modem speed, follow these steps:

1. **Right-click the connection item that you're using (host or remote), and choose Properties from the pop-up menu.**

   The Properties dialog box for the connection item appears.

2. **Click the Connection Info tab.**

   The Connection Info page appears.

3. **Click the Details button.**

   The Properties page for your modem appears, as shown in Figure 15-2.

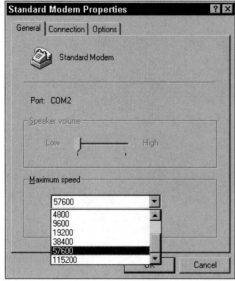

Figure 15-2:
Adjust modem speed using this dialog box.

Standard Modem Properties

General | Connection | Options

Standard Modem

Port: COM2

Speaker volume

Low High

Maximum speed

57600

4800
9600
19200
38400
57600
115200

Cancel

4. **Click the arrow in the Maximum Speed text box; from the drop-down list, select a lower speed than the one that currently appears.**

   For example, if the speed is currently set at 115,200, change it to 57,600.

5. **Click OK to close the modem properties page; click OK again to exit the Properties dialog box for the connection item.**

Other things to try

Have you dutifully tried switching video drivers and lowering your modem speed and *still* find yourself in the dark? You may be experiencing one of the following problems:

- ✔ **Your modem may be incorrectly configured:** In Chapter 5, I walk you through the process of configuring a modem on the remote PC.

- ✔ **You may be experiencing a hardware conflict:** You can find lots of information about troubleshooting hardware conflicts on the Symantec Web site at www.symantec.com. In Chapter 17, I tell you how to research this type of problem and how to contact Symantec by e-mail.

- ✔ **Another program may be accepting the call:** If you're dialing a host that's on a network; another program, such as a remote access server (RAS) or a fax program, may be accepting the call and preventing the remote from initiating a pcAnywhere session.

If the Host Won't Launch . . . Look Again

Amazingly, the help desk folks I talked to at Symantec told me that one of the most common calls they receive is from users who claim that they can't launch the host PC. As I discuss in Chapter 6, launching the host simply means opening the pcAnywhere program on the host computer. pcAnywhere must be running before the host can receive an incoming call from a remote PC.

You launch the host by right-clicking a host connection item and selecting Launch Host from the pop-up menu. When you do this, nothing much happens on your screen, except that a tiny Host Waiting icon appears on the Windows taskbar, as shown in Figure 15-3.

Host Waiting icon

Figure 15-3:
Look hard
for the
tiny icon.

The icon is supposed to be unobtrusive so that it doesn't interfere with other activities that someone may be performing on the host computer. But the icon is so miniscule that a lot of people can't seem to find it. They call the Symantec technical support people thinking that they're unable to launch the host. The help-desk person calmly directs the caller to the bottom-right corner of the screen (and bills them the minimum charge of $29.95 for the call).

The diminutive design of the Host Waiting icon is not a deliberate revenue-raising ploy. The people at Symantec are far too nice to think that way. But if you *were* just about to make that call to the help desk, this one tip just covered the cost of this book.

Speed Up a Sl-o-o-o-w Session

pcAnywhere users are typically impatient. They're the kind of folks who complain when they can't get fast Internet service in their cars. They hate anything slow — especially remote control sessions.

In this section, I give you a few pointers on how to speed things up.

Reduce the resolution of the host desktop

Resolution is a measure of the quality of an image represented by dots per inch. High-quality images have more dots per inch, which makes them appear richer and smoother. But pcAnywhere has to schlep all those extra dots per inch across the connection, resulting in slower performance.

To decrease the resolution of the host desktop images and improve performance, follow these steps:

1. **From the pcAnywhere desktop on the host PC, choose Tools➪Application Options.**

   The Application Options dialog box appears.

2. **Click the Remote Operation tab.**

   The Remote Operation page appears, as shown in Figure 15-4. The default entry in the ColorScale text box is 256 colors.

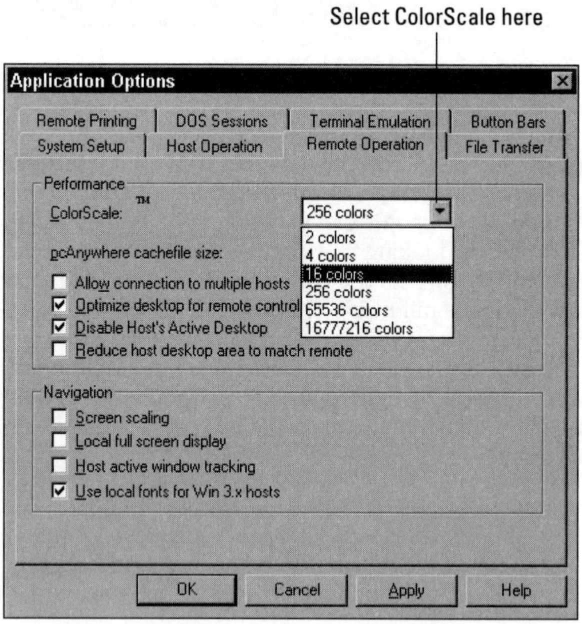

Select ColorScale here

Figure 15-4:
Adjust the
ColorScale
to reduce
the resolu-
tion on the
host screen.

3. **Click the arrow in the ColorScale box; from the drop-down list, select 16 colors, 4 colors, or 2 colors.**

4. **Click OK to save your changes and exit the dialog box.**

Unclutter the host desktop

The concept of cleaning up the host desktop serves the same purpose as reducing the resolution. Reducing clutter on the host desktop decreases the amount of image data transported from the host PC to the remote PC and improves performance. Clean up the host desktop by doing the following:

✔ **Hiding the Windows taskbar on the host PC.** Choose Start⇨Settings⇨ Taskbar and place a check in the Auto Hide check box. This causes the taskbar not to display unless you move your mouse pointer to the area of the screen where your taskbar is located (usually the very bottom). It becomes visible until you move your mouse pointer out of that area.

✔ **Minimizing all Windows except the one you're currently working in.**

Other ways to pick up the pace

The speed and performance of your remote control session depends on the quality of your connection and the amount of data being transferred across it.

Here are a few more ways to pick up the pace:

✔ **Don't use file transfer and remote control simultaneously:** Using both of these features at once really increases the traffic across the connection. Try to have only one of them open during a session.

✔ **Use toolbars instead of menus:** Menus, especially long ones, create extra traffic flowing from the host PC to the remote PC. This is another drag on the speed of your session. Toolbars require less image data to be transported across the connection.

✔ **Update your drivers:** Updating your modem and video drivers can enhance performance considerably.

✔ **Get the fastest type of phone connection that your budget allows:** Today's modems and computer processors allow for data transfer rates well in excess of what standard phone lines can accommodate. Consider a special ISDN line, as discussed in the Chapter 3 sidebar "Faster! Faster! ISDN that data now!"

When the Host Disconnects You

Here's the scenario: You connect to the host PC from the remote PC without a glitch. But before you can begin your session, you're abruptly cut off. A message appears on your screen saying that the host has disconnected you. How rude!

One common reason is that you've set your modem speed too high. You can reduce it by following the steps discussed earlier in this chapter.

Another likely explanation is that you're dialing into a host computer that uses a Windows Internet Naming Service (WINS) modem. The WINS service is a feature that helps computers and modems locate each other on the network. WINS modems were developed by AT&T and are manufactured by four or five companies to which AT&T grants the rights.

WINS modems lose connections because their drivers, the software that links them to your Windows operating system, are sometimes incompatible with pcAnywhere. The WINS driver sends a message telling pcAnywhere that the modem isn't connected, and pcAnywhere terminates the session. Sometimes this problem is resolved by requesting an updated driver from the manufacturer. Sometimes it persists even with a new driver.

pcAnywhere is aware of this problem, and makes no express or implied warranties as to its compatibility with WINS modems. It's beyond their control. Sorry.

Back Up Old Files before Synchronizing

Be careful when you're synchronizing files (see Chapter 8). You can select the "Never overwrite duplicate files" option, but sometimes pcAnywhere overwrites older files even though this option is checked.

To avoid this problem, you can do what is referred to as "synchronizing to an empty file." You create a new, empty file with the same name as the file you want to synchronize (after you change the name of the older version of the file, of course). That way, when you synchronize, the old files are not overwritten.

Synchronize Your Software Versions

Even though the older versions of pcAnywhere are pretty much compatible with the 9.0 version, you can still run into a snag on a network if the host is running an older version.

One situation occurs in which the remote PC can't see any icons under the My Computer icon on the host PC. If pcAnywhere were running properly, you'd expect to see icons for files, including the Documents folder icon. You'd also expect to see the Network Neighborhood icon. This problem has been documented on networks in which the remote PC is running pcAnywhere 9.0, but the host is running an earlier version. Another possible resolution to this problem is to change the video driver you're using on either the host or remote PC, as explained earlier in this chapter.

The obvious cure is to update the host PC to pcAnywhere 9.0. You can do this on your own if pcAnywhere was installed on the host by using a standard (as opposed to a network) installation. (The different types of installations are explained in Chapter 10.) If a network installation was used to install pcAnywhere, the network administrator needs to update the shared installation file.

After you've installed pcAnywhere 9.0, you can convert data saved using earlier versions of pcAnywhere. Choose Tools⇨Data Conversion. A wizard asks you which files you want to update and then completes the updating process.

Don't Panic if the Host Doesn't Recognize You

A common problem when you're dialing a host PC on a network from your remote PC is that the host cannot "authenticate" you. This means that the host doesn't recognize you as someone who's authorized to access files on the network. You may feel that you've been snubbed — cast out.

One possible solution is that you've been fired, and the network administrator has terminated your access privileges. If that's not the case, other possibilities include the following:

- ✔ **You've selected an incorrect connection item:** Double-check to make sure that you've selected the correct remote connection item, and not one configured to access a different host. (Remote connection items and their configuration are discussed in detail in Chapter 5.)

- ✔ **The properties for your network protocol are improperly configured:** Right-click the remote connection item you're using and select Properties from the pop-up menu. Click the Connection Info tab, and then the Details button. Make sure that the Connect to pcAnywhere Host Using Dial-Up Networking option is selected, as shown in Figure 15-5.

- ✔ **You've entered the wrong user name, password, or domain name:** This error is more common than you think. Try connecting and entering your login information again — carefully.

- ✔ **You're in a state of denial about having been fired:** My condolences. Time to pull out the want ads.

Make sure that this option is selected

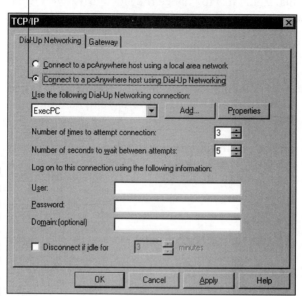

Figure 15-5:
Make sure
that the
remote con-
nection item
is properly
configured.

Make That Remote Printer Obey

Remote printing gives a lot of pcAnywhere users heartburn. The first sign of trouble is usually an error message that says, `This Printer/Driver does not Support Remote Printing`.

If you see this message, make sure that the host and remote are using *identical* printer drivers, including the same version (although not necessarily the same type of printer). In addition, Windows can't make a remote printer obey unless it has a driver that supports remote printing, so check with the printer manu-facturer on that issue. The pcAnywhere Web site lists alternative drivers for various printers.

You should also check that the host is set to use the special printer port set-ting that is installed with pcAnywhere. The host must be set to use the port called pcaw.prn. The remote can be set to use a usual port setting, such as LPT1. You can check the port setting on the host by choosing Start⇨ Settings⇨Control Panel⇨Printers. Right-click the icon for the remote printer, choose Properties from the pop-up menu, and then choose the Details tab to view or change the current port setting for the remote printer.

Troubleshooting Telephone Line Problems

No troubleshooting chapter is complete without mentioning telephone line problems. (Chapter 10 discusses these problems in detail.) The most common telephone line problems are lost or very slow connections. These types of problems are especially irritating because they often involve equipment you neither own nor fully control, such as public telephone lines.

Here are some quick fixes that can try:

- ✔ **Removing all other communications devices from the telephone line:** This includes phones, fax machines, and caller identification devices.

- ✔ **Dropping your modem speed:** I cover how to do this earlier in the chapter as a method for combating the black screen problem.

- ✔ **Asking the phone company to test your line:** It may be a good thing that you don't own the phone lines if it turns out a costly repair is needed.

If your problem is slow standard telephone lines, consider a special high-speed ISDN-line telephone. The "Faster! Faster! ISDN that data now!" sidebar in Chapter 3 gives you more information about this option.

Chapter 16

Ten Useful Tools

*p*cAnywhere comes with lots of tools that support you in using the program. These special features help you sort files, manage and replicate data, and run a program faster. The topics I discuss in this chapter contribute to the efficiency of pcAnywhere and can help maintain the health of your operating system as a whole.

The Making of a Macro

A *macro* is a type of shorthand. In only a couple of keystrokes, a macro can tell a computer to do something fairly involved, such as executing a long sequence of commands or running an entire program. When you use a macro, you don't need to specify a full command sequence or path to the program you want to run.

Macros are a personal thing between you and your remote PC. You tell your remote PC what keystroke combination you want to use, and what you want the macro to accomplish. For example, you may indicate that you want the computer to run a specific script every time you press Alt+5.

pcAnywhere creates a separate file for each macro that you create. A macro file has the extension .mk7.

To create a macro, follow these steps:

1. **Choose Tools⇨Application Options.**

   The Application Options dialog box appears.

2. **Click the Terminal Emulation tab, and then click the Macro Keys button.**

   The Select Macro Key File dialog box appears, as shown in Figure 16-1.

Specify folder   Enter filename

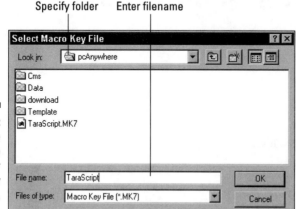

Figure 16-1:
Specify the filename and folder for the new macro.

3. **Select a folder from the Look In drop-down box.**

4. **Type a filename in the File Name text box and click OK.**

   The Macro Keys dialog box appears, as shown in Figure 16-2.

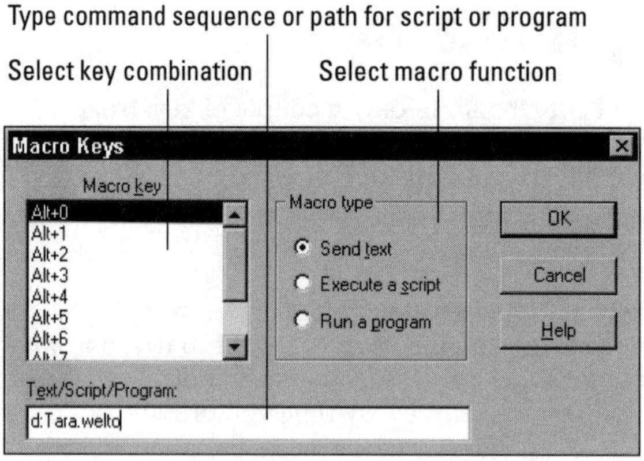

Type command sequence or path for script or program

Select key combination   Select macro function

Figure 16-2:
Specify the function, key combi-nation, and command sequence for the macro.

5. **Select the key combination that you want to use for the macro from the Macro Key drop-down list.**

6. **In the Macro Type section, select one of the following options to tell pcAnywhere the function of the macro that you're creating:**

- **Send text:** Transmits a command to the host (such as reboot)
- **Execute a script:** Tells pcAnywhere to run a script on the host PC
- **Run a program:** Tells pcAnywhere to execute a program

7. **In the Text/Script/Program text box, type one of the following:**

- The name of the command sequence that you want to execute when the macro runs
- The filename and path for a script that you want to execute when the macro runs
- The filename and path of a program that you want to execute when the macro runs

8. **Click OK to save the settings for the new macro and exit the Macro Keys dialog box.**

9. **Click OK to close the Select Application Options dialog box.**

Now when you're in pcAnywhere and press the macro key combination you entered, the command, program, or script you specified runs automatically.

Doing It in DOS

Did you think the days of DOS were over? This old dog of a program still shows up from time to time.

DOS was the first operating system designed for PCs and is still an integral part of Windows 3.1. Windows 95/98 and NT come with their own built-in versions of DOS in order to support any DOS applications that are still out there (and there are quite a few).

A problem sometimes arises in pcAnywhere when you connect from a remote PC to a host PC that's running DOS — the remote PC may have trouble viewing the host screen. Fortunately, this is one of those fixable problems that the designers of pcAnywhere anticipated perfectly.

To change the settings on the remote PC so that you can view a host PC running DOS, follow these steps:

1. **Choose Tools➪Application Options.**

   The Application Options dialog box appears.

2. **Click the DOS Sessions tab.**

3. **Select the Synchronize Display with Host option, as shown in Figure 16-3.**

4. **Click OK to exit the Application Options dialog box.**

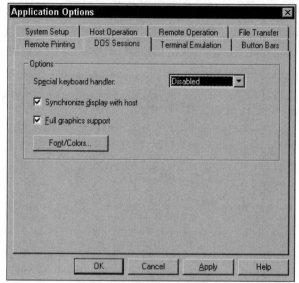

Figure 16-3:
Options to
view a host
running
DOS.

Recording a pcAnywhere Session

Recording a session enables you to replicate the session if it went well, or analyze what went wrong if the session was a bust.

There are two ways to record a session. The first method is to begin recording the session automatically upon connection. This ensures that you don't miss a single step in the process. The other method is to start the recording after the session has begun. Starting the recording later in the session can make it easier to get right to the part that interests you without having to waste time viewing the preliminaries.

Due to the way that pcAnywhere was designed, sessions are recorded only on the remote PC — not on the host.

To begin recording upon connection

To begin recording a session immediately when you establish a connection, follow these steps:

1. **Right-click the remote control connection item for which you want to record a session and choose _P_roperties from the pop-up menu.**

   The Properties dialog box for the connection item appears.

2. **Click the Automated Tasks tab.**

   The Automated Tasks page appears, as shown in Figure 16-4.

Select to begin recording upon connection

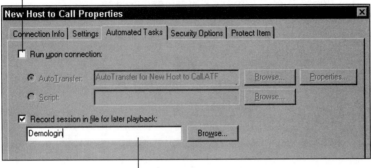

Figure 16-4:
Choose
options on
this page to
record a
session.

Enter filename for recorded session

3. **Select the Record Session in File for Later Playback option.**

   Type a name for the session in this text box.

4. **Click OK to close the dialog box.**

   pcAnywhere immediately begins recording the session the next time you connect to the host PC.

To start recording during a session

All session recording and playback options can only be accessed from the online menu or online toolbar of the remote PC. (As I discuss in Chapter 8, the online menu and toolbar are only available during an online session.) Furthermore, sessions can only be recorded on the remote PC.

To begin recording at any time during an online session, follow these steps:

1. **Establish a connection to the host; then, from the remote computer, select Recording from the online menu or the Start/Stop Session Recording button from the online toolbar.**

   The Select Recording File dialog box appears.

2. **In the Select Recording File dialog box, type a name for the session and click Save.**

   This closes the Select Recording File dialog box.

Replaying a Session

To use the pcAnywhere utility for replaying a previously recorded session, follow these steps:

1. **Choose Tools⇨Playback Sessions/Screens.**

   The Select Playback File dialog box appears.

2. **In the File Name text box, type the name of the file from the saved session that you want to review.**

3. **Select Record Files (.RCD) from the Files of Type drop-down box. (This is the default type.)**

4. **Click Open.**

   The Playback Options dialog box appears as shown in Figure 16-5.

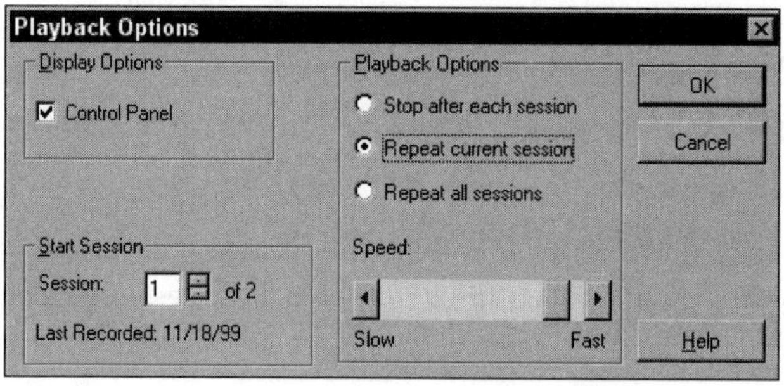

Figure 16-5:
Use this dialog box to play back a recorded session.

Playback Options		✕
Display Options	**Playback Options**	OK
☑ Control Panel	○ Stop after each session	Cancel
	⦿ Repeat current session	
	○ Repeat all sessions	
Start Session	Speed:	
Session: 1 ⊟ of 2	◄ ▶	
Last Recorded: 11/18/99	Slow Fast	Help

5. **Select Repeat Current Session and click OK.**

   The session begins playing on your screen.

   This Repeat Current Session option allows you to view only the session you selected in Step 3. Alternatively, the Stop After Each Session option allows you to play all recorded sessions and to stop after each one. The Repeat All Sessions allows you to watch all sessions that have been recorded without stopping. The Start Session field assigns a number to each session in chronological order and allows you to access and play a desired session by locating its number in the Session field.

6. **(Optional) Select the Control Panel check box to display the Control Panel dialog box on your screen during the session.**

   The Control Panel dialog box enables you to start, stop, and control the speed of the session as you are viewing it.

7. **When the session has been replayed, a dialog box appears on your screen telling you when the session is over; click OK to exit this dialog box and restore the pcAnywhere desktop to your screen.**

Saving a Screen

pcAnywhere lets you take a "snapshot" of your computer screen during a remote control session. Snapshots are useful if you want to save some information on the screen without having to copy it down or print it out.

To save a screen to view later, follow these steps:

1. **After establishing a connection to the host, choose the Save Screen option from the remote online menu or click the Save the Current Screen button on the online toolbar. (The online menu and online toolbar appear on your screen only during an active remote control session.)**

2. **In the File Name text field of the Select Save Screen File dialog box, type a filename for the screen that you want to save.**

3. **Click the Open button.**

   The dialog box disappears, and the current screen is saved under the filename that you designated.

4. **You can repeat these steps to save successive screens to the same file.**

   The screens are later replayed in the order in which they were saved.

To view a screen that you've previously saved, follow these steps:

1. **Choose Tools⇨Playback Sessions/Screens.**

   The Select Playback File dialog box appears.

2. **In the File Name text box, type the name of the file for the saved screen that you want to review.**

3. **Select Screen Files (.SCN) from the Files of Type drop-down box and click Open.**

   The screen that you selected in Step 2 appears on your desktop. You may close this screen by clicking the X in the upper-right corner, as you would for any active window.

Creating a pcA Activity Log

A *log* keeps track of how often certain events occur. For example, if you're troubleshooting a telephone line problem, you may want to record the number of connection failures or abnormally terminated sessions.

To create a log, which you can later view on either the host or remote PC, follow these steps:

1. **Choose Tools⇨Logging Options.**

   The Logging Options dialog box appears, as shown in Figure 16-6.

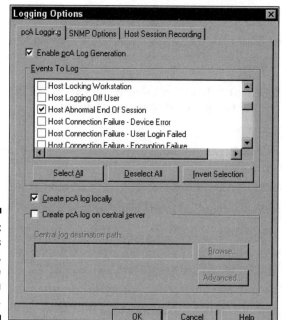

Figure 16-6:
In this dialog box, select the events you want to log.

2. **Select Enable pcA Log Generation.**

   Select the activities you want to track from the Events to Log window.

3. **Select Create pcA log locally.**

   You can also create a log on the server or specify a network path for the location of the log on another computer.

4. **Click OK to exit the Logging Options dialog box.**

Viewing a pcA Log Report

To use the pcAnywhere utility for viewing a report of previously logged events, follow these steps:

1. **Choose Tools⇨Activity Log Processing.**

   The Activity Log Processing dialog box appears.

2. **Click the Report button.**

   The Choose Input Log File dialog box appears as shown in Figure 16-7.

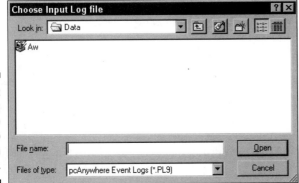

Figure 16-7:
Select a log
file to be
used to
create a
report.

3. **In the File Name text box, type the name of the log file for which you want to view a report and click the Open button.**

   The Host and Remote Session Log dialog box appears.

4. **In the Host and Remote Session Log Report dialog box, indicate a date range for the report (see Figure 16-8) and click OK.**

   The Select Destination for File Output dialog box appears, asking you to enter the name of the destination file for your output. This is the filename under which your report is saved.

5. **In the dialog box, type a name for the log report file; then click OK.**

   A dialog box appears confirming the filename that you just entered and asking if you want to view it now.

6. **Click Yes to view the log report.**

7. **When you are finished viewing the log report, click the Close box (X) in the upper-right corner of the log report window to close it. Do the same to exit the Host and Remote Session Log Report dialog box.**

   Or you can use this dialog box to repeat Steps 4 and 5 and create another report.

Host and Remote Session Log Report   ✕

Report Type
⦿ Fully Formatted
○ Data Only - Comma Delimited
○ Data Only - Fixed Fields

OK
Cancel
Help

Date Range
	Year	Month	Day
Start:	1980	01	01
End:	1999	11	18

Figure 16-8:
Specify a
date range
for the
logged data
to appear in
the report.

Creating an NT Event Log

Windows NT comes with all sorts of utilities to monitor the health of the network. For example, Windows NT Server comes with Performance Monitor,
which helps identify such things as trends, bottlenecks, and the effect of
system configuration changes.

You can record pcAnywhere events to an NT log so that you can later use
Performance Monitor (or another NT diagnostic tool) to analyze the data. To
create an NT log, choose Tools⇨Logging Options. The Logging Options dialog
box opens with the NT Event Log page visible. Select the Enable NT Event
Logging check box, and select the activities you want to track in the log.

NT event logging is only available from a computer running NT.

Windows NT takes over from there. You can find out about related NT services
for evaluating the information you've logged by using the Windows NT help
feature. For example, perform a keyword search with the words *event log*.

Enabling ISDN Channel Bonding

ISDN lines can transmit data at a rate ten times faster than standard telephone lines. (For more information, see the Chapter 3 sidebar "Faster! Faster!
ISDN that data now!")

The most common type of ISDN service is called Basic Rate Interface (or BRI).
BRI consists of three lines called *channels*. Two of the channels, called B channels, carry data at rates of 64 kilobits per second (Kbps). The third line is
used primarily for control and error checking rather than data transmission.

If you have the right equipment, you can combine two B channels to increase
the rate of data transmission to 128 Kbps. This process is called *channel
bonding*.

A special type of modem, called a CAPI modem, is required for ISDN transmissions and channel bonding. CAPI stands for Common ISDN Application Programming Interface.

If you're lucky enough to have an ISDN line and a CAPI modem, you'll be glad to know that pcAnywhere supports them. To configure a CAPI modem, right-click the connection item you're using, and select Properties from the pop-up menu. The Connection Info page appears. Select the option ISDN Via CAPI 2.0.

You can now enable channel bonding, which combines two 64-Kbps channels into a single 128 Kbps channel. Click the Details button and select the Channel Bonding option. Click Apply to save this setting, and then click OK to exit the dialog box. You're now ready to enjoy a high-speed data transfer session.

Downloading from the LiveUpdate Server

The LiveUpdate utility connects you to the Symantec LiveUpdate server so that you can quickly get updates for pcAnywhere. These updates improve pcAnywhere's performance or correct problems users have reported to Symantec.

You can access LiveUpdate by going to the Help menu and selecting LiveUpdate. The LiveUpdate dialog box offers you the option of connecting over the Internet or by modem. (There's also an option to Find Your Device Automatically, but this option isn't recommended, according to the Symantec Web site.)

After you tell pcAnywhere how you want to connect, another LiveUpdate dialog box appears describing the types of updates currently available (in other words, what problems the updates fix). Select the ones that you want to download and click Next. pcAnywhere downloads these updates directly from the server in minutes.

You can also do a manual update, which means that you download the update files from the Internet rather than via a direct connection to the update server. But LiveUpdate is the faster of the two methods. If you choose to do a manual update, you need to first download the installation files from the Symantec Web site. Generally, you want to run a manual update only if you can't establish the direct connection to the LiveUpdate server due to a peculiarity of your equipment or network.

Chapter 17

Ten Reasons to Wander the Symantec Web Site

In This Chapter

▶ Visiting Symantec's award winning Web site

▶ Taking advantage of free Web site tools

▶ Dealing with pcAnywhere problems

Symantec's Web Site Was Voted One of the Ten Best

1n 1999, the Symantec Web site was voted one of the year's ten best by the Association of Support Professionals.

The Web site isn't flashy. What it lacks in Java animation and special visual effects, it makes up for in substance. Its designers opted for ease of navigation and comprehensive troubleshooting information rather than flashy graphics.

A Toddler Could Navigate This Web Site

Well, maybe not every toddler — but certainly an above-average kindergartner. The URL address for the site is www.symantec.com.

The first thing you see when you log on is a picture of a globe and hypertext links to several countries. Click the link for your country. After you've clicked your country link, the Symantec Web site index page appears, as shown in Figure 17-1.

Click for lists of service and support options

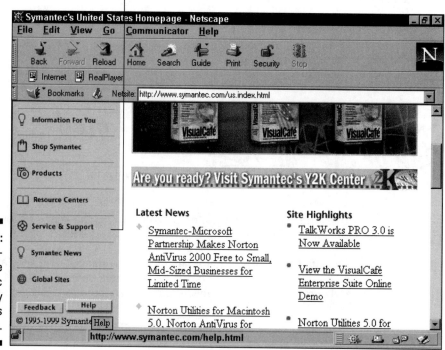

Figure 17-1:
Access features of the Symantec Web site by using this index page.

You Can Find Articles on Troubleshooting Topics

For a quick answer to an installation problem or a technical question, click the Service and Support link. This displays the Web page shown in Figure 17-2.

Select pcAnywhere from the first drop-down box, and select Version 9.0 from the second drop-down box. Then click the Go button.

The next Web page that appears, as shown in Figure 17-3, displays two lists. One list identifies technical support options and the other identifies your customer service choices.

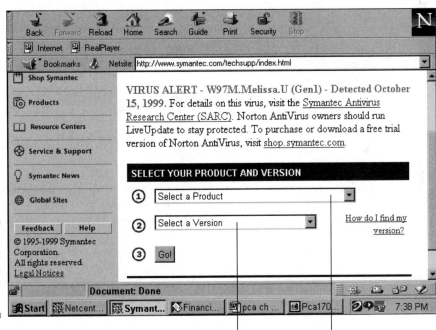

Figure 17-2: Indicate that you're using pcAnywhere Version 9.0.

Select 9.0   Select pcAnywhere

Click here to use Troubleshooter

Your technical support options

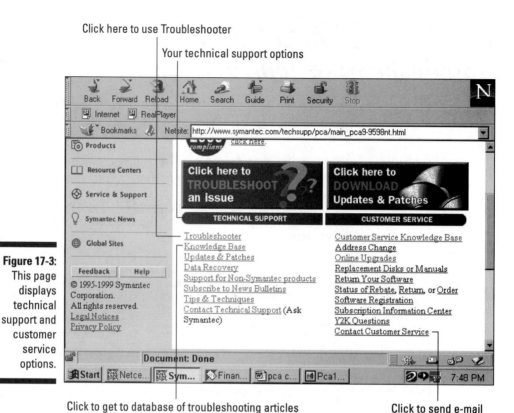

Figure 17-3:
This page
displays
technical
support and
customer
service
options.

Click to get to database of troubleshooting articles

Click to send e-mail

Click the Knowledge Base link to display a list of topics, as shown in Figure
17-4. Click any topic to show a list of technical support articles available for
that subject. To read the text of an article, click its title.

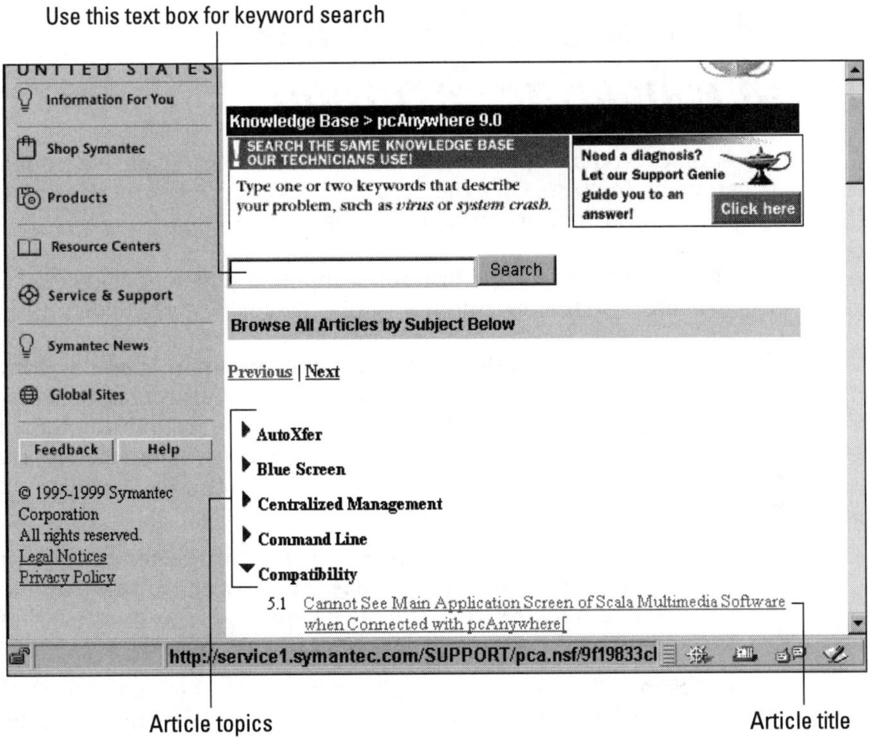

Use this text box for keyword search

Figure 17-4:
Click the
Knowledge
Base link to
display this
page.

Article topics   Article title

You Can Do a Keyword Search

What if you don't find an article that answers your question?

To find the answer more quickly, try a keyword search. Enter keywords pertaining to your question in the text box at the top of the Knowledge Base page. Click the Search button and a list of articles relevant to your question appears.

The Web Site Gives You a Troubleshooting Strategy

At times, you may prefer to use Symantec's comprehensive troubleshooting strategy. To do so, click the Troubleshooter option, which is first on the list of Technical Support options (see Figure 17-3).

After you click the Troubleshooter option, a screen appears explaining that Symantec's four step troubleshooting strategy is as follows:

✔ **Step 1:** The first line of attack is making sure that you're working with the latest version of the software. (Later in this chapter, I discuss how to download updates from the Web site.) The troubleshooter screen provides you with instructions for running LiveUpdate, a hypertext link for a manual update, and yet another link to an article explaining what problems the updates fix.

✔ **Step 2:** You can read about the current "top issues and solutions." These are the most common problems experienced by pcAnywhere users. The Troubleshooter screen provides hypertext links to articles about these topics.

✔ **Step 3:** If your question isn't one of the most common ones, the Troubleshooter takes you to a page where you can search the Knowledge Base, peruse a list of articles, or do a keyword search of articles (see Figure 17-4).

✔ **Step 4:** If the previous three steps haven't solved your problem, you're provided with a list of phone numbers and fee schedules for technical support. There's also a hypertext link for sending Symantec e-mail, which is discussed in the next section.

You Can Get a Quick Answer by E-Mail

If you can't find the answer to your question on the Web site, you can ask for a personal response from Symantec. Go to the page that displays the list of technical support and customer service options (refer to Figure 17-3). From the list of customer support options, click the Contact Customer Service link. (It's the very last one on the list.)

A list of contact options appears, including an e-mail link, which you can use to send your question via e-mail to a technical support person. The technical representative usually responds within 24 hours.

Web Site Solutions Are Free

You can save a lot of money by consistently taking your troubles to the Web site, rather than calling technical support.

Telephone support by phone currently costs $2.95 per minute for routine installation problems and $29.95 per incident for more in-depth technical questions. (You are eligible to receive limited free telephone support for the first 90 days from the date of your software purchase — but after that, you pay the big bucks.)

Access to solutions on the Web site is always free.

There's No Holding on the Web Site

If you want telephone support, and you call when the operators are busy, you're liable to waste time holding for the next available representative. On the other hand, access to the Web site is free, it's available 24 hours a day, and you won't lose time (or money) waiting on the phone.

You Can Get Live Updates

The latest versions of the pcAnywhere LiveUpdate files can often solve a problem that you're having (because everyone else is having it, too). The updates are software supplements to your existing version of pcAnywhere. You can download the updates from the Web if you're on a computer that isn't attached to a network. If you *are* on a network, the network administrator may need to update the shared installation file, as I discussed in Chapter 3.

To access the updates, click the Troubleshooter link from the list of technical support options, and the page shown in Figure 17-5 appears. This page tells you when the last update was released and provides instructions for performing either a live or a manual update. You can also click a link to access an article explaining what issues are addressed by the latest update.

A live update is quicker than a manual update (see Chapter 16 for more information). You accomplish a live update in one step by establishing a connection between the Symantec LiveUpdate server and your modem. It takes only a few minutes. If you do a manual update, you need to first download and run the installation files from the Web site. The manual installation process can take half an hour or more. Generally, you only want to run a manual update if the live update has failed. Articles that address this topic are available on the Web site.

Click here to find out about LiveUpdate   Date of last update

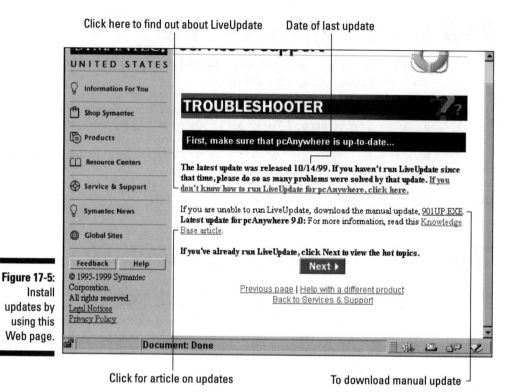

Figure 17-5:
Install
updates by
using this
Web page.

Click for article on updates   To download manual update

You Can Patch Things Up

A software *patch* is a quick fix or modification for a software program usually
distributed by the software manufacturer. You can download patches for
pcAnywhere from the Web site by clicking the Updates & Patches link from
the list of technical support options.

You can view a list of software patches currently available and a description
of the problem that they each fix. Then simply click the hypertext link (the
one that says "click here") beneath any patch that you want to download, as
shown in Figure 17-6.

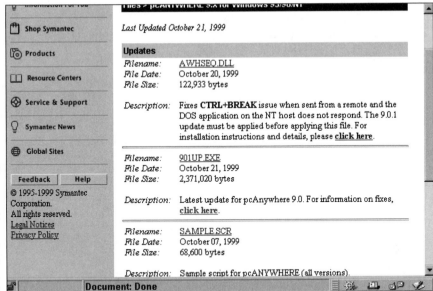

Figure 17-6:
Click a
hypertext
link for the
patch you
want to
download.

Glossary

• •

I'm providing this glossary as a quick guide to the new terms that you may run across in this book. Words that appear in italics within a definition refer to terms that I define separately in this glossary.

Access permissions

Sharing of files in Windows NT is controlled by access permissions granted to individual users. There are four types of Windows NT access permissions:

No Access: The user cannot view the file.

Read: The user may read, but not change, the file.

Change: The user may modify or delete the file.

Full Control: The user has permission to change or delete the file, as well as the ability to determine the access permissions granted to other users of the file.

Action bar

The Action bar is located at the top of the pcAnywhere main window. The Action bar contains *Action buttons,* which you click to navigate the pcAnywhere program. The Action bar contains four default Action buttons: Be a Host PC, Remote Control, File Transfer, and Be A Gateway. You can also add an Online Access Action button.

Action buttons

Buttons on the *Action bar* that are used to navigate the pcAnywhere program.

Activity log

A file that contains information about specific types of actions performed and events occurring on a computer, such as error messages, logon attempts, and accessing of various program features. The information stored in the activity log is used to generate a log report, which you can analyze for maintenance and troubleshooting purposes.

ASCII text

ASCII stands for American Standard Code for Information Exchange. It's a binary code used for text and printer control. ASCII is a common-denominator code that enables you to import and export data to and from applications that don't normally support each other. For example, you may convert a text file to ASCII and then convert the ASCII to a spreadsheet program. For pcAnywhere purposes, ASCII is used to help convert word files to pcAnywhere script commands.

AutoTransfer

Refers to the pcAnywhere commands, which automatically transfer files to or from the host computer or perform *synchronization*. You can schedule an AutoTransfer to take place immediately upon a connection with the host PC.

Bit

The smallest unit of data storage; a single binary digit (0 or 1).

bps

The abbreviation for bits per second. It's the basic measurement of the speed of data transfer.

Byte

A unit of data made up of 8 bits (and a possible ninth bit for error correction purposes).

Cache file

A special file that improves performance by storing downloaded data or images. The program doesn't have to download data or images again the next time you want them to appear on your screen. In pcAnywhere, a remote computer maintains a cache file of images that it has downloaded from the host computer.

Caller

Someone given the right to access a host computer and initiate a pcAnywhere *remote control* session. Each caller is assigned a login name and password that identifies it to the host. When you initially set up a *host connection item,* you must identify the callers permitted to access it.

Caller properties

Caller properties include the caller login name, password, and access rights.

Channel bonding

The process of doubling transmission speed by spreading it over two telephone lines. *ISDN* modems use channel bonding to transmit data over two 64 Kbps lines simultaneously to achieve a transmission rate of 128 Kbps.

COM port

Ports on a PC used to connect to a mouse or an external modem. A device attached to a COM port on a PC transmits data serially. pcAnywhere enables you to transfer data between two computers by cabling the COM ports of both PCs together.

Compression

The process of getting data to take up less space by removing spaces and identifying repeating patterns. Data is generally compressed before transmission and decompressed after.

Connection device

The hardware used to make a connection between two computers. This can be network cabling, a serial cable between two computers, or a modem. Also referred to as simply a *device.*

Connection item

A file represented by an icon on the pcAnywhere desktop that contains information used to make a connection. Information contained in a connection item includes the type of hardware used, the phone number or network address, and commands governing the connection once it's established.

Crash recovery

Crash recovery is a way to salvage data that is only partially transmitted at the time that a connection ends abnormally. pcAnywhere has a crash recovery option that can be enabled for *file transfers* and *synchronizations*.

Directory

An index on a hard drive or floppy disk used for locating files. A directory is visually represented by a file folder icon, which appears in the Windows Explorer window. Each program has its own directory containing files necessary to run the application.

DNS

Stands for Domain Name System. It's software that enables you to locate other computers on the network, or on the Internet, by translating the computer's 15-character Windows computer name (called the NetBIOS name) to a name (called an IP address) that can be interpreted by the *TCP/IP protocol*.

Domain

A group of client and server computers on a Windows NT network controlled by one security database used for authenticating users.

Drive

An electromechanical device used for viewing floppy disks, CD-ROMs, and tapes.

Driver

A software program that links a peripheral device, such as a printer, to the Windows operating system. The driver software for a device enables the Windows operating system to control it. When a new hardware device is added to a computer, the driver for that device must be installed. A driver can also link a software program to your operating system.

Encryption

A mathematical method of scrambling data to protect it from being intercepted by unauthorized persons.

Event log

A file used by the Windows NT operating system to compile data about events, such as system failures, abnormally ended sessions, and failed logon attempts.

File Manager

A pcAnywhere program feature that enables you to transfer files between a host and remote computer. The pcAnywhere File Manager options include file sorting and file overwriting preferences.

File transfer

The process of transferring files from one computer to another.

Flow control

A programming command built into the modem's driver software that signals that data transmission to the modem can occur or resume. When a modem receives data at a faster rate than it can store, the flow control method temporarily halts transmission.

Gateway

In pcAnywhere, a gateway is a computer on a local area network (*LAN*) with a modem (or other communications device) that can be used by other computers on the network that do not have modems. Computers on the network can dial outside the network or receive calls coming into the network by using the modem on the gateway computer. Gateways can be either bidirectional or unidirectional. A bidirectional gateway can both send and receive calls. A unidirectional gateway can either send or receive calls, but not both.

Host

A host, or host computer, contains files or applications accessed by another computer (called the *remote* or remote computer) during a *remote control* session. The remote computer establishes a connection with the host and controls the host during the remote control session.

Host connection item

A file maintained on a *host* computer that contains settings and other information that enables a remote computer to connect to it. The host connection item is represented by an icon on the pcAnywhere desktop. When you right-click the icon and select the Launch host option from the pop-up menu, the settings in the host connection file are activated and the host computer is ready to receive an incoming call from the *remote* computer.

Host list box

During a communication session, the list of drives and files from the host computer that is displayed on one side of the File Manager window.

Interface

A common set of design conventions, such as wiring and connection ports, that govern how a hardware device attaches to a computer.

Internal modem

A modem that plugs into an expansion slot inside the computer, as opposed to being plugged into a *COM port* on the outside of the computer.

IP address

The address used to identify each computer on a network. Also known as a *network address*.

IRQ

Stands for Interrupt ReQuest (a sloppy acronym if ever there was one). It's a signal to the computer's processor that a device needs to use its resources. Hardware devices are assigned IRQ codes that have different levels of priority to interrupt other devices that may be using the processor.

ISDN

Stands for Integrated Services Digital Network. It's an international telephone communications standard for transmitting voice, video, and data over digital lines called channels. ISDN's most common service is called the Basic Rate Interface (BRI). BRI consists of two 64 Kpbs lines and one 16 Kbps line that are used for error control. The two 64 Kbps lines can be combined to transmit data at 128 Kbps. This process is called *channel bonding*.

Kilobit

A kilobit is equivalent to 1,024 data bits.

Kilobyte

A kilobyte is equivalent to 1,024 bytes.

LAN

Stands for local area network. A LAN is a network in a confined geographical area, such as a single office building.

Launch

To start or open a program or application.

Launching the host

In pcAnywhere, launching the host means starting pcAnywhere on the host computer so that a remote computer may establish a connection to it.

List box

The File Manager window contains two list boxes: One displays the files on the host computer, and the other displays the files on the remote computer.

LiveUpdate

The pcAnywhere feature that enables you to connect to the Symantec LiveUpdate server and download the most recent updates and *patches* for pcAnywhere.

Log report

A summary of the events recorded in an activity or event log file.

LPT

LPT is an acronym for line printer port. It's a port on a computer that's generally used to establish a connection to a printer.

Macro

A series of keystrokes that you can execute to call out a previously defined command or series of commands that perform an operation, start a program, or run a script.

Mapping a drive

The process of specifying the location on a network and/or specific computer on which a drive is located when executing a command involving that drive.

Megabit

One million bits.

Megabyte

One million bytes.

Modem

A piece of equipment that makes it possible for a computer to communicate by using a telephone line. It translates telephone signals (analog signals) to digital signals used by a computer.

Network installation

A network installation is used to install pcAnywhere in a file on a drive that all computers on the network can access. This makes the process of installing and updating pcAnywhere much simpler because it doesn't have to be done on each individual PC.

Null modem cable

A cable used to connect two computers together so that they can transfer files and send and receive data without the use of modems.

Online menu

The online menu contains all options necessary to manage a pcAnywhere *remote control* session. It's visible only during the session. Because the *remote* computer is in control of the *host* during the online session, the online menu options are much more extensive on the remote computer.

Online service

A service (often provided for a fee) that users can access using a modem and a special phone number to obtain information, exchange messages, receive technical support, and download files.

Online toolbar

The online toolbar is visible on the screen of the *host* and *remote* computers only during the pcAnywhere *remote control* session. It contains buttons with icons for all the online menu options. Because the remote computer is in control of the host during the online session, the online toolbar options are much more extensive on the remote computer.

Parallel data transfer

Moves eight or more bits of data at one time, as opposed to *serial data transfer,* which moves data one bit at a time.

Parameter

Any value assigned to a program in order to customize that program for a particular purpose. In pcAnywhere parameters are used to provide information that a pcAnywhere script needs to execute a command. Examples of parameters are the time frame for the program to be executed, or the location of data to be copied.

Parity

Parity refers to a method of checking for errors in data transmission. In a remote control session, the receiving computer checks for errors in the data by checking for the number of 1 bits, making sure that they follow a prescribed pattern.

Partitions

Logical divisions or sections on a computer that are assigned letters for identification and access. For example, on many computers, a CD-ROM drive is assigned the letter D.

Patches

A patch is computer code that provides a quick or temporary solution for a problem with a program. You can download patches for pcAnywhere from the Internet or use the Symantec LiveUpdate Server.

Peripheral device

A device attached outside the computer that sends and receives data. Computers, modems, mice, and printers are examples of peripheral devices.

Ports

A connection point on a computer used to connect a *peripheral device* (for example, a printer), or to transmit data in and out of the computer.

Protocol

A set of rules governing the transmission and receipt of data.

Pseudocode

Pseudocode is a fancy term for plain English. When writing pcAnywhere *scripts,* you first use psuedocode to write out the steps to be performed. You later translate them into scripting commands.

Public key

A public key encryption system uses a public key code to *encrypt* (or scramble) data being transmitted to ensure its security. The user must have a private key code to unscramble the data. The private key code is unique to, and known only by, the party for whom the transmission is intended.

Remote

A PC that connects to a *host* computer and controls it during a *remote control* session.

Remote control

A connection in which a *remote* computer establishes a connection with a *host* computer and controls it.

Remote control connection item

A file located on the *remote* computer, which contains information needed to establish a connection with the *host* computer, such as the connection device to be used and security information.

Remote list box

During a communication session, the list of drives and files from the remote PC that is displayed on one side of the File Manager window.

Remote networking

A connection in which a *remote* computer connects to a *server* and operates as a *workstation* on the network. Remote networking (also referred to as dial-up networking) is available only on networks.

Resolution

A measure of the quality of an image based on the number of dots per inch.

Resources

Any hardware, software, or data files on a computer.

Rights

Rights authorize all users on an NT network to perform actions on the network, such as backing up files whether or not you have access to those files. In contrast, *access permissions* are specific to individual files.

Scripting

A set of instructions to a program, such as pcAnywhere. Scripts are written using a set of rules that enables the instructions to be read by the program.

Serial data transfer

The transmission of data one bit at a time over a single line.

Server

A computer on a network that has resources that it shares with other computers on the network.

Shared network drive

A drive on a computer that other computers on a network can access.

Standard installation

The type of installation you perform when you install pcAnywhere on a single computer, as opposed to on an entire network. A standard installation may be used even if the computer is attached to a network.

Synchronizing

The process of simultaneously copying a folder on the host and remote computer so that files contained within the folders are identical to each other at the end of the synchronization process. If two files have the same name, pcAnywhere, by default, copies the file with the most recent date and time to both folders.

Syntax

The set of rules that govern how a command in a particular program can be written. An incorrect application of these rules, when writing a pcAnywhere script, results in a syntax error.

TAPI

An acronym for Telephony Applications Programming Interface. TAPI is a feature available on Windows 95 and NT 4.0 that automatically detects and configures communications hardware that uses telephone lines.

TCP/IP

Stands for Transmission Control Protocol/Internet Protocol. TCP/IP is a common network protocol that enables dissimilar computers to communicate with each other. TCP/IP is used on the Internet.

Voice First

A type of connection where a remote user can have a traditional verbal telephone conversation, and then begin a *remote control* session between the *host* and *remote* computers without terminating the initial connection.

WAN

A wide area network with workstations spanning distances greater than one kilometer.

WINS

An acronym for Windows Internet Naming Service. This is a type of software produced by Microsoft that runs on a Windows NT server and converts Windows names to names recognized on a network (IP addresses).

Workstation

A computer on a network that isn't a server.

Index

• R •

IDG BOOKS WORLDWIDE
BOOK REGISTRATION

We want to hear from you!

Visit **http://my2cents.dummies.com** to register this book and tell us how you liked it!

✔ Get entered in our monthly prize giveaway.

✔ Give us feedback about this book — tell us what you like best, what you like least, or maybe what you'd like to ask the author and us to change!

✔ Let us know any other *...For Dummies®* topics that interest you.

Your feedback helps us determine what books to publish, tells us what coverage to add as we revise our books, and lets us know whether we're meeting your needs as a *...For Dummies* reader. You're our most valuable resource, and what you have to say is important to us!

Not on the Web yet? It's easy to get started with *Dummies 101®: The Internet For Windows® 98* or *The Internet For Dummies*, 6th Edition, at local retailers everywhere.

Or let us know what you think by sending us a letter at the following address:

...For Dummies Book Registration
Dummies Press
10475 Crosspoint Blvd.
Indianapolis, IN 46256

BESTSELLING
BOOK SERIES